CIVIC ENGAGEMENT
IN GLOBAL CONTEXTS

CIVIC ENGAGEMENT IN GLOBAL CONTEXTS

International Education, Community Partnerships, and Higher Education

EDITED BY
JIM BOWMAN AND JENNIFER DEWINTER

UTAH STATE UNIVERSITY PRESS
Logan

© 2021 by University Press of Colorado

Published by Utah State University Press
An imprint of University Press of Colorado
245 Century Circle, Suite 202
Louisville, Colorado 80027

All rights reserved

 The University Press of Colorado is a proud member of the Association of University Presses.

The University Press of Colorado is a cooperative publishing enterprise supported, in part, by Adams State University, Colorado State University, Fort Lewis College, Metropolitan State University of Denver, Regis University, University of Colorado, University of Northern Colorado, University of Wyoming, Utah State University, and Western Colorado University.

ISBN: 978-1-64642-122-0 (paperback)
ISBN: 978-1-64642-123-7 (ebook)
https://doi.org/10.7330/9781646421237

Library of Congress Cataloging-in-Publication Data

Names: Bowman, Jim, 1968– editor. | DeWinter, Jennifer, editor.
Title: Civic engagement in global contexts : international education, community partnerships, and higher education / edited by Jim Bowman and Jennifer deWinter.
Description: Logan : Utah State University Press, [2021] | Includes bibliographical references and index.
Identifiers: LCCN 2021015370 (print) | LCCN 2021015371 (ebook) | ISBN 9781646421220 (paperback) | ISBN 9781646421237 (ebook)
Subjects: LCSH: Service learning. | Writing centers. | Rhetoric—Study and teaching (Higher)
Classification: LCC LC220.5 .C576 2021 (print) | LCC LC220.5 (ebook) | DDC 808.0071/1—dc23
LC record available at https://lccn.loc.gov/2021015370
LC ebook record available at https://lccn.loc.gov/2021015371

Cover illustrations © VLADGRIN/Shutterstock (*foreground*), © Pure Imagination (*background*)

Jennifer deWinter would like to thank her excellent colleagues at WPI, who have worked tirelessly through the Interdisciplinary and Global Studies Division to bring students to work on community projects all over the world. While many people are part of this project, she would especially like to thank, in no particular order, Lorraine Higgins, Kris Boudreau, Jennifer Rudolph, Constance Clark, Candace Ruta, Julie Richards, Erin Bell, Greg and Kumiko Snoddy, Anne Ogilvie, Aarti Madan, Esther Boucher, Paula Quinn, and Rick Vaz. Additionally, she would like to make a special shout-out to Aaron McGaffey, Freya deWinter, and Rowan McGaffey for joining her on many an adventure.

Jim Bowman would like to thank his many colleagues at St. John Fisher College for their support for civic engagement and foreign study. He also dedicates this book to the spirit of students, faculty, staff, and their families as they seek meaningful connections across the world in uncertain times. And to Meg, Chloe, and Dominic—we will get to Turkey one day, inshallah.

CONTENTS

Introduction: Rethinking Service Learning, Citizenship, and Democracy in Global and International Learning Environments
Jim Bowman and Jennifer deWinter   3

PART 1: ADMINISTRATIVE CONSIDERATIONS AND APPROACHES

1. Literacy and Civic Engagement in a Transnational WPA Practice: The Case of Russia
   Olga Aksakalova   23

2. Whose WPA?: Collaborative Transnational Development of Writing Programs
   Susan V. Meyers and María de Lourdes Caudillo Zambrano   44

3. International Project Centers and Global Civic Engagement
   Jennifer deWinter   68

PART 2: US STUDENTS AND INTERNATIONAL EXPERIENCES AT HOME AND ABROAD

4. The Use of Writing for Transfer in Study Abroad
   Kathryn Johnson Gindlesparger   95

5. Reflections on an Emergent Entremundista Pedagogy: Teacher-Researchers in Engaged Transdisciplinary Public Scholarship
   Adela C. Licona, Stephen T. Russell, and The Crossroads Collaborative   111

6. Service Learning as an Agent of Local and Global Social Change: Building Civic Engagement in Central America through Literacy and Sustainability
   Patricia M. Dyer and Tara E. Friedman   133

7. Intercultural Complications in a "Glocal" Community Project
   Joyce Meier   152

PART 3: SERVICE LEARNING AND CIVIC ENGAGEMENT PEDAGOGIES IN NON-US CONTEXTS

8. Student-Driven Service Learning: Fostering Academic Literacy and Civic Engagement in Croatia

    Rebecca Charry Roje   177

9. An Oasis of Civic Engagement? Considering Critical Dispositions Developed within the American University in Cairo

    James P. Austin   198

10. Experiences Learned from Fostering a Critical and Creative Writing Culture among Youth in Qatar

    Sadia Mir and Ian Mauer   218

11. Geopolitical Turbulence and Global Civic Engagement: Forensics of an Unfulfilled Fulbright Suggest Challenges Ahead

    Jim Bowman   235

    Afterword: The Practice of Knowledge Mobility: Rewriting Global Civic Engagement

    Bruce Horner   251

    Index   261
    About the Authors   271

CIVIC ENGAGEMENT
IN GLOBAL CONTEXTS

Introduction

RETHINKING SERVICE LEARNING, CITIZENSHIP, AND DEMOCRACY IN GLOBAL AND INTERNATIONAL LEARNING ENVIRONMENTS

Jim Bowman and Jennifer deWinter

This collection was imagined as one featuring work from scholars in the fields of rhetoric, composition, and literacy studies that would interrogate global partnerships and the structures that shape them. We sought analysis that would question some of the assumptions about reciprocity, equity, and implicitly democratic norms valued by most universities in Western societies. These essays demonstrate the vibrant, collaborative efforts at civic engagement occurring around the world in higher education. Unfortunately, the landscape for global cooperation, exchange, and engagement looks and feels even more uncertain and challenging following the geopolitical tumult manifest in events of 2016 and beyond. The rise of populist, nationalist political movements both in the United States and abroad is a lens through which it is difficult *not* to read these studies and narratives about global civic engagement.

On January 27, 2017, as one of his first actions as president, Donald Trump signed an executive order to ban people of several Muslim majority countries from traveling to the United States. Though the policy has been resisted by many and challenged in courts, it has created a chilling effect on many would-be immigrants and potential visitors, including foreign students (Wall and Carey). Early results of the ban suggest that people are more reluctant to come to the United States than before, and a similar phenomenon appears to be occurring among Americans seeking opportunities abroad. The climate for foreign travel had been deteriorating for years as the fighting in Syria, the subsequent refugee crisis, and years of spectacular attacks by Islamic State fighters around the world has impacted perceptions of safety in foreign travel, whether for academic, professional, or recreational reasons. Though the world was facing great challenges leading up to the US 2016

DOI: 10.7330/9781646421237.c000

presidential election, such as violent conflicts in the Middle East and the looming threats posed by the planet's rapidly changing climate, at least structures for cooperation exist to provide some response to these considerable difficulties. As we write this introduction today, the same threats remain, yet the means of unified global response have weakened, and traditional US partnerships, agreements, and understandings have been rendered unstable and in some cases ruptured. The United Kingdom has voted to leave the European Union and seen political chaos in its aftermath; a campaign fueled by demagoguery and nationalistic critiques of "globalism" has also propelled Donald Trump into the presidency; subsequently, US foreign policy has become hostile toward traditional democratic allies in Europe and sought to improve relations with authoritarian regimes in Russia, Turkey, Egypt, the Philippines, and elsewhere; the United States has pulled out of the Paris Agreement and ceded its role as a leader in addressing the challenge of fossil fuel reduction. Within populist, nationalist movements around the world, globalism has become a fashionable—and in many cases, politically effective—target of discontent and a scapegoat for economic stagnation.

Geopolitical backlash against trade and climate agreements appears to have buckled the very landscape of global cooperation. In such a climate, faculty and administration in institutions of higher education face new and greater uncertainties and a host of difficult questions: Is this the time to invest resources in sustaining ongoing relationships between universities and community partners of different countries? Should new relationships and programs be initiated in such a climate? With xenophobia rising around the world, especially in the United States, will people still want to invest in the United States and its colleges and universities?

We want to believe that, now more than ever, the answers to such questions should be a resounding "yes." The essays in this collection certainly demonstrate the value of global engagement and the important role universities can play in connecting people from different societies to respond to twenty-first-century challenges, located in the field of rhetoric and composition but broadly applied in our engaged activities. Global civic engagement has never been the easy path, and the obstacles to forging successful programs appear to be increasing in type and degree.

If we take global civic engagement in the context of higher education to mean the practice and reflection upon academic work and experiences involving intentional, ethical encounters among people and institutions of higher education from different societies, then we have to acknowledge that these efforts are already too established to disappear; if anything, their value should be confirmed in these times where more, not less, contact and understanding need to be developed and sustained. The works assembled here reassert the value of global cooperation and illustrate the role of universities in efforts to promote global civic engagement—in the form of service learning, foreign study, faculty and student exchanges, and bilateral and transnational projects. These projects have material consequence as practices of everyday life, where we see agency, action, and transformation. Nevertheless, many aspects of such programs continue to struggle with best practices to connect universities and local communities to each other and to partners around the world.

In the decades leading up to our current moment, many US colleges and universities embarked on ambitious projects abroad in an effort to enhance their work in an increasingly globalized world. These efforts have been fueled by both pragmatic and idealistic motives. Some institutions seek to develop a global brand that brings prestige and perhaps even a pipeline of international students to the United States (Pon and Ritchie). Others seek to immerse students in diverse cultural contexts and thus realize college-wide learning goals pertaining to global awareness (Hovland). Yet others develop initiatives that afford students and faculty opportunities to practice civic engagement on a global scale (Bringle et al.). Engagement efforts of this type involve work within international communities that represent service and strive for social change in both professional and educational contexts. Colleges and universities may partner with international NGOs, such as Engineers without Borders, Doctors without Borders, and Presidents United to Solve Hunger (PUSH), the latter in a project described by Patricia Dyer and Tara Friedman in this collection. Community literacy and service learning—with their focus on place-based learning, reciprocity, pragmatic outcomes, and sustainability—appear to make sense as frameworks for such initiatives. These projects demonstrate their efficacy in realizing institutional goals, yet additional effects, not always or entirely positive, are likely to occur for the people and institutions involved. National and international power structures and conflicts can infuse reading, writing, and learning at the level of the individual, local communities, regions, and nations.

Writing and literacy practices remain crucial to the efficacy and ethics of global civic engagement projects. The design of the projects, their outcomes (often written products), and student and community partner reflections become important in measuring impact and success. Thus, writing programs are particularly well-positioned to contribute meaningfully to civic engagement in higher education in diverse global contexts. Emerging scholarship has productively examined how writing programs and campus-wide initiatives involving writing and learning more broadly operate in comparative contexts (Thaiss et al.). The collection *Transnational Writing Program Administration*, edited by David S. Martins, includes several essays that feature in-depth explanation of how sociopolitical contexts of universities shape the construction of writing programs. Still, research in these areas is new, and many of the complexities of this work remain under-theorized in important ways. Civic engagement, for instance, is a movement that naturally reflects US neoliberal attitudes and implicit norms of democratic citizenship: service-learning projects and pedagogies may not always travel well given how university, faculty, student, and community relationships may differ markedly across diverse societies with distinct political systems and circumstances.

This collection examines the role of writing, rhetoric, and literacy programs and approaches in the practice of civic engagement in global contexts. Writing programs have experience in civic engagement and service-learning projects in their local communities, and their work is central to developing students' literacy practices. Further, writing programs compel student writers to attend to audience needs and rhetorical exigencies as well as reflect on their own subject positions. Thus, they are particularly situated to partner with other units on college campuses engaged in global partnerships. These types of projects are important and valuable, but only with critical self-reflection and iteration with community partners.

Civic Engagement in Global Contexts provides practical pedagogical and administrative approaches for writing studies faculty engaging with global learning projects, as well as nuanced insight into how to navigate contact zones from the planning stages of projects through to the hard work of self-reflection and change. Partnerships and projects across national borders compel us to think through the ethics of writing studies program design and teaching practices. Doing this difficult work can disrupt presumptive notions of ownership that faculty and administrators hold concerning the fields involved in these projects and can even lead to decentering rhetoric/composition and other assumptions held by US-based institutions of higher education. We organized the chapters loosely around three main groupings: administrative considerations and approaches; US students and international experiences at home and abroad; and service learning and civic engagement pedagogies in non-US contexts. The challenge that any collection has in grouping like chapters is that there is a lot of overlap between content and themes. Therefore, in the following section, we offer four themes through which this collection can be additionally read and understood:

1. Focusing on students learning global perspectives and communicative competencies through rhetoric and composition practice;
2. Developing faculty while decentering US ideological practices for a more inclusive and ethical engagement in international and global contexts;
3. Understanding how universities can work within and across international contexts and the role that scholars and practitioners in rhetoric and composition can play in facilitating this collaborative approach; and
4. Looking to the ethics and practices of international service learning and community literacy as a geopolitical endeavor.

These four themes run throughout the book, and highlighting them here makes clear the argument that our field's engagement with international service learning and community literacy is an important democratic intervention in the formation of educated citizens who must understand their place in relation to international and global politics, identities, and ethical forms of engagement.

STUDENT LEARNING OF GLOBAL PERSPECTIVES AND COMMUNICATIVE COMPETENCIES

University-wide and program-specific student learning outcomes centered on global knowledge and communicative competencies tend to drive global partnerships and curricula. These outcomes are well-intentioned, as well as inherently abstract. According to the initiative from the American Association of Colleges and Universities titled "Shared Futures: Global and Social Responsibility," created by dozens of faculty from diverse disciplines, students should strive to achieve the following:

1. "Become informed, open-minded, and responsible people who are attentive to diversity across the spectrum of differences
2. Seek to understand how their actions affect both local and global communities
3. Address the world's most pressing local and global issues collaboratively and equitably"

Though ambitious articulations of this sort identify students' behavioral expectations and desired learning outcomes, they provide much less guidance concerning the roles that faculty, students, and administrators must play in producing such outcomes within complex global learning environments. The task at hand can be daunting. Barnett et al., in "Diversity, Global Citizenship, and Writing Transfer," suggest the extent of the efforts necessary for success in global civic engagement projects: "To achieve learning outcomes common to . . . articulations of global citizenship and to make these global learning initiatives most effective . . . universities need innovative learning structures and pedagogical approaches to help students make meaning from these encounters with and studies of human difference" (60). The chapters in this collection demonstrate the depth of knowledge among scholars and program administrators working in writing studies, a field that concerns itself with the teaching of critical communication skills and regularly produces academic leaders focused on student learning. Innovation of the sort referenced above compels us to consider the training and knowledge of faculty charged with designing and delivering programs with the capacity to reach such important student learning outcomes.

This collection provides descriptive and theoretical accounts of efforts to support students in developing global perspectives and competencies in and through writing. We have in mind several different contexts. In one common scenario, US colleges and universities sponsor students through foreign study projects and programs, in which students are often tasked with writing prompts that help them develop self-awareness as they engage in diverse global environments (Gindlesparger; Dyer and Friedman). Katie Gindlesparger, in her chapter "The Use of Writing for Transfer in Study Abroad," takes an intimate look at the capacity of reflective writing to increase the value of foreign study experiences for students by helping them connect the learning with their (future) careers. Her follow-up interviews with foreign study alumni at her professionally oriented institution demonstrate that writing tasks of this sort may fail to do more than reflect students' relationships toward their future careers. She calls, instead, for a more structured reflection on global learning experiences tied to a dynamic understanding of their future career practices and contexts. In her study, a more critically self-aware understanding of one's own career path shapes the potential impact on students' global learning.

Student learners examined in two chapters develop their writing skills as they address US and foreign audiences in order to respond to global challenges facing communities abroad (Dyer and Friedman; deWinter). As they undertake these sorts of personal and professional writing tasks, students face complexities typical of all college writers, yet compounded by the considerable difficulty of writing about and sometimes for communities with distinctly different cultures, histories, and traditions, especially about learning and higher education. Overcoming these challenges might account for the high impact of international service learning on lifelong learning, which deWinter reports based on a longitudinal study. Similarly, Patricia M. Dyer and Tara Friedman's "Service Learning as an Agent of Local and Global Social Change" operates at the intersection of global civic engagement and literacy studies. Their contribution offers a rich narrative of a multi-year project in the United States and Honduras in which reflective, professional, and academic writing tasks are deployed to support student engagement in addressing global problems that challenge both societies. Writing represents a key component in students' involvement before, during, and after their participation in the project. The tireless efforts of writing faculty have led to substantial cultural shifts on their campus toward global engagement and the promotion of writing, critical thinking, civic engagement, and sustainability.

FACULTY DEVELOPMENT AND DECENTERING US PRACTICES

Though universities around the world have seen increased interest in writing studies and rhetoric in recent decades, the field itself continues to be a largely US-centered discipline. PhD-granting institutions in rhetoric and composition by and large reside in the United States. As a result, most writing pedagogies reflect US approaches to teaching, writing, and identity formation—hegemonically defined as mostly white and middle-class. In other words, many US-educated writing faculty involved in global civic engagement deploy pedagogies that have emerged from decades of theorizing and practice within predominantly North American contexts. Within universities and communities outside the United States, however, many of these practices—service learning, collaborative learning, reflective writing, and other student-centered pedagogies—may appear to be alien and even at odds with conventional practices within these societies. Thus, they become a potential source of confusion, misunderstanding, and conflict that requires careful coordination and engagement with global partners, a theme that appears throughout this collection. Aksakalova, for example, discusses the political history of education and writing in Russia, cautioning writing teachers and administrators working in non-US contexts to "be mindful of the socio-economic and political forces that shape educational policies and inform the notions of citizenship and civic engagement." More strongly, Charry Roje reflects on a US satellite campus in Croatia, asserting that "it seems more imperative than ever to avoid even the perception of paternalistic or neocolonial intentions, particularly in societies unfamiliar with the concept of service learning and skeptical of the efficacy of grassroots social change movements in general." The very act of working in these international spaces, in other words, functions to challenge and sometimes decenter US-based pedagogies, opening spaces in international collaborations while also transforming US-based or trained faculty in their quotidian practices.

Preparing faculty for these experiences can be as important as engaging students with the literature and theories of contact zones, cosmopolitanism, or voluntourism. While work with communities via service learning and community literacy generally sees the positive effects of sustained, engaged educational practice that energizes all of the stakeholders (cf. Cella; Flower), scholars in the field are already warning about the ethical challenges of working with community partners. For example, Ervin argues in her chapter "Composition and the Gentrification of 'Public Literacy'" that compositionists professionally and materially benefit from work in public and community literacy, and that we are doing the middle class "gentry" work in reorganizing social orders to the benefit of faculty, students, and institutions (39). This critique rings especially poignant in international community partnerships, which are not always geographically located near the partner institution. The danger, of course, is a type of cultural imperialism, often critiqued in the literature surrounding voluntourism (Banki and Schonell; Wright), which notes that traveling to destinations with the intention of volunteering is often more beneficial to the tourist-volunteer than the hosting community.

Faculty training, then, must be cognizant of the ways in which faculty must be prepared, both for themselves and as ambassadors in different international contexts, as well as fulfilling their student learning objectives in the classroom and around the assigned coursework. Meyers and Zambrano in this collection attend to this challenge by focusing on faculty development, particularly on faculty exchanges between the United States and Mexico. Meanwhile, chapters from both Dyer and Friedman as well as deWinter note that service-learning tours where US institutions are sending US students to volunteer in other nations and nonadjacent communities need long-term commitment from the faculty and institutions. In Dyer and Friedman's chapter, the authors outline a faculty fellows program that partners US faculty with faculty from Honduras to facilitate student volunteer work in rural areas. DeWinter discusses the logistics of running service-learning programs at over forty project centers all over the world and engaging over half of the undergraduate body of a small-midsized STEM university in this work. Both discuss the need for focus on faculty training and development through mentorship, and both echo service-learning research that calls for long-term, sustained engagement with these communities through institutionalizing partnerships.

Practically speaking, the best work possible for truly decentering inherently US-centric pedagogies and curricular practices involves commitments beyond those we are trained to imagine. Rather than faculty-to-faculty partnerships, we should be striving to link programs, departments, colleges, and community partners with one another. Rather than semester- or academic year–long projects, we should be building multi-year collaborations that bake in periodic self-reflections of stakeholders seeking to understand and develop sustainable, equitable relationships with one another (see, for example, Cushman; Vogel et al.; Stewart and Alrutz). These prescriptions for success align squarely with what we know to be best practices in service learning and civic engagement. They are also easier said than done, especially given how engrained power dynamics can be between, for example, universities and local communities, as well as between middle-class university students and community partner organizations. Information, perspectives, and resources should be flowing in both directions as these relationships grow and evolve. Further, faculty involved in designing, delivering, and evaluating such transnational collaborations need to continue making their voices heard and sharing their stories in professional conferences and in the journals and forums. As this occurs, more experienced faculty leaders as well as graduate students and ultimately undergraduates can appreciate and acknowledge the (North American) particularity of so much of what we learn and how we learn it. In doing so, each party and person involved can promote and practice better, deeper, more ethical global learning.

UNIVERSITIES WORKING IN AND ACROSS INTERNATIONAL COMMUNITIES

Global civic engagement is an extension of traditional US university values that see one of the primary purposes of higher education as educating a civically engaged population. In many ways an evolution of John Dewey's civic education, civic engagement has often provided the underpinning of community literacy and service-learning work in rhetoric and composition (Flower; Adler-Kassner et al.; Delano-Oriaran et al.).

Jacoby speaks to this in quoting the Coalition for Civic Engagement and Leadership (2005):

> Civic engagement is acting upon a heightened sense of responsibility to one's communities. This includes a wide range of activities, including developing civic sensitivity, participation in building civil society, and benefiting the common good. Civic engagement encompasses the notions of global citizenship and interdependence. Through civic engagement, individuals—as citizens of their communities, their nations, and the world—are empowered as agents of positive social change for a better world. (qtd. in Jacoby 9)

Jacoby builds from this to note that the phrase "civic engagement" is a "'big tent' that allows individuals and initiatives representing a range of perspectives to gather beneath it for the purpose of creating a cohesive whole that advances responsibility for the common good" (10). Universities, then, are tasked with educating not just a future, educated workforce but also a thoughtful citizen who can critically define a "good" and find the discursive ethos necessary to work collectively toward that good.

This ideology runs throughout this collection, with writing and rhetoric programs often acting within these university values in engaging students and defining and working with diverse communities. Dewey's philosophies have long influenced rhetoric and composition; writing courses ask students to consider audiences, write with purpose, write reflectively, and write to form an identity for oneself and in relation to others. Thus, multiple essays in this collection ask readers to consider rhetoric and writing practices enacted in non-US locations. Aksakalova challenges the reader to critically engage with writing pedagogy in a Russian university, linking critical thinking and academic integrity to teaching civic responsibility both within the nation-state and within larger international intellectual communities. In other words, values about ideas and plagiarism are as formative in civic consciousness in the underlying logic of knowledge as a sense of "good" might be. Austin, Mauer and Mir, and Charry Roje likewise look to rhetoric and composition pedagogy in non-US sites as a US-trained method to teach civic engagement, service, and ethics to university students in Croatia, Egypt, and Qatar. Such global campuses are in the United States as well, as Licona et al.'s article explores: Their work at The University of Arizona and funded by the Ford Foundation looks to bring together "university colleagues from distinct personal, disciplinary and epistemological backgrounds, [who] share an interest in social justice and transdisciplinarity [to begin] discussion about the possibility for a deliberate move to experimental approaches to co-teaching, co-research, and co-writing." The project outlined in this collection engages with Tucson youth, sexual health, and the rhetorics of the body as a form of participatory service learning within the always already international and global context of the US-Mexican border. And as Meier reminds readers in this volume, most classrooms are already international in nature, with non-US citizens in service-learning composition classes and doing work in US communities as international visitors.

While the civic has historically been limited to the civic body in which voting rights were associated (city-states, nation-states, etc.), global interconnectedness through travel, economies, and world problems causes this sense of civic engagement and the common good to necessarily expand. Thus, multiple universities are adopting language concerning global civic engagement in programs or outcomes, such as the University of North Carolina's Global Civic Engagement program for international service-learning opportunities or Penn State's statement on civic engagement and its connection to global activities, or the Center for Communication and Civic Engagement at the University of Washington. At the university level, the discourse around global civic engagement tends to fall within four categories:

1. Global service learning with students studying abroad or doing service learning in international contact zones
2. Global problem solving large challenges that transcend geopolitical borders
3. International campuses comprised of faculty, students, and staff from diverse national backgrounds
4. International collaborations between faculty and researchers

Universities are able to claim these activities categorically under global engagement or global impact, extending the reach of the university into other domains, whether or not they have satellite campuses in other nations.

As Deans argues in *Writing Partnerships: Service-Learning in Composition*, writing studies, with its emphasis on engagement, reflection, and social justice, is functionally a complementary outgrowth of the history of higher education in the United States: "Throughout the history of US higher education, service to the community, be it the local, national, or global community, has been integral to the missions of a wide range of colleges and universities, whether motivated by an ethic of public service, a mandate to extend research to the general public, or a commitment to particular religious beliefs" (10–11). What has been true for universities in general has also been the case for writing programs and English departments. Deans continues,

> English studies has a long-standing tradition of concern for social justice. Much of our theory is propelled by commitments to democracy, equality, critical literacy, and multiculturalism. Moreover, much of our classroom practice is motivated by a commitment to prepare all students for reflective and critical participation in their personal, cultural, working, and civic lives. (11)

Ultimately, then, universities benefit from the international and global civic service projects of writing studies and can claim the positive effect on the university brand, the positive impact on faculty, the opportunities for students, and the long-term positive influences on alumni, communities, and the learning situations.

Unsurprising, then, is that rhetoric and composition scholars participate in university initiatives vis-à-vis global civic engagement and international service learning. If not run within a rhetoric and composition program directly, what we see in this collection is rhetoric and composition scholars fully involved in university-wide programs, bringing with them expertise in writing and reflection within the often-challenging situations of non-university communities or international contact zones. In this collection, for example, Gindlesparger discusses a summer study tour in Europe, focusing on student learning and writing development, but also on faculty development. DeWinter's chapter looks to a different model—service learning with community partners in international contexts—and presents the assessment data on learning outcomes in writing, communication, engagement with the project, and ethics. Important in this chapter is not just what students and faculty learn in the process of international service learning but also the long-term impact on alumni surveyed years after graduation. Meyers and Zambrano's chapter pivots from students abroad to discuss the need for faculty development at the level of international exchange of faculty, with the United States and Mexican universities sending faculty to one another's campuses to learn, engage, and build sustainable relationships. Such an exchange is beneficial to faculty and the university profile. While desirable positive effects on faculty and universities can energize such projects, Bowman's chapter reminds readers that the often volatile politics of different geopolitical regions can disrupt well-planned exchanges in his discussion of past Fulbright-Hayes trips, and, more recently, his abandoned Fulbright grant to Turkey in response to growing unrest in the country.

Read as a collection about writing studies within larger university missions concerning global activities and presence, what emerges in this collection is a series of activities and projects that can be adapted for different university contexts. The chapters provide evidence that writing and reflection are beneficial to both students and faculty in defining themselves within global communities. They offer thoughtful interrogation of the challenges of international research and engagement, both theoretically and in everyday practices. Pulling from Marginson's 2011 work that imagines a "networked and more egalitarian university world patterned by communication, collegiality, linkages, partnerships and global consortia" (422), Boni and Calabuig imagine that higher education "may foster a democratization of knowledge, which implies the participation of more and more actors in the social construction of reality" (23). Here, the authors in this collection support the university's role in building a cosmopolitan worldview through engagement, audience empathy, reflection, and writing by bringing to bear the theories and practices of rhetoric and composition to their quotidian engagement with international and global communities.

EDUCATION AS A (GEO)POLITICAL ENDEAVOR

As should be clear from this introduction, the civic engagement work of US-based writing studies programs represents political work undertaken with a goal of developing critically literate national citizens. The shift to global civic engagement alters the dynamic and needs to account for how we imagine citizenship, especially if we explicitly aspire to producing not just national citizens but global citizens. In many ways, each contribution to this collection speaks to this challenge. The matter of so-called global citizenship—a well-intentioned if ill-defined cousin to cosmopolitanism—carries potential value and deserves more attention than can be provided here. The larger concern in considering political dimensions of global civic engagement is that too often our work either neglects to consider, or insufficiently examines, how citizenship differs across borders and national contexts. Yet participation in a democracy has always been tied to the political and national structures of other countries—now more so than ever. As we understand ourselves better, we may hope to come to know others across important lines of difference.

Civic engagement and service-learning projects are always inherently political, and sometimes explicitly so. A closer look inward at the cultural dynamics of writing programs demonstrates the political nature of their work for not just students and faculty but the institutions themselves, especially in the context of community service. Our field knows rhetorical education and composition involve political literacy and action. Such edited collections as *Going Public* attest to how much attention has been devoted to citizenship and public writing within writing programs and higher education. In his chapter from *Going Public*, "Infrastructure Outreach and the Engaged Writing Program," Jeffrey Grabill argues that writing programs "constitute a powerful and potentially transformative infrastructure for outreach and engagement. Transformative for students and teachers certainly, but—just as importantly—transformative for universities as a location for high impact experiences and not 'merely' service" (16). How might universities, which are committed already to a mission of serving students as well as local and global communities, be transformed by this work? Outreach and service have been typically undervalued by institutions, due in no small part to a failure in imagination. Grabill understands writing programs as "emergent" and capable of value beyond conventional place-based ways of thinking. Instead, the value comes in producing work made possible through relationships to other departments, programs, communities, and, in the case of the global projects outlined in this book, in exposure to different national contexts, traditions, and people, especially in the current epoch of populism. The contributions of Meyers and Zambrano, Dyer and Friedman, and deWinter highlight how crucial these relationships among institutions can be to students and programs. In the context of global civic engagement, these exposures to difference carry a value intrinsically linked to the content and skills of project work.

Writing programs emerge from a particular political space and reflect cultural assumptions about what constitutes a public or a community—as well as which priorities higher education institutions should focus on in their efforts to develop students. Shamoon and Medeiros's chapter "Not Politics as Usual: Public Writing as Writing for Engagement" illustrates how democratic norms concerning public space and citizenship are embedded within US culture and its institutions of higher education. Thus, these interests need to be carefully accounted for in the work US universities imagine engaging in with global partners. They note that, "public writing . . . focuses squarely on another common goal of writing for engagement, namely writing for civic and political engagement in the community. . . . Many service-learning organizations embrace civic responsibility or the development of social responsibility and citizenship skills as an important outcome of the community engagement experience" (Shamoon and Medeiros 178–179). This explicit attention on the citizen goes so far as to posit that courses in their writing program with a public writing and community engagement focus will "position students firstly as citizens in a democracy who have the potential for political agency" (179). Even within universities in the United States, where noncitizen residents and international students represent a not insignificant number of the university population, this assumption should be recognized more openly as problematic—a point that is evident when examining, for example, Joyce Meier's compelling contribution to this collection on her community-based learning project involving international students at her university. Not all societies are democratic, not all democracies are comparable, and the rewards of democratic cultures are never distributed equitably within societies. Global partnerships of today and into the future extend across US borders into a world where democratic norms and protected public speech cannot be taken for granted. Most of the projects described in this collection involve collaborations between institutions of the United States and societies where democratic politics and public speech are either absent or not vigorously protected. Chapters in this book by Austin, Licona et al., Mauer and Mir, Aksakalova, Charry Roje, and Bowman testify to the complexity and range of diverse political cultures that faculty and students experience in global community-based learning work. Project design itself needs to be ready to address such differences in assumption that undoubtedly affect the terms and nature of engagement.

CONCLUSION

As we review this collection in its entirety, we are reminded that scholars in rhetoric and composition, as in other fields, have rightly directed attention to place, especially in the context of service learning and civic engagement. Ashley Holmes's *Public Pedagogy in Composition Studies* demonstrates the deep historical links between higher education and its local communities. She advocates for more public writing in partnership with communities, while recognizing how such work is often fraught with political conflict as students and universities engage with partners in projects where differences over values, resources, language practices, and worldviews can be commonplace. Like Grabill's work, she posits a transformative power to public pedagogy and civic engagement initiatives, rationalized according to feminist ethics: "public pedagogies attempt to shift the loci of power and authority, positioning students and community partners as teachers and teachers as learners, blurring traditionally defined roles" (Holmes 150). Obviously, community-based learning projects of this sort would represent inherently political work in any context. Across lines of difference, the multiple sources of conflict are likely to be configured in ways we may struggle to recognize, requiring sensitive cultural preparation and stakeholder buy-in, extensive ongoing project support, and critical self-reflection of students, faculty, and administrators. Failure to approach such work in these ways could easily exacerbate the underlying problems that fuel increased authoritarianism, nationalism, and populism.

It is with this political warning ringing in our ears that we edited this volume, the purpose of which is to provide a praxis of engagement in such international civic endeavors. While we have provided multiple thematic ways to read with this volume, each chapter can be taken on its own—case studies of driving ideologies, motivations, and commitments from our field that speak to challenges of globalization and internationalization in our times. Such a case study approach, too, offers an opportunity for us as editors and for any reader to compare the chapters, seeing homologies as well as important variations that are bound up in location, time, and the political structure of the situation. They invite us to imagine possibilities for our own future teaching, to reflect on our own engagement with students and with local and global community stakeholders, and to grow as scholars and educators through shared practice.

WORKS CITED

Adler-Kassner, et al. *Writing the Community: Concepts and Models for Service-Learning in Composition. AAHE's Series on Service-Learning in the Disciplines.* American Association for Higher Education, 1997, p. 208.

American Association of Colleges & Universities. "Shared Futures: Global and Social Responsibility." *AACU*, no date, https://www.aacu.org/global-learning/outcomes.

Banki, Susan, and Richard Schonell. "Voluntourism and the Contract Corrective." *Third World Quarterly*, vol. 39, no. 8, 2017, pp. 1475–1490.

Barnett, Brooke, et al. "Diversity, Global Citizenship, and Writing Transfer." *Understanding Writing Transfer Implications for Transformative Student Learning in Higher Education*, edited by Jessie L. Moore and Randall Bass, Stylus Publishing, 2016.

Boni, Alejandra, and Carola Calabuig. "Education for Global Citizenship at Universities: Potentialities of Formal and Informal Learning Spaces to Foster Cosmopolitanism." *Journal of Studies in International Education*, vol. 21, no. 1, 2015, pp. 22–38.

Bringle, Robert G., et al. *International Service Learning Conceptual Frameworks and Research.* Stylus, 2011.

Cella, Laurie. "Introduction: Taking Stock of Our Past and Assessing the Future of Community Writing Work." *Unsustainable: Re-Imagining Community Literacy, Public Writing, Service-Learning and the University*, edited by Jessica Restaino and Laurie Cella, Lexington Books, 2013, pp. 9–21.

Cushman, Ellen. "Sustainable Service Learning Programs." *College Composition and Communication*, vol. 54, no. 1, 2002, pp. 40–65.

Deans, Thomas. *Writing Partnerships: Service-Learning in Composition*. National Council of Teachers of English, 2000.
Delano-Oriaran, Omobolade, et al., editors. *The SAGE Sourcebook of Service-learning and Civic Engagement*. SAGE Publications, 2015.
Ervin, Elizabeth. "Composition and the Gentrification of 'Public Literacy.'" *The Locations of Composition*, edited by Christopher J. Keller and Christian R. Weisser, State University of New York Press, 2007, pp. 37–54.
Flower, Linda. *Community Literacy and the Rhetoric of Public Engagement*. Southern Illinois UP, 2008.
Grabill, Jeffrey. "Infrastructure Outreach and the Engaged Writing Program." *Going Public: What Writing Programs Learn from Engagement*, edited by Shirley K. Rose and Irwin Weiser, Utah State University Press, 2010, pp. 15–28.
Holmes, Ashley J. *Public Pedagogy in Composition Studies*. National Council of Teachers of English, 2016.
Hovland, Kevin. "Global Learning: What Is It? Who Is Responsible for It?" *Peer Review*, vol. 11, no. 4, Association of American Colleges and Universities, Sept. 2009, pp. 4–7.
Jacoby, Barbara. *Civic Engagement in Higher Education: Concepts and Practices*. United Kingdom, Wiley, 2009.
Marginson, Simon. "Higher Education and Public Good." *Higher Education Quarterly*, vol. 65, no. 4, 2011, pp. 411–433.
Martins, David S. *Transnational Writing Program Administration*. Utah State University Press, 2015.
Pon, Kevin, and Caroline Ritchie. "International Academic Franchises: Identifying the Benefits of International Academic Franchise Provision." *London Review of Education*, vol. 12, no. 1, UCL IOE Press, Mar. 2014, pp. 104–120, doi:10.18546/LRE.12.1.10.
Shamoon, Linda K., and Eileen Medeiros. "Not Politics as Usual: Public Writing as Writing for Engagement." *Going Public: What Writing Programs Learn from Engagement*, edited by Shirley K. Rose and Irwin Weiser, Utah State University Press, 2010, pp. 177–192.
Stewart, Trae, and Megan Alrutz. "Meaningful Relationships: Cruxes of University-Community Partnerships for Sustainable and Happy Engagement." *Journal of Community Engagement and Scholarship*, vol. 5, no. 1, University of Alabama Press, Apr. 2012, pp. 44–55.
Thaiss, Christopher, et al. *Writing Programs Worldwide: Profiles of Academic Writing in Many Places*. Parlor Press and the WAC Clearinghouse, 2012.
Vogel, Amanda L., et al. "What Influences the Long-Term Sustainability of Service-Learning? Lessons from Early Adopters." *Michigan Journal of Community Service Learning*, vol. 17, no. 1, Fall 2010, pp. 59–74.
Wall, Robert, and Susan Carey. "Travelers Stopped in Transit to U.S. After Trump Order; Executive Order Suspends Entry of Anyone from Iran, Iraq, Libya, Somalia, Sudan, Syria and Yemen for at Least 90 Days." *Wall Street Journal (Online)*, Jan. 28, 2017.
Wright, Hayley. "Volunteer Tourism and Its (Mis)Perceptions: A Comparative Analysis of Tourist/Host Perceptions." *Tourism and Hospitality Research*, vol. 13, no. 4, 2013, pp. 239–250.

PART 1

Administrative Considerations and Approaches

1
LITERACY AND CIVIC ENGAGEMENT IN A TRANSNATIONAL WPA[1] PRACTICE
The Case of Russia

Olga Aksakalova

The current scholarly conversation about transnational writing projects and pedagogies recognizes that the teaching and learning of writing are conditioned by geopolitical, historical, social, and institutional dispositions of a given setting, as well as by globalization (Anson and Donahue; Horner; Martins; Thaiss et al.; Muchiri et al.). Building on this premise, my essay offers a close look at how the practices of a transnational writing program can reveal synergies and potential tensions between local political and academic cultures. I discuss the adoption of some features of the US-based writing pedagogy in Russia, where higher education has become an important vehicle for enhancing the country's global competitiveness and national pride. Higher education also provides a space where, historically, definitions of citizenry and civic engagement have been propelled. In the recent Soviet past, the notion of civic responsibility translated into a uniform, state prescribed "civic position" steeped in Communist ideology. Presently, because the country is in transition, it is not uncommon to include "the betterment of Russia" in universities' mission statements,[2] a rhetorical move that links higher education with the sociopolitical needs of the country.[3] At the same time, universities sometimes define their missions in slightly oppositional terms. For example, St. Petersburg University proudly claims that it follows its own educational standards that are higher than the federal standards (my translation, https://spbu.ru/universitet). The mission of Moscow University for the Humanities includes the statement "We are not waiting to be told what and how to do [fulfill our mission]" (https://www.mosgu.ru/about/missiya/).

A common cause of many universities is to place the country on the map of internationally competitive education through internationalization initiatives (Maltseva; West and Frumina) that have included, with increasing frequency, implementations of US-based writing pedagogies.[4] I view one such implementation against the backdrop of Russia's changing sociopolitical and educational landscape. I concentrate on the bilingual writing program, Writing and Communication Center (WCC), that I founded at Moscow's New Economic School (NES) in 2011. Conceptually and methodologically informed by US composition principles and writing center theory, the program has always been led by US-trained WPAs, but it employs both Russian and American consultants. During my leadership, the work of the WCC comprised curriculum development and Writing Across the Curriculum (WAC) / Writing in the Disciplines (WID) faculty development, as well as writing and oral communication tutoring for students and professional development projects in collaboration with other universities.[5]

I investigate the foundational framework, pedagogical approaches, and administrative decisions of the WCC in its first two years of existence (2011–2013), concentrating on those aiming to facilitate independent critical inquiry and academic integrity through student-centered practices. My analysis suggests that these two common features of writing instruction when practiced abroad—particularly in a post-Soviet state—can function as vehicles for developing students' civic responsibility necessary for contributing to the democratization of local political and social structures and for participating in the academic and professional cultures globally. The teaching of critical thinking through writing and ethical integration of sources encompass a range of practices that may place a transnational WPA into highly contested, interrelated terrains of pedagogy, policy, and politics but they also instill a civic dimension in her practice. In addition, I have found that strong institutional support is essential for the productive fostering of a teaching and learning environment where literacy habits are developed in connection with civic habits.

Following this introductory section, I provide a sociohistorical context for understanding the link between literacy practices and civic values in Russia to illuminate how writing pedagogies that facilitate autonomous thinking and academic integrity promote civic engagement. Specifically, in the first section, I distill how the teaching of autonomous thinking and academic integrity through writing, especially at the undergraduate level, can assist students in recognizing and challenging the dominant ideology. Through my analysis of Russia's current crisis of plagiarism, I also illustrate that these two pedagogical foci are essential for building a more civically conscious and uncorrupt society. In the second section, I offer a close look at the academic and civic missions of the New Economic School. In the third section, I explain how these missions are realized through specific practices of the WCC. I argue that these practices exemplify ways to promote a shift in Russian academic culture toward student-centered learning and civic consciousness. In the conclusion, I summarize the ways in which the writing program at NES combines academic and civic features and then consider the implications of my analysis for transnational writing programs. Throughout the essay, I use the term "transnational" to refer broadly to the "programs, activities, and institutions that involve students and faculty from two or more countries working together" (Martins 2). In other words, the term should signal a collaborative rather than hierarchical partnership between countries.

LITERACY AND CITIZENSHIP IN CONTEMPORARY RUSSIA

The constructs of citizenship and national identity have remained central to Russia's ideological apparatus since the collapse of the Soviet Union in 1991. As scholar of Slavic languages and literatures Kevin Platt points out, "authoritative visions of history and identity during the 1990s were predicated on the notion that 1991 marked a moment of radical social transformation, erasing geopolitical divisions between Russia and the west" ("The Post-Soviet" 6). However, Vladimir Putin, who came to power in 2000, has worked to redefine Russia's national identity. As political scientist Lilia Shevtsova suggests: "Putin's 'Russian national identity' has a clear agenda: to undermine the process of transforming individuals into citizens, and to return the nation toward total submissiveness and the status of 'poddanye,' that is, state slaves" (37). The growing opposition to the West and efforts aimed at "linking the Russian present with the Soviet and pre-Soviet eras" (Platt 6) have become the current government's ideological tools to unify public opinion while sharpening national vigilance and pride.

One important platform where these state efforts have become evident is secondary and postsecondary education. Platt notes the surge of "patriotic and apologetic textbooks to Russian children" (7), which Putin hoped would "foster a sense of pride in one's history, in one's country" (qtd. in Platt 7). Institutions of higher education have been tasked with a different agenda for enhancing national power, ironically through international recognition, by increasing the rate of scholars' publications in high caliber international journals.[6] English for Academic Purposes (EAP) courses have become prominent in universities, as have academic writing centers and initiatives that offer services to scholars in pursuing international publications (Butler et al. 206–207). This attention to academic writing illustrates that the link between literacy and citizenship is particularly strong in volatile historical moments. Amy J. Wan articulates this point in her book *Producing Good Citizens: Literacy Training in Anxious Times*: "Literacy becomes defined, shaped, and distributed in ways that mediate the relationship between the sponsoring institution and larger social trends. That is, literacy becomes a tool to shape citizenship in response to societal shifts" (11). In Russia, socioeconomic changes affect literacy objectives. As the country has shifted to a market economy, the state has become increasingly determined to increase academic participation in the global arena. It is expected that students' international mobility and faculty's increased participation in the global research space will help Russian education attain international prestige. Thus, the teaching of academic writing in Russian higher education is in large part a response to the state's imperative to raise global competitiveness of Russian universities. As a result, WCC director Ashley Squires explains, "Most Russian writing centers prioritize faculty and graduate students." She confirms, "The reason why appears fairly straightforward: given the current pressure on Russian faculty and institutions to generate published research in international journals, the case for establishing centers to address the writing needs of researchers is fairly self-evident" (66).

When universities commit to the goal of advancing their research output and employ writing pedagogies solely to this end, they reiterate the role of higher education as propagator of a prescribed civic duty—very reminiscent of Russia's Communist past—to improve the country. However, when writing pedagogies are linked to critical thinking and emphasize student-centered practices, they perform a different kind of civic duty, not necessarily at odds with, but not in service of the state's priorities. Socratic methodology and writing-to-learn practices can help undergraduate and graduate student writers construct their own ideas and contributions to a disciplinary discourse; in this way, writing practices bound to facilitate critical thinking help to forge a space for reexamining existing notions of citizenship and for constructing new ones. Ann George notes, citing James Berlin, "Because language and thought are inextricably linked, language instruction becomes a key site where dominant ideology is reproduced—or disrupted" (78). In a writing classroom or tutoring session where students engage in active meaning-making, the teacher functions as a facilitator of critical thinking, and academic integrity is emphasized, which makes it possible to imagine knowledge-making habits different from those propagated by the state. When practiced in both first language (L1) and second language (L2) as well as across disciplines (rather than solely in English classes, as is the case with NES), this learning model gives legitimacy to autonomous thinking, free expression, and explicit recognition of the intellectual property of others. As such, it can consequently provide students with confidence to implement these habits and practices not only in educational but also in civic situations. The higher education, then, not only propels a dominant ideology but also empowers students to evaluate and challenge its premises. James Austin shows how this empowerment can be possible also in Cairo, where undergraduate students at the American University have "opportunities for civic engagement in a nation where this form of engagement is often discouraged and can be dangerous. Such engagement included critiques of political power structures and cultural-religious practices, as well as consideration of the ways in which Islamic charity organizations can better serve local communities" (199).

In countries where higher education has a long history of serving the state, academic professionals may find it difficult to discern and challenge their role in carrying out the state's mandates, especially when the state provides funding. Private institutions are in a better position to do this, but in Russia, very few do. Even fewer endorse pedagogies that aim to train students to think autonomously and to feel empowered to recognize and question the pervasiveness of the state. Perhaps the most striking example of how challenging it is to distance oneself from the dominant ideology in Russia is that the state controls a vast majority of media channels, a trend that increased in 2014 with Russia's annexation of Crimea: "Media outlets became more firmly incorporated into the Kremlin's policy efforts, moving from supporting the government with biased news to actively participating in an 'information war' with its perceived adversaries" ("Russia"). As a result, many intellectuals who were opposing Putin's regime became supporters of his expansionist policy (Platt, "Russia's Powerful").

One danger of this development is the public's renewed faith in, rather than resistance to, an authoritative state. The trust in strong leaders—and by extension in authoritative teachers—dates back to the Soviet and Tsarist times. As the media situation illustrates, in volatile times, the Russian public may latch on to familiar constructs and knowledge-making tools well described by journalist Nataliya Rostova: "When you ask an average Russian if freedom of the press is important to him, he'll say no. In general, they're ok with the idea of censorship. They're ok with the idea of state-owned media" (Rostova, qtd. in Gordts). In such an environment, practicing a teaching philosophy wherein the authority of knowledge-making emerges from students through autonomous or collaborative practices might be increasingly challenging; however, it is all the more civically important in helping students develop, own, and articulate meaning and consequently recognize and resist any attempts to turn them into "state slaves" (Shevtsova 37). By introducing a set of transferrable habits of mind such as autonomous expression, transnational WPAs and their host institutions in Russia on the one hand support the movement toward Russian education's global competitiveness, but on the other, they participate in a larger civic project of democratizing local sociopolitical and educational structures.

To ascertain how a transnational writing program can provide a point of contact—and contention—between political and (within) academic worlds, it is important to consider the ongoing crisis of plagiarism in Russia and the intellectual community's attempts to address this crisis. In the Soviet era, it was not uncommon for academics and politicians to plagiarize their dissertations, monographs, and articles. In the post-Soviet period, the prestige attached to academic publications became increasingly appealing not only to academic and political leaders but also to business professionals: "For many officials and business people, having a doctorate is a matter of prestige that testifies to one's high status and capabilities. In many cases, it has been easy for influential people to make arrangements with academic institutions (and dissertation reviewing committees) through various pressures or rewards" (Golunov and Kurilla 2). Scholarly work can be produced by "a host of entrepreneurs who render such services openly and practically legally." Their efforts may vary:

> While many of these service providers economize their efforts by simply copying, pasting, and slightly editing texts from the Internet, some provide texts that are harder to trace, such as theses written during the Soviet period. Others offer to write original texts at a premium cost. Some offer "all inclusive" services, which include writing a dissertation *and* writing and publishing a number of associated articles and monographs, often necessary as part of the degree qualification process. (Golunov and Kurilla 2)

The so-called purge of falsified academic documents was launched by Prime Minister Dmitry Medvedev in 2012, and under Igor Fedyukin's leadership, theses from Moscow Pedagogical University were examined: "The result was the closing of the university's dissertation council, the firing of head professor Alexander Danilov, the revocation of 11 doctoral and candidate degrees, and the enactment of a set of recommendations to improve all procedures for awarding postgraduate degrees" (Golunov and Kurilla 3). Medvedev's campaign against plagiarism had a strong political dimension, as it "could be a way of hitting back at the conservatives surrounding Putin, who have mounted a campaign against Medvedev" (Shuster). In fact, Clifford Gaddy from the Brookings Institution found that Putin's own dissertation had been plagiarized (Golunov and Kurilla 2). The national initiative to expose plagiarism, "Dissergate," named after Nixon's "Watergate," met a mounting opposition from high-powered politicians, later leading to Fedyukin's resignation from his post.

Anti-plagiarism efforts have also spurred a heated discussion in the academic world. Konstantin Sonin, a leading economist who served as faculty and former vice-rector at NES, explained in his blog the roots of pervasive plagiarism in Russia:

> The roots of the crisis go back to the Bolshevik Revolution of 1917, when the best scholars in Russian were forced out of universities and Marxist-Leninist dogma came to dominate every discipline in the humanities. Cut off from their international peers, Russian academics suffered "a return to the Middle Ages," says Sonin. After four generations of isolation, many of the scholars who emerged from behind the Iron Curtain could offer little more than "indecipherable blather," Sonin says. At the same time, the arrival of capitalism turned doctoral degrees into a status symbol, like a Lamborghini or a Rolex. "So our academics learned to do one thing well," Sonin says. "They churn out these dissertations." (qtd. in Shuster)

Other academic leaders have also discussed the flourishing of plagiarism among graduate students and faculty (Zenkin; Golunov). A widely-accepted solution has been the voluntary online community "Dissernet," whose members investigate and expose fraudulent dissertations, activities that have led to degree revocations.[7] Other recommended solutions include instituting concrete plagiarism policies at universities, specifying definitions for different forms of plagiarism and disciplinary consequences for each, and issuing financial compensation to faculty who detect plagiarism (Golunov 254).

Perhaps because academic discussions about intellectual property are so tightly linked to and fueled by corruption in sociopolitical spheres, Russian scholars have focused mainly on (1) what historical and current trends in the culture cause plagiarism (Enikolopov et al.; Zenkin), and (2) how to police unethical textual borrowing (Golunov). In other words, there is an attempt to understand the problem and prevent it.

The language used in these discussions of plagiarism can be deeply steeped in shame and clinical metaphors, such as "isolated case of illness" or "epidemic" (Abalkina 200). This disciplinary stance toward intellectual property reveals a strong recognition that the anti-plagiarism fight in Russian academia contributes to a larger anti-corruption effort in the country.

Finding effective pedagogies to address plagiarism becomes a civic act on the part of the institution and WPAs in Russia because when "cheating is blossoming both among students and faculty," it "reinforc[es] corruption practices outside of the academia" (Chirikov 10). A WPA working in this setting will find that not unlike the case in the United States, the efficacy of plagiarism policies in Russian universities is measured by the seriousness and practicality of disciplinary actions, not always by pedagogical philosophies and approaches. Because the topic of plagiarism is so politically charged there, the challenge of steering policy-making conversation toward "pedagogical remedies" and away from "punitive responses" (Howard and Watson 121) may be steeper in Russia than in the United States. The trick for a WPA, then, is to remain attuned to the political ramifications of plagiarism, to consider the factors behind university plagiarism policy—or lack thereof[8]—and promote pedagogies in curricular and cocurricular spaces that facilitate students' content generation and ethical source integration.

Russian humanities scholar Sergei Zenkin observes an interesting correlation between passive learning and plagiarism: "If it is permissible to repeat verbatim after the teacher, why is it not permissible to copy someone else's text?" (195, my translation). Thus, Zenkin suggests that there is something inherent in the current educational system that might create mental conditions for plagiarism. He calls for a paradigm shift from product-oriented to process-oriented teaching as a way to promote ethical borrowing. This attention to pedagogy, of course, underpins a bulk of US-based plagiarism scholarship (Fink) and thus indicates a common ground between Russian and international scholar-teachers of composition. It also highlights what can potentially attract Russian colleagues in the US composition scholarship as they begin to generate a discourse on plagiarism: a substantial body of pedagogical and theoretical approaches to plagiarism.

Before turning to the implementation and possible ramifications of my WPA practices with regard to autonomous thinking and academic integrity at the New Economic School, I provide below a brief institutional description of the school.

CIVIC CONSCIOUSNESS AND LEVELS OF INTERNATIONALIZATION AT NES

New Economic School (NES) is a small, private research university in Moscow, Russia, with 400–500 students. The school's international orientation dates back to its inception in 1992 when international economics scholars joined forces with their Russian colleagues to build an innovative graduate institution. International faculty were invited to bring modern approaches to teaching and studying economics in Russia. Financial support came from philanthropist George Soros, Eurasia Foundation funded by the US government, the Ford Foundation, the MacArthur Foundation, and the World Bank. NES was a part of a larger emergent current that is "one of quite a few attempts to build an economics capacity by the international donor community in developing and transition countries" (Guriev, "Research Universities" 719). Thus, global consciousness lies at the root of the school's history. NES maintains openness toward international colleagues and students, although tensions between Russia and the West have intensified since 2014.

The NES mission is to provide modern economics education and research to the Russian society, business sector, and government (my translation, https://www.nes.ru/about/?lang=ru). Currently, NES offers several master's programs and a liberal arts undergraduate program run jointly with Federal Research University, Higher School of Economics. Courses are taught in both Russian and English in accordance with international curricular and research standards. Economics faculty are often hired on the international job market and held to tenure requirements compatible with those in research institutions abroad. Faculty in English and other disciplines are hired locally and internationally; they are highly competent and innovative teachers who participate in national and international research communities. Students graduating from MA and BA economics programs at NES are often admitted to top tier graduate programs in economics, including Ivy League schools.

Standing in the forefront of Russian economics studies, NES faculty have openly discussed Russia's anti-democratic course and its state-controlled economy and media (Guriev, "In Russia: More Proof"), corruption (Enikolopov et al.), and have supported initiatives to increase anti-corruption efforts and civil liberties (Guriev, "Why I Gave"). Faculty's criticism of the regime, however, has not placed the school into a strictly left corner of organized opposition. In fact, NES does not align itself with a particular political platform or civic position. Rather, NES faculty have shown that it is possible to behave democratically in a society where democracy remains volatile[9]: to speak constructively and responsibly about the regime and analyze corruption in their research and journalism while at the same time use their sterling expertise to offer constructive and open support to the government for improving economic and social aspects of the Russian society.

The most striking example is the role of the school's former rector Sergei Guriev in the government of President Medvedev: "He wrote speeches for Mr. Medvedev, sat on numerous advisory bodies and served on the boards of state companies" (Barry). At the same time, Guriev donated funds to support opposition leader Alexei Navalny because he believed in the country's need for increased political competition (Guriev, "Why I Gave"). Another former NES employee, Igor Fedyukin, a historian with a PhD from the University of North Carolina, Chapel Hill, who served as NES director for policy studies and was a key member of the search committee for the writing center founding director, took the post of deputy minister of education and science in 2012. As I mentioned in the last section, in his new role, Fedyukin headed the campaign against pervasive plagiarism in Russian academia. These civic acts on the part of the academic community do not come without challenges in contemporary Russia,[10] but they are important to note here for two reasons. First, they demonstrate that university policy makers who value independent and civically responsible thinking are the ones likely to institute active learning pedagogy and a coherent writing program to facilitate it. Secondly, they shed light on the overall character of the cultural climate in which institutions of higher education are functioning in Russia.

While the mission of NES remains oriented inward—toward economic and academic prosperity in Russia—the means by which the mission continues to be realized are derived from international engagements. Gur Ofer, one of the school's founders, explains,

> The general goal was to bring "modern" economics, a euphemism for Western economics, to Russia by establishing in Russia "a graduate center offering a high level of teaching, study, and research in economics as practiced in the West and training teachers of economics as well as professional economists and researchers in economics for Russia (and other constituents of the Commonwealth of Independent States)." (17)

From its inception, NES has recruited international faculty as visiting or tenure-track professors. Sergei Guriev, who served as the school's second rector between 2004 and 2013, points out an important tendency in NES's effort to hire internationally: "reversing the brain drain and bringing back those who left Russia for PhD programs" (Guriev, "The Miracle Worker" 10). Indeed, many of the permanent and visiting faculty at NES have been returnees (myself included) who share the dream of making their native country better. This approach to internationalization highlights not blind westernization but a concern for the country's former, current, and future citizens. The returnees are invited to bring their expertise acquired abroad to the current educational reform supported by the Russian government:

> Russia has a desperate need for new, competitive research universities—to create conditions and incentives for competitive research and for training new generations of researchers.
>
> This has been recognized by the government, which has begun an ambitious overhaul of the university system. The reform is to make the system more open, mobile, and competitive. (Guriev, "Research Universities" 716)

In turn, what makes NES attractive to international faculty is a considerable amount of academic freedom, generous provisions for research time, research centers, and opportunities to contribute to program and curriculum development.

NES has another major facet that may be appealing to international faculty, donors, and students: familiar approaches to teaching that emphasize student-centered learning, academic ethics, professional development for teachers, and support services for students. These features distinguish NES from many other universities in Russia. Educational reform to achieve "democratization and modernization of Russian society and the country's economy"[11] has been implemented across higher education. Yet, a need for "active learning techniques as a method of instruction" and a "greater cooperation between academic staff and students" remains vital (Maltseva 59).

In the rest of this essay, I explore how approaches to writing at NES's liberal arts undergraduate (BA) program create an effective model for fulfilling this need and help to shape national and global citizens.

WRITTEN AND ORAL COMMUNICATION IN THE LIBERAL ARTS UNDERGRADUATE PROGRAM AND CIVIC ENGAGEMENT

Academic writing and oral communication have always been taught at NES in the graduate-level English and economics courses. Prior to 2011, English instructors were highly competent and innovative graduates of prestigious linguistic universities in Russia with years of experience. They taught academic writing, business writing, and presentation skills using EAP approaches. In addition, economics faculty who publish widely in international journals have been in a great position to teach Russian graduate students disciplinary writing conventions. Likewise, the school has always had a strict plagiarism policy articulated through an explanatory handout and regulations, such as public warnings, disciplinary meetings with program administrators, and expulsion. Importantly, these resources emerged not from the English Department, but economics faculty. So, writing had not become affiliated strictly with a language department, but with a discipline-specific knowledge. Meyers and Zambrano note a similar way of disseminating writing expertise from *within* disciplines in Mexico; I second their invitation to turn to these international models that can "help programs in the United States revisit and possibly revise their own practices" in regard to WAC/WID by eliciting "expertise . . . from individual disciplines and departments and moving towards a consensus model for the teaching of writing across a campus, as opposed to a central department (like an English department) that stewards such work on a campus" (n.p.).

At NES, the need for a more comprehensive and centralized writing program emerged in 2011 when the school launched a bachelor's program (BA) in economics, offered jointly with Federal Research University, Higher School of Economics. While students work toward receiving a degree in economics, the program is structured in the liberal arts tradition, emphasizing a multidisciplinary and multicultural curriculum featuring elective courses. Courses are offered in Russian and English, and pedagogical approaches are largely steeped in active and project-based learning achieved through a range of writing and speaking practices. One of the teaching and learning values of the program is to develop critical thinking and communication skills in Russian and English and to perform creative problem-solving (my translation, https://www.nes.ru/bachelor-of-arts-in-economics/).

BA program directors and school administrators decided that their innovative pedagogical goals would be best accomplished by hiring a US-based compositionist, who preferably also knew Russian, to head the Writing and Communication Center (WCC). In the fall of 2011, concurrently with the launch of the BA program, I began working with NES students and faculty as founder and director of the WCC, a bilingual entity, and as an English lecturer. The WCC was conceptualized as an independent department, separate from the English Department, though many consultants in the first two years were English faculty. Our commitment to bilingualism helped to shape the WCC not merely as a language center, but as a place where thinking could be generated, cultivated, and challenged irrespective of the language in which it occurs. During 2011–2013, the WCC followed two main directions: supporting faculty in integrating writing and speaking practices into their courses and supporting students in their curricular and cocurricular projects through tutorials and workshops.[12] As WCC director, I was also asked to build undergraduate and graduate English writing- and communication-enhanced curricula. Very soon after the WCC began functioning, colleagues from other universities expressed interest in learning about US-based composition pedagogy. This resulted in several collaborative initiatives[13] and occasioned rich learning opportunities for me.

In the discussion that follows, I focus on the WCC's bilingual work within the BA program because our practices here illustrate best how learning and civic habits are intertwined, as well as the institutional resources necessary to cultivate them.

First, it is important to note that BA directors introduced writing- and communication-enhanced student-centered pedagogies as integral to the program's educational philosophy. Space was provided for me to introduce our services and WAC/WID resources at faculty meetings, and some faculty later requested assistance with assignment design and feedback strategies. Faculty also often referred students to the WCC for tutoring. This level of institutionalization helped to articulate that student-centered learning achieved through discussion and writing rather than through lectures was the program's pedagogical staple. Without institutional support, implementing a pedagogical model that potentially decenters a teacher's authority (in the classroom as well as in the WCC tutoring sessions) can be particularly challenging in an environment where, traditionally, knowledge-making is expected to emerge from teachers and where political rhetoric instills respect for authority. From colleagues teaching at other universities, I learned that teachers wanting to experiment with yielding some authority to students are hesitant to do so because of insufficient institutional support and student preference for a prescriptive teaching model.[14] Active learning has been found to cultivate civic consciousness in Russia: "The more students are involved in the learning process, the higher their Civic Engagement characteristics are" (Prutskova). Yet not many undergraduate institutions commit to it: "Undergraduate student experience is primarily organized around passive learning" (Chirikov). This reliance on older teaching models can be explained by tradition and lack of financial and ideological incentive from the Ministry of Education. Thus, an institution that invests in developing a process-oriented and student-centered writing program occupies a pioneering position and depends on its own resources, both financial and academic. It also has to have a strong commitment to the pedagogies it promotes and understand the civic role they can play.

One way in which NES demonstrated its commitment to a civically conscious literacy model is by promoting writing and communication pedagogies that develop student agency in putting forth inquiries. Taking a position and supporting it with evidence was the goal of many course projects across the curriculum. For example, at the end of the course Social and Economic History of Russia, students completed a research paper addressing a clear research question and containing a literature review, hypotheses, discussion, conclusion, and bibliography. Likewise, intermediate and advanced English courses, as well as economics courses, included at least one argumentative assignment. As an academic genre, argumentation is relatively new in Russia, so it was important to scaffold assignments through in-class and out-of-class low-stakes tasks. To further support students in their efforts, WCC designed course-specific writing seminars and workshops and provided tutoring.

Workshop settings featuring debates, collaborative brainstorming, and peer reviews revealed not only students' enthusiasm to express their opinions and put forth arguments, but also their discomfort and resistance to active forms of learning. For example, in my writing seminar, one student was reluctant to share his work with a peer out of concern for plagiarism. Another student was very uncomfortable letting me use her writing anonymously for a class exercise. One-on-one conferences were absolutely essential for alleviating at least some of their discomfort. Additionally, I found it crucial to discuss pedagogical rationale for our practices, especially when these practices seemed new to students.

As students worked toward producing their own inquiries and theses, they also required guidance with source integration. Our approach to citing and plagiarism combined practical policy steps with pedagogy. Early in the semester, the WCC sent students several documents concerning citation: (1) a memo prepared by an economics professor prior to the launch of the WCC that defined forms of plagiarism as improper citation of sources that occurs on three levels: verbatim, paraphrasing, and attribution; (2) citation guides in Russian and English; and (3) MLA, Chicago, and APA style sheets. Students learned best practices for paraphrasing and citing to avoid plagiarism both in their classes and at the WCC. Also, by engaging in the writing process in various courses while receiving support at the WCC, students were well positioned to understand the value of *the process* of obtaining knowledge, not solely the knowledge itself.

Their time at the WCC yielded several important results. Historically, in Russian higher education, good teaching has been equated with informative and expressive lecturing.[15] One-to-one consultations at the

WCC dealing with content generation are especially rich opportunities for students to develop confidence in putting forth ideas and to redefine their understanding of efficacy in teaching and learning. Studying with tutors who facilitate thinking and allow for quiet time to engage in the writing process primes students to rethink their position as learners. The sense of agency students acquire in the process can potentially lessen their dependence on other thinkers as authority. It can instead allow for an alternative, analytical, and evaluative approach to authority, thus enriching students' ways of thinking academically. Often students who were referred to the WCC to use proper citation showed some detachment and discomfort. Partially this reaction can be explained by the shaming associated with plagiarism (students who plagiarize receive public warnings). A more interesting reason, as I gathered from cursory remarks and body language, was that sometimes students felt they were expected to unlearn their prior knowledge. In high school, plagiarism conversations occurred rarely and students were taught to trust experts more than themselves. WCC consultants and faculty had to find ways to foreground academic integrity so that it did not threaten the pillars established by previous literacy sponsors, but rather, widened them.

Moreover, consultations at the WCC devoted to explicating and citing other writers' ideas help to destigmatize plagiarism. Upon recommendation of their professors or on their own accord, students sought assistance with citation and paraphrasing. The fact that their professors and WCC consultants were available to support them in learning how to borrow ideas in academically acceptable ways could help to transform the notion of educational process from being fear-driven (as the current plagiarism policy suggests) into nourishing and collaborative. Redefining power relations between students and teachers in this way can transfer productively to students' social experiences within and outside of Russia; it suggests to students that it is possible to foster relationships and make progress not through force and fear, but through communication, empathy, respect, and responsibility.

IMPLICATIONS FOR RUSSIAN HIGHER EDUCATION AND TRANSNATIONAL APPROACHES TO WRITING

By constituting a structured approach to academic writing in two languages, NES offers to Russian evolving higher education a functional middle ground between a conservative call for the "revival of institutions of moral control" (Yurevich 83) and entrepreneurial vision of higher education as " 'a product' to be 'purchased' " (Zajda 21). The experience at NES illustrates that introducing a US-informed writing pedagogy in a non-Western setting may have positive implications for students' participation in both local and global environments. As a result of becoming active agents in their own education, they can develop confidence in putting forth ideas and learn to challenge assumptions. Academic and career paths available to NES students after they graduate will surely bring financial success, along with global and local prestige. However, the habits of mind they acquire through curricular and cocurricular writing practices instill an understanding that these forms of success come with personal and public responsibility.

My experience at NES suggests a few implications for transnational approaches to writing. First, in countries going through socioeconomic and political transitions, higher education can be a particularly contested space for fulfilling political agendas, developing academic values, and (re)defining civic engagement, its scope and form of existence. The same conclusion surfaces in Jim Bowman's chapter that illustrates an attempted coup's tremendous impact on Turkish higher education: "All the deans of Turkey's universities were required to resign and thousands of academics and graduate students have been fired or expelled. The failed coup appears to have been a pretext for the government to act against any people perceived to be hostile to its rule" (13–14).

Second, a transnational WPA quickly learns that her work with the local faculty, students, and administrators may not only raise the university's academic and potentially national and/or international prestige but also establish a philosophy of teaching that engages with the social and political realities in shaping students' civic consciousness. Thus, as transnational WPAs are continuing to develop pedagogies relevant for satellite campuses, visiting appointments, consultancies, and other forms of literacy brokerage, they must be mindful of the socioeconomic and political forces that shape educational policies and inform the notions of citizenship and civic engagement. What helped me to see the full scope of the relationship between writing pedagogy and civic values in my transnational work was a continuous conversation with Russian, European, and American educators—in person as well as on paper, as evidenced in numerous citations here from international scholars—on the subjects of literacy and citizenship. In Moscow, I was fortunate to have students and colleagues who eagerly reflected with me on how new pedagogies fit into the Russian educational tradition and the civic role they might play in the rapidly changing country. This kind of collaborative reflection that crosses the boundaries of teacher-student-administrator hierarchy was ongoing and productive.

As writing programs in the United States are growing increasingly transnational and translingual, they can also benefit from such collaborative practices, especially ones that consider student voices in the programmatic and pedagogical decisions.

As a bilingual WPA, I certainly had an advantage to grasp the context of my students' literacy histories and sociopolitical implications of teaching writing as a thought-generating process. I initiated informal conversations as well as formal faculty development seminars to discuss writing pedagogies and their civic implications. My Russian colleagues helped me immeasurably to realize the value of providing a rationale to students and faculty when introducing new pedagogical directions. For example, in my literature class, students openly questioned my Socratic pedagogy and requested interpretations established by literary experts. As novice literary readers, they did not think their interpretations were correct or complex enough, nor did they think that they mattered. I found myself explaining the rationale for my teaching frequently and, in these discussions, asking students to consider the value of autonomous thinking in and outside of academic contexts. I also actively sought advice from my Russian colleagues, who helped me understand the root of my students' resistance. For example, I learned that argumentation or independent inquiry building was a relatively new mode taught in high schools. I also learned that citation was not widely taught in secondary or higher education. These conversations usually touched on plagiarism as a pervasive feature of Russian academia and the political scene. As a result, I quickly realized that it is impossible to be thinking about education and writing pedagogies as separate from civic responsibilities.

Thus, as WPAs and writing instructors take the dialogue on teaching and learning writing into the global context, it is important to expand our emphasis on how pedagogical and administrative decisions of a transnational WPA entwine with civic responsibility and global ethics. Studies concerning this would in turn assist transnational WPAs in shaping their work and their understanding of their role not only as literacy sponsors but also as citizenship sponsors.

NOTES

1. I use the term WPA to describe my work at NES for two reasons: (1) writing center directors are members of the Council of Writing Program Administrators (http://wpacouncil.org/aws/CWPA/pt/sp/about) and (2) curriculum design, assessment, and faculty professional development, including WID/WAC resources, fall under a WPA's purview (http://wpacouncil.org/aws/CWPA/pt/sp/about).

2. See the "About" ("О Вышке") web page of Higher School of Economics in Russian: www.hse.ru/info/; see also the "About" ("О МГИМО") page of Moscow State Institute of International Relations in Russian: mgimo.ru/about/.
3. This pronounced alignment between education and national growth is rooted in the ongoing Russian education reform. In 2000 and 2001 respectively, the Russian government passed the National Doctrine of Education in the Russian Federation 2000–2025 and the Concept of the Modernization of Education in Russia until 2010. Both "declared that education should reflect the needs of the labour market and the nation's socio-economic growth. For the first time, education has thus been defined in economic terms as 'a long-term investment' and 'the most effective capital investment'" (Maltseva 64–65).
4. US writing specialists organized the seminar Establishing Effective Writing Centers: Goals, Methods, and Structure in December 2015: awuc.misis.ru/establishing-effective-writing-centers-goals-methods-and-structure/. In my position as founding director of the Writing and Communication Center at NES, I led professional development programs for Russian faculty on writing pedagogy, including in the Fulbright Summer School for the Humanities (see Schleifer et al.). Smolny College in St. Petersburg implements Bard College's Language and Thinking Program (Peoples).
5. Three essays have been published about the NES WCC. First, former WCC Associate Director Kara Bollinger's "Introducing Western Writing Theory and Pedagogy to Russian Students" in Pavel Zemliansky and Kirk St. Amant's *Rethinking Post-Communist Rhetoric* examines specific pedagogies implemented at the WCC and student learning preferences in light of the changing economy of Russia. Second, current WCC Director Ashley Squires's "The NES Writing and Communication Center and the Case for Student-Oriented Writing Centers in Russia" discusses the importance of giving priority to student rather than faculty writers in Russian writing centers. Squires's other essay "Writing Centers and Academic Professionalization in Russia" appears in the collection *Western Curricula in International Contexts*.
6. In 2012, President Putin signed Decree #599, "On measures to realize government policies in education and research." This federal directive required an increase in scholarly publications in international journals listed in the Web of Science database ("Yukaz").
7. For more on Dissernet, see www.dissernet.org.
8. See Golunov as well as Chirikov on lack of plagiarism policies in Russian universities.
9. Joan DeBardeleben offers a close look at the political and social forces that determine the course of democracy in Russia.
10. See Guriev's *New York Times* Op Ed "Why I Am Not Returning to Russia" and Golunov and Kurilla's "Academic Integrity in Russia Today."
11. For details on the government-mandated reform to higher education, see Maltseva; and Guriev, "Research Universities in Modern Russia."
12. For details on the WCC current services, visit the WCC website at nes.ru/wcc.
13. For example, I was invited to conceptualize and co-organize a faculty development seminar, Fifteenth Fulbright Summer School for the Humanities in 2013, Writing Pedagogy: Perspectives from Russia and the US (see Schleifer et al.). The WCC also offered a course for faculty from different Moscow universities that focused on composition and writing center theory and practice entitled Writing Pedagogy: Theory and Practice.
14. This view was shared by English instructors from several Moscow universities who attended WCC's faculty development course, Writing Pedagogy: Theory and Practice.

15. Froumin found that "[i]n their relationships with students a majority of teachers do not abide by democratic norms, are authoritarian, and resolve conflicts which arise in accordance with their notions of common sense" (137).

WORKS CITED

Abalkina, Anna. "Некорректные заимствования в журналах: отдельные случаи болезни или эпидемия?" Edited by Sergei Zenkin. *Russian Sociological Review*, vol. 13, no. 3, 2014, pp. 200–203.

"About." *New Economic School*, www.nes.ru/en/about/. Accessed 22 May 2016.

Anson, Chris M., and Christiane Donahue. "Deconstructing 'Writing Program Administration' in an International Context." *Transnational Writing Program Administration*, edited by David Martins, Utah University Press, 2014, pp. 21–47.

Austin, James. "An Oasis of Civic Engagement? Considering Critical Dispositions Developed within the American University in Cairo." *Civic Engagement in Global Contexts* edited by Jim Bowman and Jennifer deWinter, Utah State University Press, 2021.

Barry, Ellen. "Economist Flees as Russia Aims Past Protesters." *The New York Times*, 29 May 2013, www.nytimes.com/2013/05/30/world/europe/economist-sergei-guriev-leaves-russia-abruptly.html.

Bollinger, Kara M. "Introducing Western Writing Theory and Pedagogy to Russian Students: The Writing and Communication Center at the New Economic School." *Rethinking Post-Communist Rhetoric: Perspectives on Rhetoric, Writing, and Professional Communication in Post-Soviet Spaces*, edited by Pavel Zemliansky and Kirk St. Amant, Lexington Books, 2016, pp. 19–42.

Butler, Donna Bain, et al. "Student and Teacher Perceptions of Academic English Writing in Russia." *The Journal of Teaching English for Specific and Academic Purposes*, vol. 2, no. 2, 2014, pp. 203–207, doi.org/10.2139/ssrn.2735380.

Chirikov, Igor. "The Mystery of Russian Students: Poor Learning Experience, High Satisfaction." *Higher Education in Russia and Beyond: Challenges for Student Experience in Russia and Eastern Europe*, vol. 1, no. 3, 2015, pp. 10–11.

DeBardeleben, Joan. "The 2011–2012 Russia Elections." *Russia after 2012: From Putin to Medvedev to Putin—Continuity, Change, or Revolution?* edited by J. L. Black and Michael Johns, assisted by Alanda D. Theriault, Routledge Taylor & Francis Group, 2013, pp. 3–18.

Enikolopov, Ruben, et al. "Social Media and Corruption." *Social Science Research Network*. Nov. 2016, pp. 1–50, dx.doi.org/10.2139/ssrn.2153378.

Fink, Thomas. "Reconfiguring the Representation of Plagiarism and Misuse of Sources." *Journal of Teaching Writing*, vol. 30, no. 1, 2015, pp. 1–23, journals.iupui.edu/index.php/teachingwriting/article/view/20756/20288.

Froumin, Isak D. "Democratizing the Russian School: Achievements and Setbacks." *Educational Reform in Post-Soviet Russia: Legacies and Prospects*, edited by Ben Elkof et al., Frank Cass, 2005, pp. 129–152.

George, Ann. "Critical Pedagogies: Dreaming of Democracy." *A Guide to Composition Pedagogies*, edited by Gary Tate et al., Oxford University Press, 2014, pp. 77–93.

Golunov, Serghei. "Студенческий плагиат как вызов системе высшего образования в России и за рубежом." *Voprosy obrazovaniya / Educational Studies*, vol. 3, 2014, pp. 243–257, cyberleninka.ru/article/n/studencheskiy-plagiat-kak-vyzov-sisteme-vysshego-obrazovaniya-v-rossii-i-za-rubezhom.

Golunov, Serghei, and Ivan Kurilla. "Academic Integrity in Russia Today: The Political and Social Implications of Thesis Falsification and Education Reform." *PONARS Eurasia: New Approaches to Research and Security in Eurasia*, memo no. 246, Mar. 2013, pp. 1–5, www.ponarseurasia.org/memo/academic-integrity-russia-today-political-and-social-implications-thesis-falsification-and.

Gordts, Elina. "Putin's Press: How Russia's President Controls the News." *Huffington Post*, 24 Oct. 2015, www.huffingtonpost.com/entry/vladimir-putin-russia-news-media_us_56215944e4b0bce34700b1df. Accessed 21 May 2016.

Guriev, Sergei. "In Russia: More Proof of the Internet's Power." *The New York Times*, 18 Mar. 2013, www.nytimes.com/roomfordebate/2011/12/12/is-the-kremlin-loosening-its-grip/in-russia-more-proof-of-the-internets-power.

Guriev, Sergei. "The Miracle Worker on Miracles." *Miracle of NES: The Foundations of Modern Economics in Russia*, New Economic School, 2012, pp. 9–11.

Guriev, Sergei. "Research Universities in Modern Russia." *Social Research*, vol. 76, no. 2, Summer 2009, pp. 711–728, www.jstor.org/stable/40972282?seq=1#page_scan_tab_contents.

Guriev, Sergei. "Why I am Not Returning to Russia." *The New York Times: Global Opinion*, 5 June 2013, www.nytimes.com/2013/06/06/opinion/global/sergei-guriev-why-i-am-not-returning-to-russia.html.

Guriev, Sergei. "Почему я дал деньги Навальному" ["Why I gave money to Navalny."] *Slon.ru*, 15 May 2012, Slon.ru. Accessed 22 May 2016.

Horner, Bruce. "Transnational Writing Program Administration." Afterword. *Transnational Writing Program Administration*, edited by David S. Martins, Utah State University Press, 2014, pp. 332–41.

Howard, Rebecca Moore, and Missy Watson. "The Scholarship of Plagiarism: Where We've Been, Where We Are, What's Needed Next." *WPA: Writing Program Administration*, vol. 33, no. 3, Spring 2010, pp. 116–124, wpacouncil.org/archives/33n3/33n3howard-watson.pdf.

Maltseva, Elena. "The Challenges and Prospects of Reforming Russia's Higher Education System." *Russia after 2012: From Putin to Medvedev to Putin—Continuity, Change, or Revolution?* edited by J. L. Black and Michael Johns, assisted by Alanda D. Theriault, Routledge Taylor & Francis Group, 2013, pp. 57–72.

Martins, David S. "Transnational Writing Program Administration: An Introduction." *Transnational Writing Program Administration*, edited by David S. Martins, Utah State University Press, 2014, pp. 1–18.

Meyers, Susan V., and María de Lourdes Caudillo Zambrano. "Whose WPA?: Collaborative Transnational Development of Writing Programs." *Civic Engagement in Global Contexts*, edited by Jim Bowman and Jennifer deWinter, Utah State University Press, 2021.

Muchiri, Mary N., et al. "Importing Composition: Teaching and Researching Academic Writing Beyond North America." *CCC*, vol. 46, no. 2, 1995, pp. 175–198, doi.org/10.2307/358427.

Ofer, Gur. "Miracle of NES: The Foundations of Modern Economics in Russia." *New Economic School*, 2012, last updated 16 Jan. 2015, documents.mx/documents/the-miracle-of-nes-the-foundations-of-modern-economics-in-russia.html.

Office of the President of the Russian Federation. "Указ Президента Российской Федерации от 7 мая 2012 г. N 599 'О мерах по реализации государственной политики в области образования и науки'" ["Presidential Decree on Methods to Realize Government Policies in Education and Research"]. *Российская газета* [*Russian Newspaper*], 9 May 2012, http://rg.ru/2012/05/09/nauka-dok.html. Accessed 21 May 2016.

Peoples, Peg. "Empowering Students Through Language and Critical Thinking: The Bard College Language and Thinking Program." *Voprosy obrazovaniya / Educational Studies*, vol. 4, 2015, pp. 116–131, doi.org/10.17323/1814-9545-2015-4-116-131.

Platt, Kevin. "The Post-Soviet Is Over: On Reading the Ruins." *Republics of Letters: A Journal for the Study of Knowledge, Politics, and the Arts*, vol. 1, no. 1, May 2009, rofl.stanford.edu/node/41.

Prutskova, Yelena. "Civic Effects of Higher Education in Russia: The Impact of Educational Programs." *Higher Education in Russia and Beyond: Challenges for Student Experience in Russia and Eastern Europe*, vol. 1, no. 3, 2015, pp. 14–15, herb.hse.ru/en/2015-1(3)/141967418.html.

"Russia." *Freedom House.* Country Report: Freedom of the Press, 2015, freedomhouse.org/report/freedom-press/2015/russia.

"Russia's Powerful Media Bubble." *Background Briefing with Ian Masters*, narrated by Ian Masters and featuring Kevin Platt, KPFK, Los Angeles, 20 Mar. 2014, http://archives.ianmasters.com/content/march-20-russias-powerful-media-bubble-vermonters-push-public-bank-latest-outrageous-corpora.

Schleifer, Roland, et al. "Под строгим взглядом Ломоносова: учебная сессия по развитию академического письма в России" ["Under Lomonosov's Watchful Gaze: A Case Study of an Early Faculty Development Writing Workshop in Russia."] *Сопоставительная лингвистика* [*Contrastive Linguistics*], vol. 5, 2016, pp. 298–309, https://bit.ly/3hhAxkz.

Shevtsova, Lilia. *Interregnum: Russia Between Past and Future.* Carnegie Endowment for International Peace, 2014, carnegie.ru/2014/05/13/interregnum-russia-between-past-and-future-pub-55578.

Shuster, Simon. "Putin's Ph.D.: Can a Plagiarism Probe Upend Russian Politics?" *Time: World*, 28 Feb. 2013, world.time.com/2013/02/28/putins-phd-can-a-plagiarism-probe-upend-russian-politics/

Squires, Ashley. "The NES Writing and Communication Center: The Case for Student-Oriented Writing Centers in Russia." *Высшее образование в России*, vol. 8–9, 2016, pp. 66–73, www.ashleysquires.com/wp-content/uploads/2016/04/Squires-Центр-письменной-и-устной-коммуникации.pdf.

Thaiss, C., et al. *Writing Programs Worldwide: Profiles of Academic Writing in Many Places.* Parlor Press, 2012.

Wan, Amy J. *Producing Good Citizens: Literacy Training in Anxious Times.* University of Pittsburgh Press, 2014.

West, Richard, and Elena Frumina. "European Standards in Russian Higher Education and the Role of English: A Case Study of the National University of Science and Technology, Moscow (MISiS)." *European Journal of Education*, vol. 47, no. 1, 2012, pp. 50–63, doi.org/10.1111/j.1465-3435.2011.01507.x.

Yurevich, Andrei V. "The Phenomenon of Freedom in Contemporary Russia." *Russian Social Science Review*, vol. 54, no. 6, 2013, pp. 69–87.

Zajda, Joseph. "Reforms in the Higher Education in the Russian Federation: Implications for Equality and Social Justice." *European Education*, vol. 39, no. 2, Summer 2007, pp. 20–36, doi.org/10.2753/eue1056-4934390201.

Zenkin, Sergei. "Специфика академического плагиата." *Plagiarism in Science Russian Sociological Review*, vol. 13, no. 3, 2014, pp. 193–196. Materials from the Round Table Held in the Russian State University for the Humanities, 11 June 2014.

2
WHOSE WPA?
Collaborative Transnational Development of Writing Programs

Susan V. Meyers and María de Lourdes Caudillo Zambrano

Several Mexican universities have recently begun to develop academic literacy in higher education, showing concern for the way that students can improve reading and writing skills in academic disciplinary contexts (Carlino; Albarrán et al.). Similarly, many Mexican researchers have begun inquiring into different aspects of academic literacy, such as "b-learning" environments, pedagogical models, and the relationship between critical thinking and writing (Albarrán et al.; Hernández-Rojas et al.; Hernández Zamora et al.). These initiatives had generated spaces for shared good practices and research in academic networks like the "Written Culture and Discursive Communities Network" (Red de Cultura Escrita y Comunidades Discursivas). Nevertheless, in only a few cases have these efforts been integrated into institutional writing projects across curriculum, and many institutions continue to treat students' needs in remedial courses that are typically disassociated from real literacy practices. Structures like writing programs and writing centers are practically nonexistent in Mexico and throughout the Latin American higher education context in general (Carrasco and Hernández; Carlino; Galán Vélez and Ormsby). As Mexico, among other Latin American nations, looks toward addressing this gap, many institutions are looking outward for models and collegial collaborations—though the shape of such working relationships has yet to be determined, especially in important but highly politicized contexts like the United States and Mexico—particularly since the 2016 US presidential election.

First steps have been taken through our recent binational collaboration in which faculty from a US university and a Mexican university conducted a research project on both of their campuses to develop a model for a Mexico-based writing program. In this way, our project attends to gaps in the literature—and in practice—on both sides of the border. First, in conjunction with this anthology, our project presses

DOI: 10.7330/9781646421237.c002

forward the interest that US-based compositionists have increasingly expressed interest in international contexts (Bazerman; Donahue; Thaiss et al.). Second, this focus likewise attends to a specific gap in the literature and practice on the Mexican side of the border as interest in writing-based courses as such has developed only recently. Jointly, both authors addressed the key question of how WPAs can collaborate with international colleagues to build and design programs—and to help programs in the United States revisit and possibly revise their own practices. Implicit in this line of inquiry are deeper questions about the nature of knowledge transfer in an international context. Through the process of a year-long, action-research project that took place on both sides of the border, we considered these questions, as we have attended to issues both of how these programs can be shaped in Mexico, and how such international relationships can be formed in order to reach goals at both institutions.

The findings from this project also include insights that will be significant to other Mexican and Latin American institutions that wish to establish writing programs, as well as for further binational collaborating teams involved in the development of such programs. Specifically, in contrast to the general education–driven context of the United States, which focuses on a combination of First-Year Composition (FYC) and WAC/WID, the specific needs/model of Mexican universities like the Universidad Iberoamericana in Mexico City cause us to refocus our attention on a model that relates more to expertise being shared outward from individual disciplines and departments and moving toward a consensus model for teaching writing across a campus, as opposed to a central department (like an English department) that stewards such work on a campus. Further, this nuanced model also helps us to reframe our understanding of the movement of information and expertise within the shared knowledge economy in which we now find ourselves. This reframed understanding of knowledge/expertise highlights the way information circulated through hybrid "third spaces" can be adopted and repurposed, more accurately representing the real flow of ideas/information in an overlapping political/economic space, like Mexico and the United States today. As such, it stands to help improve relationships between the two countries, especially in/through higher education. Finally, this frame of "expertise in specific contexts" spread collaboratively *across* contexts also provides a model for international collaboration because it can encourage participants to share information freely without holding on to expectations about how it will be used. For instance, when Dr. Caudillo Zambrano first approached

Dr. Meyers about this project, Dr. Meyers agreed, though warily, because she was concerned about sharing information about writing programs in a way that would be overly authoritative or top-down. (Indeed, the inherently politicized context of writing instruction has been noted by other authors in this volume. In particular, see Olga Aksakalova's "Literacy and Civic Engagement in a Transnational WPA Practice: The Case of Russia" and James P. Austin's "An Oasis of Civic Engagement? Considering Critical Dispositions Developed Within the American University in Cairo.") However, it turned out that the project itself was most successful when each of us shared freely with each other from the relative areas of expertise that we have—and listened accordingly. (See also Patricia M. Dyer's and Tara E. Friedman's discussion of US–Latin American collaborations in this volume, "Service Learning as an Agent of Local Change and Global Social Change: Building Civic Engagement in Central America through Literacy and Sustainability.") Further, we were helped by the fact that, due to the good fortune of available funding, we were able to visit each other's campuses and engage in sustained conversations with each other's colleagues, leading to more brainstorming and cross-pollination of expertise. In the end, we were able to develop a suitable model for the Universidad Iberoamericana, inspired by our conversations—and particularly by Dr. Caudillo Zambrano's observations at Seattle University—but still specific and suitable for its own context.

SHARED VALUES, DIFFERENT OUTCOMES: COMPARISONS BETWEEN THE UNIVERSIDAD IBEROAMERICANA AND SEATTLE UNIVERSITY

Part of the success of our project relates both to the nature of our collegial relationship and to a consensus of values between our two home institutions: Seattle University (SU) in Seattle, Washington, and the Universidad Iberoamericana (Ibero) in Mexico City. Our collaboration began when we met briefly at an academic lecture in Mexico City in late 2014. A few months later, while planning her upcoming sabbatical, Dr. Caudillo Zambrano reached out to Dr. Meyers to seek institutional support at Seattle University for a study that she wanted to do on US-based writing programs. Dr. Meyers secured her a courtesy faculty appointment, and Dr. Caudillo Zambrano came to Seattle in the fall of 2015 in order to spend her sabbatical observing composition classes, conducting interviews with writing faculty, and reading related background texts from the field of rhetoric and composition. Her goal was to gather enough information from this context to help her home institution develop a structure for its own writing program. Throughout this work, the two of us—both keenly interested in cross-cultural and comparative perspectives—became quite intellectually connected, and we decided to extend our work together into a more formal study of international collaborations related to building writing programs. Therefore, after Dr. Caudillo Zambrano returned home, she hosted Dr. Meyers on her campus in June 2016 in order to extend the conversations. We also benefited from both of our universities being Jesuit and thus sharing some educational values and common learning objectives, such as social justice, education of the whole person, and reflection. These points of underlying pedagogical commonality were useful, though there were certainly many points of difference as well. What our shared value systems did allow us, though, was an agreed upon value in writing curriculum that is both practical and critically minded, such that it prepares students to write meaningfully for the real-world professional and civic contexts in which they will find themselves after graduation (Kirsch).

The most significant difference is the shaping and placement of writing courses at the two universities. On the one hand, a foundation of Seattle University's general education curriculum is a first-year writing course called the Academic Writing Seminar. Thereafter, at higher levels of general education classes, students take courses within the disciplines that engage them in extended writing projects. In addition, Seattle University has a robust writing center that has historically held a strong tie to WAC/WID initiatives on campus—although the recent retirements of the WAC/WID faculty leader and the Writing Center director have created some instability in writing leadership on campus, making the present project useful to Seattle University as it provides a means of carefully considering our current structures. In contrast, writing and communication skills are handed across a more diverse set of courses.

CURRICULUM COMPARISON

In this decentralized structure, it is common for instructors of the course to feel unclear about expectations. This lack of coherence to the curriculum—in terms of both content and structure—constitutes one of the central reasons that Ibero sought collaboration with its sister institution, Seattle University, to explore options for developing a more solidified writing program.

Given the fact that our goal was to draw on comparative analysis to help inform Ibero's needs and projects, it was important for us to

Table 2.1. Curriculum comparison

	Seattle University	Universidad Iberoamericana
Common Learning / General Competencies	Common Learning Objectives in the Core: -Jesuit, Catholic, and intellectual tradition -Disciplinary knowledge and integrative learning -Communication -Global engagement	General Competencies: -Oral and written communication -Thought leadership -Teamwork -Creativity and innovation -Whole humanist commitment -Discernment and responsibility
Communication	Communication Learning Objective: Students will be able to communicate effectively in a variety of genres and for different audiences and purposes through writing, speaking, and visual expression. (SU, Course Descriptions and Guidelines University Core Curriculum, Fall 2013)	Oral and Written Communication General Competencies: The capacity to express ideas and feelings in oral and written form, to interact with clarity and veracity (veracidad) (Universidad Iberoamericana)
Mandatory courses to develop Communication	-Academic writing seminar -Core courses (general education) -Capstone course (WAC and WID Model)	-Oral and written communication course (COE Course), with five different versions, tailored for different programmatic undergraduate areas. The current policies surrounding the course are general and do not, for instance, include specific learning outcomes. (Remedial Model)
Other relevant curricular features		University reflection area: -Four mandatory courses focus on Jesuit aspects of the university's pedagogical focus: "Person and Humanism," "History and Society," "Transcendence," and "Person and Praxis." Synthesis and evaluation curriculum area: -Three mandatory courses related directly with the discipline or profession.

adopt a careful and appropriate methodology: one that allows for the sharing of ideas without the expectation that an entity like Ibero would adopt a model like Seattle University's wholesale. As we considered how aspects of the US-based composition field (and its related writing programs) could be used to inform these conversations, it was important for us to keep in mind the particular material history of the composition discipline within the United States because the specific ways that composition studies has been shaped in the United States has related to key developments in higher education in this context, as well. Moreover, other comparative perspectives are likewise available now. For instance, there have been some interesting initiatives to develop more integrated literacy models in Argentina, Brazil, and Colombia (Moyano and Natale; Motta-Roth; Narváez; Carlino), and, more recently, in Mexico (Galán Vélez and Ormsby). These initiatives were inspired by WAC and WID models from the United States, and these efforts are trying to focus the teaching of reading and writing not on remedial actions like spelling and grammar but rather on truly integrated curriculum with real impact on disciplines across the curriculum. However, only a few of these projects have institutional support and/or are a part of institutional policies. Two relevant examples include a writing center at a Mexican university based on the North American Model (Galán Vélez and Ormsby; Carlino) and a faculty development program in Argentina that promotes longitudinal teacher training for the integration of the teaching or writing across courses. This latter model is based on a collaborative interdisciplinary team structure with membership among both writing instructors and other professors in their disciplines (Moyano and Natale).

A common feature among current initiatives—both those with and without institutional support—is the fact that they are driven by faculty of different disciplines (such as humanities, social sciences, and sciences) rather than by writing professors. Because higher education curriculum in Latin America normally doesn't have a general education area, there does not tend to be a centralized location for such writing courses on campus. Nevertheless, these curricular characteristics constitute "fertile ground" for the development of writing programs, perhaps particularly along the line of a Writing in the Disciplines model. For example, the University of Buenos Aires developed a related initiative more than a decade ago, called the Group for Inclusion and Quality Education by Taking Care of Reading and Writing in all Subjects, that is a multidisciplinary team comprised of pedagogues, linguists, psychologists, biologists, and math teachers (GICEOLEM). Other relevant examples include the literacy program across the university (PRODEAC) designed at the Universidad Nacional General de Sarmiento in Argentina (Moyano and Natale); the interinstitutional research project promoted by the Colombian Department of Science (Narváez); and the research initiatives about genre, discourse theory, and multiliteracies developed in the Brazilian National Council for Scientific and Technological Development (Motta-Roth). These various nuances cast important questions about the development of further writing programs in Latin America.

THEORY AND METHOD: HOW TO APPROACH BINATIONAL COLLABORATIONS

Scholars affiliated with composition studies in the United States and the United Kingdom have made valuable contributions to our understanding of literacy and how it works and changes in the context of nation states. Of particular relevance to our project are Brian Street's theories of literacy, particularly his belief that literacy is deeply tied to ideology and does *not*, as is so often assumed, function as a neutral, unchanging entity. Further, US scholar Deborah Brandt argues that "literacy sponsors" are ideologically charged institutions that change over time. For instance, the contributions of literacy scholars to the foundations of our project include the significance not only of resisting the temptation to move a model wholesale from one context to another but also the reminder that contexts themselves are constantly shifting. Therefore, we need to be looking at literacy, including writing programs, as living, breathing entities. As the field of composition studies has expanded to a consideration of literacy in international contexts, scholars like Kate Vieira have likewise helped us to expand our notion of how knowledge—and literacy—are affected by movement across international borders. In Vieira's research, literacy and information become dynamic goods that shift purpose as they shift context and often become liberatory in the process, especially for communities like immigrants ("American by Paper"; "On the Social Consequences of Literacy"). Similarly, migration scholar Roger Waldinger argues that transnationalism is not the experience of belonging to one place or another but rather to both places simultaneously. In a very real way, he argues, they become citizens of a provisional "third space." This third space is neither legitimate nor illegitimate; rather, it reflects the reality of these people themselves. Similarly, as we consider means of collaborating across national borders to build writing programs, it is important to think about not only comparing and/or adapting to contexts but also to thinking about how information—and information transfer—function within this third context in which we find ourselves as shared members of a functional shared economic structure. In this way, all written forms become part of a greater knowledge economy that exists between the two nations.

Action-Based Methodology

Given the potential for political—and possibly transformative—impacts of our work, we were mindful of choosing a methodology in line with our shared values around civic engagement (Crabtree and Sapp).

Further, because this project focused both on research into the nature of international collaborations and on developing the proposal for a program on the Iberoamericana campus, an action-based methodology was the most appropriate approach. (For further discussions of this approach, see Adela C. Licona's and Stephen T. Russell's "Reflections on an Emergent Entremundista Pedagogy: Teacher-Researchers in Engaged Transdisciplinary Public Scholarship" in this volume.) Action-based research has been shown to be valuable for both the extensiveness of data gathered, as well as its resistance to the traditional hierarchy that can emerge in research dynamics (Henning et al.; Juergensmeyer). Indeed, in certain contexts like ours, its mindfulness toward action can even initiate a form of civic engagement for faculty themselves, as it becomes a form of "service learning" for these faculty members (Lorimer and Stock).

In our case, our action research approach involved site visits to both of our campuses, based on travel availability. In the case of Dr. Caudillo Zambrano, the visit to Seattle University was for six months during the second half of 2015 (with a one-month follow-up in spring of 2016) as it constituted her sabbatical time. For Dr. Meyers, the visit was briefer—just two weeks during June 2016—though Dr. Meyers had previously traveled to Mexico City several times for academic projects and therefore was able to transition quickly into the culture of the Iberoamericana campus. Without this preexisting familiarity, US faculty members could still make effective trips to Mexico, though they may require more and longer visits. In addition, this methodological approach attended to our two principal project goals. First, we sought to identify needs on the Iberoamericana campus with respect to academic writing. This goal focused on defining the steps of building a writing program at Ibero and identifying common steps for building academic writing programs in the Mexican context overall. Second, we aimed to develop a model for creating international collaborative partnerships focused on writing program development and innovation. This work included both participant observation during programmed components of each site visit as well as more traditional data collection.

In the first mode, participant observation, each of us participated in professional development workshops and meetings of faculty who teach writing-related classes at Seattle University and the Universidad Iberoamericana. Attending faculty-driven workshops and meetings on each other's campuses allowed us both to immerse ourselves directly into the kinds of conversations that characterize each campus and gave us each a means of creating collegial relationships with international colleagues working in a parallel area. In addition to these participatory activities, during her time at the Universidad Iberoamericana, Dr. Meyers also gave a total of five presentations and workshops to introduce faculty to the history and central theories of the field of composition and rhetoric as it exists in the United States. Ibero faculty members' responses and questions during and after these activities likewise served as a channel for insight and analysis related to our research project.

In terms of traditional data gathering techniques, we used both ethnographic field techniques and review of institutional documents and pedagogical materials. First, a total of seventeen semi-structured interviews were conducted with faculty members in both Seattle and Mexico City. In Seattle, six of twelve total composition instructors were interviewed about their experience teaching the Academic Writing Seminar, Seattle University's required first-year writing class. In Mexico City, eleven of twenty-one faculty teaching the course "Oral and Written Communication" were interviewed about their teaching experience and pedagogical approaches. In both cases, interview questions included twenty items organized into three general areas: personal goals and course content, general curriculum, and best practices of teaching and learning (appendix 2.B). All interviews were conducted in the interviewee's native language, and they focused on a comparison of teaching writing practices in both contexts for the purpose of informing the development of a writing program at the Universidad Iberoamericana. The results of these interviews were coded using the Analysis of Free Texts approach (Fernández Núñez; Ryan and Bernard), along with Constant Comparison Analysis (Glaser and Strauss). Through this method we identified several categories, including the following, which were the most salient:

- Institutional writing goals
- Curriculum model
- Teaching-learning outcomes
- Teaching practices in composition pedagogy and learning evaluation

In addition, six Academic Writing Seminar classes were observed by Dr. Caudillo Zambrano as part of her visit to the Seattle University campus. Finally, beyond these interviews and observations, institutional documents and pedagogical materials were reviewed and analyzed. These materials, generated by professors from both universities, constituted both contextual information and direct evidence of assumptions about and approaches to the teaching of writing.

FINDINGS AND POSSIBILITIES FOR FUTURE WORK

Broadly, we have gained insight into important factors at the national, institutional, and instructional levels. At the national level, two significant structural differences have implications for the shapes and possibilities for writing programs in each context. First, higher education admissions processes are different between the two nations. For instance, as several faculty and administrators at Ibero pointed out, the way that the standardized college entrance exam is used in Mexico (known as the Examen Nacional de Ingreso a la Educación Superior or National Evaluation Center for Education) does not take into consideration details beyond general knowledge and verbal reasoning. Therefore, universities like Ibero find it difficult to know if incoming students have particular needs, as in the need for a basic writing course to fill in more localized gaps in their academic preparation that may have been left over from secondary school. Second, as is the case at most Latin American universities, Ibero does not have a large general education component to its curriculum. Therefore, as is often the case at Latin American universities, the curriculum at Ibero is more disparately located with no preexisting pathway to draw connections among different areas of curriculum, as is often the case in US general education programs. Therefore, Ibero faculty experience challenges related to how best to deliver writing curriculum. Because there is no overarching general education structure, such as Seattle University's Core Curriculum, wherein both first-year writing and WAC/WID components are embedded, writing courses at Ibero are isolated. Further, there are currently five different versions of the course because writing itself does not have an official "home" at Ibero, as well as the fact that two different departments teach the course for five different types of student groups, as seen in table 2.2.

Moreover, because these courses are not tied explicitly to learning outcomes, instructors are often unclear about course expectations. As our interviews showed, they may feel unsupported, or they may create their own course designs, leading to even looser connections among sections of the same course. This lack of a central focus can also lead to a focus on the more concrete, visible attributes of writing (grammar and mechanics) and concern about remedial aspects rather than more complex critical thinking and rhetorical academic writing. Many Ibero instructors do indeed value rhetorical learning, even if it is not explicitly embedded in the outcomes. However, while this investment exists, it is challenging for COE instructors to fully integrate rhetorical learning, due to the absence of a stated learning outcome that focuses on this area in the curriculum as a whole.

Table 2.2. Writing course ownership and purpose at Ibero University

Course name	Features
Communication Workshop	Designed and taught by Communication Department. Linked to engineering programs.
Oral and Written Communication Oral and Written Communication Workshop Drafting Workshop Narrative Workshop	Designed and taught by Literature Department. Linked to all other undergraduate programs.

More specifically, at the level of individual instructional approaches, we noticed four general patterns:

1. The curriculum built around rhetorical contexts, and the focus is more on students' interest in the United States and on social contexts in Mexico.
2. Both groups of faculty also identified the importance of the writing process. Without question, for instance, all of the instructors who were interviewed believe in the importance of revision.
3. We found more scaffolding of assignments and rubrics in the SU classes, and relatively little of this approach in the Ibero classes, though Ibero instructors did mention a desire to see more connection *among* classes.
4. We found that, at SU, when classes are connected, it is possible to connect more to students' lives, and to help them become more self-actualized and focused on their own lines in inquiry. Ibero would like to strive toward that goal, which is in line with its Jesuit mission.

Finally, beyond these multi-layered insights, drawn from the interviews and institutional document review that we conducted at both institutions, it is important to note the ways that our own participant observation highlighted and deepened some of the patterns described above. Specifically, Dr. Caudillo Zambrano saw that teachers get more opportunities to be creative and proactive and build deeper teaching-learning environments when institutions of higher education (in this case, Seattle University) offer clarity of educational purpose and learning outcomes. In these cases, faculty do not spend as much energy on isolated efforts trying to define their own goals through "trial and error," as some teachers at Ibero attested. She also noticed the positive effect of adopting learning outcomes from the Council for Writing Program Administrators as she noticed how writing instructors at Seattle University used those ideas to structure curriculum that is focused not only on functional skills but also on critical thinking. In particular, she gleaned many useful ideas from her classroom observations at SU that will help her attend to the Jesuit mission on her own campus: using academic writing skills to help promote the "whole person" of the student, increasing students' capacity to think and judge through writing, and using writing to open spaces for reflection on civic engagement.

Further, while in Mexico, Dr. Meyers noticed particularly the alternate approach to sharing expertise. Coming from the US context, with its strong emphasis on WAC and on maintaining expertise in a single department, such as English or writing studies, she has been accustomed to thinking in terms of guiding faculty development across contexts via WAC/WID. But in Mexico, what was evident was the way that a WID approach is strong and more sustainable, and that an approach to expert prose is the predominant mode, fostering a sense of WID across the disciplines. This offers a new way of thinking about how WAC/WID work: WID need not be so siloed. Rather, what happens in Mexico offers a fresh perspective on what we're doing, more like a Writing-Enriched Curriculum (WEC). This is more likely to be the kind of model that works in Mexico, and it may offer US programs—particularly those without formal WAC leadership, as Seattle University has found itself recently—something to rethink about the way they have been doing their work, particularly as WAC programs have been the point of comparison across international contexts so far. This new work is suggesting the need for more consideration of WID, and a reframing thereof—potentially toward increased consideration of how it functions with initiatives such as civic engagement (Kells).

A NEW PROGRAM FOR IBERO—AND RECOMMENDATIONS FOR FUTURE WORK

The Universidad Iberoamericana's goal is to transition from a remedial perspective to a more integrated curricular model based on WAC and WID approaches: one that assumes that all teachers have responsibility for literacy practices in their own courses. Drawing on best practices from the WPA, SU, and other US and Mexican institutions of higher education, Ibero has decided to adopt a new "stretch" model in its curriculum (appendix 2.D). In the United States, this kind of approach typically stretches composition curriculum over additional hours or semesters to accommodate more time for students' learning curves (Glau). At Ibero, this new stretch model will add time to the existing COE course for those students who need it. Typically, students take one COE course, which meets for four hours per week. However, under this new proposal, students identified during the admissions process as needing additional

Table 2.3. Curricular Models Proposal

Curricular Models Proposal					
Writing Level	1 Stretch		2 Basic+ Intermediate		3 Basic+Others
Advanced	Sea-III		Sea-II	Sea-III	Sea-III
Intermediate	Ura (4 Courses)	Sea-II	Owc-Intermediate		Ura (4 Courses) Sea-II
Basic	Owc Owc Stretch		Owc-Basic		Owc-Basic

writing assistance will take the stretch version of the course, adding two additional hours of contact time per week. At the same time, learning goals will remain uniform between the traditional versus stretch sections of COE so the new stretch courses will not slip into a remedial category. Further, Ibero's new stretch model will also require students to continue taking writing curriculum integrated at intermediate and advanced levels, first through a course in the University Reflection Area (ARU) and next through two courses in the Synthesis and Evaluation Area (ASE1 y ASE2), the latter of which constitute the capstone courses across Ibero's undergraduate curriculum.

In addition, two other models were also considered: one that proposed to add a basic writing course and another that proposed the addition of both a basic and advanced writing course.

However, the committee reviewing the three proposals felt that the stretch model would best meet Ibero's needs because it is a simple and efficient pedagogical model that attends to and solves the problems related to the current "remedial" Spanish course. Further, it allows students to practice different writing levels across the curriculum, depending on their own learning needs—and potentially to identify the more liberatory aspects of academic writing, as a form of preparation for future civic engagement (Taylor). Finally, this model provides enough curricular space to develop writing-enriched curriculum at the other two levels, thereby bringing Ibero's new curriculum into alignment with many of the goals of WAC/WID theories. All the same, while pedagogical leaders at the Universidad Iberoamericana are pleased with this newly designed model for writing curriculum and plan to begin implementing it in January 2017, they are still aware of related ongoing needs, such as the need to review the university's admission process in a way that will provide more diagnostic insight into the writing needs of newly admitted students, as well as the need to fully support those students once they arrive, as through the creation of auxiliary services like a writing center.

Beyond these specific successes related to the development and adoption of a new writing program model at the Universidad Iberoamericana, this project has also resulted in general lessons for other pairs of binational colleagues who wish to collaborate in similar ways. Two of the most important lessons include recognition both of the need for any newly developed writing program to include adequate support for all stakeholders—including both students *and* faculty—and of the need for multiple players to be involved in the process of building a new kind of writing culture in a given area. First, whereas Ibero's initial goal was simply to develop a new curricular approach to organize and better define its existing courses, the process of conducting this project expanded interest on the Ibero campus to the development of coursework innovations and of professional support (e.g., WAC/WID workshops) and a writing center for student support. Writing centers in particular were nowhere in Ibero's initial set of plans, and an interest in professional training increased significantly as a result of this project. In both cases, the interest in support mechanisms in addition to curriculum development itself was both influenced and supported by peer institutions in Mexico. For instance, due to a set of workshops offered on the Ibero campus in June 2016, colleagues from across various campuses in Mexico City learned of each other's early initiatives in the development of writing centers. And while the development of a writing center from the ground up can be a challenging task in a context where training in writing center pedagogy isn't immediately available, networking and sharing models and resources is likely to aid multiple institutions in Mexico City in the development of their own centers. In this way, the development of a much broader "culture of writing" throughout the city—and eventually throughout the country—is perhaps the most necessary foundation for the development of Mexican university writing programs, particularly as Mexico's own version of the field of composition and rhetoric develops out of these increasing cross-institutional collaborations among both Mexican and non-Mexican university partners.

A further pair of important findings from this project relate to the goals and shapes of the kinds of programs that are likely to develop in this context of Mexico's developing writing culture. First, as we have considered the best means of shaping a program at Ibero, it has been important for us to recognize the contrasting ways that outcomes get developed in cultural contexts. Second, with respect to the shape of programs that can be built off of these outcomes, one of the most important insights of this project is the way in which the Mexican context necessitates a shift in orientation toward WAC and WID. Whereas the US context often favors an intersection between these two modalities, the Mexican context—particularly as is becoming increasingly evident on the Ibero campus—weighs more heavily in the direction of WID in the sense that, without a general education requirement with a composition component, such as most US universities have and, moreover, without a specific academic discipline focused on the delivery of such courses, Mexican institutions of higher education are more steadfastly focused on faculty from across disciplines being involved in the teaching of written communication skills. On the Ibero campus, for instance, faculty who are most heavily involved in the Oral and Written Communication courses come from a variety of disciplines. So, rather than a WAC-oriented initiative being stewarded by a composition expert, the developing program will be built by colleagues in an interdisciplinary fashion. In this way, they are engaging in the use of best practices related to writing in their own disciplines and are working together across campus. They are drawing *from* disciplinary expertise in order to create a network *across* campus. This model uses expertise from various contexts (that is, academic disciplines, national contexts, and so forth) as a means of deepening and organizing programs and best practices, and it is an alternate approach that perhaps American scholars and teachers could learn from as we continue to consider the shape of our programs in the context of increasing transnational contexts.

RECOMMENDATIONS FOR BUILDING BILATERAL COLLABORATIVE PARTNERSHIPS

Finally, beyond these specific outcomes toward the development of a writing program at the Universidad Iberoamericana, this project has informed several procedural recommendations for other collaborative partners who wish to engage in this kind of binational project. First, although we recognize the necessary tie to a resource base for travel costs, we do believe that, whenever possible, international collaborative projects should include contact with colleagues on both campuses and in both countries. Ideally, these interactions should be conducted in person in order to help build a trusting bilateral, collegial relationship; to allow both parties to fully engage with and learn about the other's context; and to help facilitate deeper, more extended and generative conversations. However, when funding or other dynamics prohibit travel, Skype is a strong secondary means of achieving this kind of connection. Regardless of the connection type, however, it is important for bilateral connection to occur fully and authentically in order to avoid an unequal power dynamic. In our case, a strong personal and intellectual connection, a shared set of educational values, and a mutual need for exploration into the conditions of writing programs on both of our campuses helped to create a deep and sustained connection that made us both invested in the project and trusting of each other's judgment, insights, and integrity.

Second, because travel is costly, it is helpful to have a representative faculty member do initial research and then return to work directly with colleagues on the home campus to make changes and updates. Third, US consultants who are trying to help should be willing to provide information directly, without worrying about being too "top-down." Indeed, in a shared knowledge economy, it is important to keep in mind that information does not "belong" to one entity. Rather, it takes on meaning and utility as it is shared and circulated, so it is best for each participant to offer information openly and to trust that it will be used—or discarded—as is most useful. Finally, an additional strategy that is quite helpful for ongoing connection is the direct collaboration between two (or more) instructors from the two different nations. In our case, this work is being achieved first through course-based online interactions that get students from paired courses in the United States and Mexico involved in curricular activities and second, through an ongoing research collaboration between two faculty members.

APPENDIX 2.A

HIGHER EDUCATION EXAM STATISTICS FROM MEXICO

According to the *EXHALING (Examen de Habilidades Lingüísticas)* diagnostic exam given to incoming students at universities throughout Mexico City in 2011, more than 50 percent of students obtained a test result that was at or below medium (table 2.4).

Results of the EXHALING exam vary significantly by institution (table 2.5).

Table 2.4. Proportion of students by level that passed or did not pass the exam (González Robles 82)

Ability	Levels below Passing			Levels above the Minimum		
	Deficient	Medium	Median	Medium High	High	Total
Auditory Comprehension	12.5%	44.6%	65.14	29.0%	13.8%	100%
Reading Comprehension	16.7%	36.5%	54.33	26.7%	20.1%	100%
Linguistic Knowledge	12.4%	39.5%	49.84	30.3%	17.9%	100%
Writing	16.4%	35.3%	49.57	35.2%	13.1%	100%

Table 2.5. Differences among average scores by institution (Obdulia, et al. 93)

IES	N	Tukey-Subconjunto para alfa = 0.05				
		1	2	3	4	5
TESE	500	48.4285				
UIC	154		51.8165			
UPN	344		52.5003			
UAM	759		52.8747			
Anáhuac	578			54.8569		
UIA	527			54.8972		
INBA	235			56.0245	56.0245	
UNAM	919			56.1287	56.1287	
ENAH	201				56.9328	
CIDE	58					62.1986
ITAM	76					62.4938
Md=54.15						

APPENDIX 2.B

INTERVIEW QUESTIONS FOR SEATTLE UNIVERSITY WRITING INSTRUCTORS
QUESTIONS

Goals and content of the Academic Writing Seminar (AWS) at SU, and goals and contents in your own course:
1. Describe in your own words the main goals of your course.
2. In your opinion, how do these goals correspond with general AWS objectives and with SU's mission to develop the whole person through reading and writing knowledge in multiple social contexts?

Curriculum:
3. Do students arrive in your course with the necessary knowledge and skills? If not, what previous work, content, courses, etc., could be missing, in your opinion?
4. Do you agree with the existence of a first-year composition requirement in undergraduate programs? Why?
5. What is your opinion about the current AWS curricular model? Specifically, is the Academic Writing Seminar too broad or too narrow to help students develop writing skills in multiple social contexts?
6. If you had the opportunity to build an undergraduate curriculum (including the core curriculum), what would you do or change to improve academic skills for critical reading and writing (e.g., change the writing seminar content or length, add links among courses across the curriculum, add methods, alter assessment, etc.)?

Teaching and Learning: Good Practices and Challenges:
7. For how long have you been a writing instructor?
8. Why do you like to teach reading and writing skills?
9. In your experience, what kind of academic work arouses students' interest in reading and writing?
10. What is the most important kind of learning that your students do in your course? (Please name two or three distinct skills and/or areas of knowledge.)
11. Can you name some meaningful teaching practices that relate to these important learning outcomes?
12. What kind of learning activities work best in your classes: questions about readings, internships, the presence of writers in class, portfolios, peer review, small groups, workshops, etc.?
13. How do you teach for transfer?

14. Do you use teaching materials made by yourself or by others (e.g., rubrics, frameworks, exercises, etc.) that help improve critical reading and writing?
15. Have you identified levels among students (i.e., differences among novice and expert students)? If yes, could you describe some of these features?
16. In your experience, what is the biggest challenge for writing teachers?
17. Regarding faculty development, what kind of resources are most helpful for improving teaching practices (e.g., faculty workshops related to the Academic Writing Seminar, academic activities to improve teaching and/or update oneself in their discipline or profession, other sources)?
18. Do you recommend any specific practices or instruments for evaluating learning outcomes, either during or at the end of a course?
19. In your experience, what would be a good practice for an institutional assessment project aimed at getting relevant information for learning outcomes in writing skills?

About the Writing Center (Learning Commons Partnership):
20. How does this work for you and for your students? Is it a relevant form of learning support? What do you recommend to improve their services?

APPENDIX 2.C

INTERVIEW QUESTIONS FOR WRITING INSTRUCTORS AT THE UNIVERSIDAD IBEROAMERICANA

GUÍA DE ENTREVISTA PARA PROFESORES DE LAS MATERIAS DE COMUNICACIÓN ORAL Y ESCRITA

Universidad Iberoamericana, Ciudad de México. Febrero de 2016.

PREGUNTAS

Objetivos y Contenido:
- Describa en sus propias palabras los principales objetivos de su curso.
- Relación de los mismos con pensamiento crítico y argumentación.

Curriculum:
- ¿Llegan los estudiantes con el nivel requerido (conocimientos y habilidades)?
- ¿En caso de que no, qué trabajo previo, contenidos, cursos, etc. haría falta en su opinión (Remedial)?
- ¿Considera útiles, pertinentes estos cursos de 1er año sobre escritura? ¿Por que?
- ¿Qué observaciones tiene sobre el contenido de la material, qué funciona, qué hace falta?
- ¿Si tuviera la oportunidad de construir un programa de licenciatura para desarrollar la escritura, qué sugeriría (contenidos del taller, vinculación entre asignturas, etc.)?

Cuál es su percepción sobre:
- La relación entre la capacidad de argumentación y el ejercicio de escritura y lectura académica.
- La relación entre el pensamiento crítico y el ejercicio de escritura y lectura académica.
- Cuál es su experiencia sobre:
  - El nivel académico de los alumnos al ingreso y su experiencia sobre el actual curso remedial de español.
  - El que la escritura académica actualmente está enmarcado en una asignatura en el plan de estudios.

Enseñanza y Aprendizaje: Buenas Prácticas y Retos
1. ¿Por qué le gusta enseñar escritura y lectura?
2. ¿Qué tipo de actividades académicas despiertan el interés y mejoran el nivel de lectura y escritura de los universitarios?

3. ¿Cuál es el aprendizaje más importante que sus estudiantes deben adquirir, según usted?
4. ¿Recuerda alguna práctica de enseñanza representativa, relacionada con este aprendizaje?
5. ¿Qué actividades funcionan mejor en su clase?
6. ¿Considera que usted enseña para la transferencia?
7. ¿Utiliza algún material (por ejemplo rúbricas de evaluación) diseñados por usted o por otro profesor?
8. ¿Ha identificado niveles de aprendizaje, diferencias entre novatos y expertos, ¿podría describir esas características?
9. ¿Cuál considera que es el mayor reto para los profesores de escritura?
10. ¿Sobre la formación docente: ¿qué tipo de apoyo le resulta de utilidad para mejorar su práctica docente (por ejemplo, talleres, jornadas académicas, etc.)?
11. ¿Recomienda algunas prácticas e instrumentos para la evaluación de los niveles de logro de los alumnos?

APPENDIX 2.D

CURRICULAR PROPOSALS FOR A WRITING PROGRAM AT THE UNIVERSIDAD IBEROAMERICANA

Table 2.6. Proposed stretch curricular model at the Universidad Iberoamericana

Writing Level	Model 1 COE Stretch	
Advanced	ASE3	
Intermediate	ASE2 or equivalent	Aru
Basic	COE	
	COE Stretch	

Table 2.7. Proposed "basic + intermediate" curricular model at the Universidad Iberoamericana

Writing level	Model 2 COE basic+ intermediate	
Advanced	ASE2 or equivalent	ASE3
Intermediate	COE intermediate	
Basic	COE-basic	

Table 2.8. Proposed "basic writing" curricular model at the Universidad Iberoamericana

Writing Level	Model 3 COE Basic	
Advanced	ASE3	
Intermediate	ARU	ASE2
Basic	COE basic	

WORKS CITED

Albarrán, Claudia, et al. "Memoria del III seminario internacional de lectura en la universidad. II Congreso nacional de expresiones de cultura escrita en instituciones de educación superior; IV Seminario internacional de cultura escrita y actores sociales." Evento de la Red de Cultura Escrita y Comunidades Discursivas, Consejo Puebla de Lectura, México, 2012. Address.

Bazerman, Charles, ed. *International Advances in Writing Research: Cultures, Places, Measures.* Parlor Press, 2012.

Brandt, Deborah. *Literacy in American Lives.* Cambridge University Press, 2001.

Carlino, Paula. "Who Takes Care of Writing in Latin American and Spanish Universities?" edited by C. Thaiss et al., *Writing Programs Worldwide: Profiles of Academic Writing in Many Places*, The WAC Clearinghouse, 2012, pp. 485–498, http://wac.colostate.edu/books/wpww/chapter41.pdf.

Carrasco, A., and K. González Hernández. "Dificultades de escritura entre estudiantes universitarios." *XI Congreso Nacional de Investigación Educativa / 5. Educación y Conocimientos Disciplinares / Ponencia*, 2013.

Crabtree, Robbin, and David Alan Sapp. "Technical Communication, Participatory Action Research, and Global Civic Engagement: A Teaching Research and Social Action Collaboration in Kenya." *Reflections: A Journal of Writing, Service-Learning, and Community Literacy*, vol. 4, no. 2, 2005, pp. 9–33.

Donahue, C. "'Internationalization' and Composition Studies: Reorienting the Discourse." *College Composition and Communication*, 2009, pp. 212–243.

Fernández Núñez, L. "¿Cómo analizar datos cualitativos?" *Butlletí LaRecerca*. Universitat de Barcelona Institut de Ciències de l'Educació, 7 Oct. 2006.

Galán Vélez, Rosa Margarita, and Lilyth Ormsby Jenkins. "El centro de escritura como puente en la educación superior: El Centro de Aprendizaje, Redacción y Lenguas del ITAM." *Memorias del II Seminario Internacional de Lectura y Escritura en la Universidad*, edited by Guadalupe Ruiz Cuellar et al., *Universidad Autónoma de Aguas Calientes*, 2010.

GICEOLEM. *Grupo Para la Inclusión y Calidad Educativas a Través de Ocuparnos de la Lectura y la Escritura en Todas las Materias.* 2010, https://sites.google.com/site/giceolem2010/.

Glaser, Barney, and Anselm Strauss. *The Discovery of Grounded Theory: Strategies for Qualitative Research.* Aldine, 1967.

Glau, Gregory. "'Stretch at 10': A Progress Report on Arizona State University's Stretch Program." *Journal of Basic Writing*, 2007, pp. 30–48.

González Robles, Rosa Obdulia, editor. Habilidades lingüísticas de los estudiantes de primer ingreso a las instituciones de educación superior del área metropolitana de la Ciudad de México. Asociación Nacional de Universidades e Instituciones de Educación Superior (ANUIES), Consejo Regional del Área Metropolitana (CRAM), Ciudad de México, 2014.

Henning, John E., Jody M. Stone, and James L. Kelly. *Using Action Research to Improve Instruction: An Interactive Guide for Teachers.* Routledge, 2009.

Hernández-Rojas, G., et al. "Un entorno b-learning para la promoción de la escritura académica de estudiantes universitarios." *Revista Mexicana de Investigación Educativa*, vol. 19, no. 61, 2014, pp. 349–375.

Hernández Zamora, G., et al. "Pensamiento crítico y literacidad académica en la UAM Cuajimalpa: perspectivas docentes." *Memorias ITAM*, 2012.

Juergensmeyer, Erik. "Sharing Control: Developing Research Literacy through Community-Based Action Research." *Community Literacy Journal*, vol. 5, no. 2, 2011, pp. 153–167.

Kells, Michelle Hall. "Writing across Communities: Deliberation and the Discursive Possibilities of WAC." *Reflections: A Journal of Writing, Service-Learning, and Community Literacy*, vol. 6, no. 1, 2007, pp. 87–108.

Kirsch, Gesa E. "From Introspection to Action: Connection Spirituality and Civic Engagement." *College Composition and Communication*, vol. 60, no. 4, 2009, pp. 827–828.

Motta-Roth, Désirée. "Academic Literacies in the South: Writing Practices in a Brazilian University." *Writing Programs Worldwide: Profiles of Academic Writing in Many Places*, edited by Chris Thaiss et al., The WAC Clearinghouse, 2012, pp. 105-116.

Moyano, Estela Inés, and Lucia Natale. "Teaching Academic Literacy Across the University Curriculum as Institutional Policy: The Case of the Universidad Nacional de General Sarmiento (Argentina)." *Writing Programs Worldwide: Profiles of Academic Writing in Many Places*, edited by C. Thaiss et al., The WAC Clearinghouse, 2012, pp. 23-34.

Narváez, Elizabeth. "Training Experiences in Reading and Writing in a Colombian University: The Perspectives of a Professor." *Writing Programs Worldwide: Profiles of Academic Writing in Many Places*, edited by Chris Thaiss et al., The WAC Clearinghouse, 2012, pp. 147-156.

Ryan, Gery W., and H. Russell Bernard. "Data Management and Analysis Methods." Collecting and Interpreting Qualitative Materials. 2nd ed., edited by Norman K. Denzin and Yvonna S. Lincoln, Sage, 2003, pp. 259-309.

Taylor, Tim N. "The Research Paper as an Act of Citizenship: Possibilities and Pragmatism." *Teaching English in the Two-Year College*, vol. 33, no. 1, 2005, pp. 50-61.

Thaiss, Chris, et al. "Writing Programs Worldwide: Profiles of Academic Writing in Many Places." *Perspectives on Writing. The WAC Clearinghouse and Parlor Press*, 2012.

Universidad Iberoamericana. "Normas particulares para el diseño de planes de estudios de licenciatura de la Universidad Iberoamericana." Ciudad de México (UIA CM), aprobadas por el Comité Académico en la 1ª sesión extraordinaria de 2012. Conference.

Vieira, Kate. "'American by Paper': Assimilation and Documentation in a Biliterate, Bi-Ethnic Immigrant Community." *College English*, vol. 73, no. 1, 2010, pp. 50-72.

Vieira, Kate. "On the Social Consequences of Literacy." *Literacy in Composition Studies*, vol. 1, no. 1, 2013, pp. 26-32.

Waldinger, Roger. "Immigrant Transnationalism." *Current Sociology*, vol. 61, no. 5-6, 2013, pp. 756-777.

3

INTERNATIONAL PROJECT CENTERS AND GLOBAL CIVIC ENGAGEMENT

Jennifer deWinter

According to the Association for International Educators (NAFSA), only 1.5 percent of all US students enrolled in higher education are studying abroad. While this report notes that study abroad numbers are increasing according to 2014–2015 data, the same report notes that 40 percent of companies surveyed missed international business opportunities because their workforce was not adequately internationally competent (Farmer). Within these data, the subset of engineers is often called upon to communicate across cultures and disciplines. According to The National Academy of Engineers, US engineers will need area studies training, as they "will be based abroad, will have to travel . . . around the world to meet customers, and will have to converse proficiently in more than one language" (152; see also Riemer). Moreover, "US engineers will represent a minority culture and, thus, will have to be open to different religions, different ways of thinking, and different social values. Flexibility and respect for ways of life different from ours will be critical to professional success" (National Academy of Engineers; see also Johnson et al.). Despite engineering students' need for global experience, however, only 16 percent of study abroad students are STEM majors, and of those, only 3 percent are from engineering fields (Chow and Bhandari 7). Dessoff attributes this lack of participation in study abroad programs to engineers' curriculum load—students need to fit too many required courses into an already tight four-year degree plan. Moreover, he notes that many engineering schools do not prioritize study abroad experiences for their students (26).

At Worcester Polytechnic Institute (WPI) in Massachusetts, faculty have integrated a study away component—combined with writing intensive, project-based learning—into its curriculum for over four decades. Study away is defined as an off-campus learning experience within the university's institutional structure (see, for example, Sobania and

Braskamp). The experience is often project-based but also includes many of the international and community engagement outcomes found in traditional study abroad. WPI created "The Plan" in 1970 to introduce a project-based curriculum that articulated engineering and science more closely with humanities, arts, and social science. Part of The Plan requires students to complete three projects: a sophomore humanities and arts project, a junior-year Interactive Qualifying Project (IQP), and senior Major Qualifying Project (MQP), which is similar to a senior research project or thesis. It is predominantly in the IQP that students work off campus at community-embedded project centers, although a smaller percent of senior projects and humanities and arts projects are also carried out at off-campus locations. The off-campus option has grown in popularity over the years. Of WPI's 2015 graduating class, for example, 63 percent opted to complete at least one of the required projects off site, and the university is moving toward "Global Projects for All," which aims to send 100 percent of the undergraduate student body off campus to complete a university project at a project center. To facilitate the off-campus option, WPI has, over the years, created over 60 Project Centers on six of the seven continents, where students can visit each year to complete senior MQPs (14 centers), junior IQPs (38 centers), and/or sophomore humanities and arts projects (3 centers).

The IQP asks students to apply social science methods to community-driven problems, developing a written report and other communication skills in the process. Students may complete this project on campus with a faculty advisor or they may apply to a domestic or international project center off campus. The majority of students take the latter option. In 2014, for example, 65 percent of enrolled juniors completed IQPs at an off-campus site, and 62 percent of current rising juniors have committed to completing future IQPs off campus ("WPI: 2014 Fact Book" 14).

In this chapter, I argue that off-campus global projects have demonstrable benefits in student writing performance, sociocultural literacies, and ethical understandings. I start with a summary of a description of our project centers and a brief explanation of how they are administered. I then present a summary of two self-studies conducted at WPI: The most recent IQP Report study, which is completed every three years, and the alumni survey, an externally funded and administered assessment that surveyed 2,532 WPI alumni who graduated between 1974 and 2011. These self-studies point to the strength of the global project centers in overall project achievement, writing, global competency, and ethical and social reasoning, achieved precisely because students are working in what they consider "real-world" contexts with sponsors embedded in communities, often in cultures that destabilize and help shape a sense of international and cosmopolitan self. I conclude with a summary of what other writing programs might do to adapt this program to different institutional contexts. Ultimately, I provide here a data-driven argument for global civic engagement and its connection to increased student achievement.

THE INTERACTIVE QUALIFYING PROJECT: STUDY AWAY AND SERVICE LEARNING IN INTERNATIONAL COMMUNITIES[1]

The goal of the IQP is to provide students with problem-solving experience relevant to actual communities. As such, the IQP aims to help students see the connection between technology development and sociocultural contexts. This is necessary both for the development of future, "appropriate technologies" that are sustainable and ethical for their users and for students' professional development as citizens and engineers working in a global context. The faculty-approved learning outcomes for the IQP requirement indicate that students should:

1. Demonstrate understanding of the project's technical, social, and humanistic context.
2. Define clear, achievable goals and objectives.
3. Critically identify, integrate, and cite multiple sources of relevant information.
4. Select and implement a sound interdisciplinary approach to meeting objectives.
5. Analyze and synthesize results from social, ethical, humanistic, technical, or other perspectives, as appropriate.
6. Maintain effective working relationships within the project team, community collaborators, and project advisor(s), recognizing and resolving problems that arise.
7. Demonstrate the ability to write clearly, critically, and persuasively.
8. Demonstrate strong oral and visual communication skills.
9. Demonstrate an awareness of the ethical dimensions of their project work.

Clear in these goals is a focus on critical literacy as well as formal and interpersonal communication, and underlying these goals is an understanding that cultural context matters. Students at WPI fulfill the IQP requirement in one of two ways: (1) they can stay on campus and fit the project into their course curriculum as an independent study advised by a willing faculty member (typically spreading the work over three 7-week

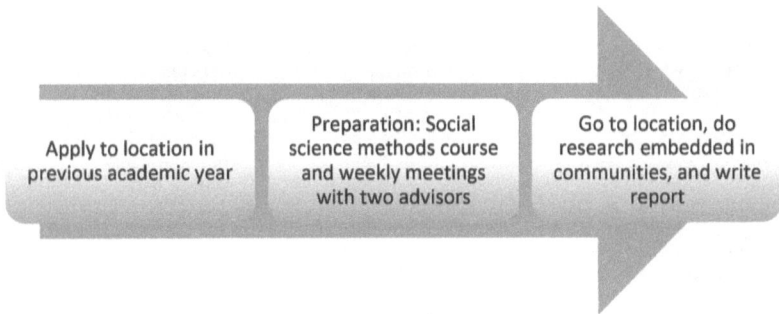

Figure 3.1. Off-campus IQP student workflow

terms) or (2) they can apply for an off-campus global project experience in which they spend seven weeks engaged in preparatory research on campus and then another seven-week term at one of the IQP-focused project centers (see figure 3.1), where under the guidance of two faculty advisors, they do hands-on work with sponsors and local communities.

Administering Off-Campus Centers

Established project centers run, on average, one 7-week term per year with twenty-four enrolled students (six groups of four) and two faculty advisors. The centers are administered by a faculty director, who has local autonomy over project types and sponsors, and some international centers also employ a liaison who lives in the region. The issues students work on are determined by both the interests of the director and the cultural and social needs of area communities, represented by partnering sponsors. The faculty director and liaison identify local sponsors (e.g., government agencies, NGOs, or community organizations) and develop short one-paragraph descriptions of potential projects for students. They also find housing and workspace for students, and they support on-site faculty advisors who oversee student work. For example, the center in Cape Town, South Africa, is directed by a social geographer who works closely with NGOs and residents of informal human settlements, often on water and sanitation issues. Projects in Venice, Italy, meanwhile, focus on preserving the city's historical and cultural treasures in the face of climate change and the crushing impact of tourism on local residents. Wellington, New Zealand, and San Jose, Costa Rica, emphasize environmental projects, and teams in northern India investigate how new technologies might improve quality of life and income for sustenance

Table 3.1. WPI Project Centers that organize student IQPs

NORTH AMERICA	SOUTH AND CENTRAL AMERICA	EUROPE
Bar Harbor, ME	Asuncion, Paraguay	Copenhagen, Denmark
Bedford, MA	Buenos Aires, Argentina	London, England
Boston, MA	Cuenca, Ecuador	Moscow, Russia
Cambridge, MA	Panama City, Panama	Thessaloniki, Greece
Lexington, MA	San José, Costa Rica	Tirana, Albania
Nantucket, MA		Venice, Italy
San Juan, Puerto Rico	ASIA-PACIFIC	Worcester, England
Santa Fe, NM	Bangkok, Thailand	
Washington, DC	Beijing, China	
Worcester, MA	Hangzhou, China	
	Hong Kong, China	
AFRICA	Kyoto, Japan	
Cape Town, South Africa	Mandi, India	
Rabat, Morocco	Melbourne, Australia	
Windhoek, Namibia	Wellington, New Zealand	

farmers, small tea-growing operations, and migratory herders in the Himalayan foothills. Students at the London Project Center often work with museums on public education projects or with local agencies on urban planning in an increasingly diversified city.

Faculty who are interested in advising at one of these project centers apply for these advising positions by ranking the different locations by preference, and if selected, they are given course release for their term away with students. Since these projects prioritize interdisciplinarity, the two selected faculty often come from different departments. This has the added benefit of increasing connectivity in campus culture among faculty.

Preparatory Term

Students who desire off-campus IQP experience must rank the centers they are most interested in, submit an essay, and have historically interviewed with site directors. This is not without some difficulty on the part of student choices (see, for example, Meldrim et al.). Nevertheless, once accepted to a site, students are typically placed into teams of four, and these teams are assigned to a sponsored project. The students take a social science course in the prep term in which they learn about the sponsor and stakeholders, get an overview of the culture, and receive training in social science methodologies relevant to their project. In the methods course, which has an assigned instructor of record, students define the problem and their objectives, research literature relevant to their work, and write a formal proposal, including the methods they will use on site as they collaborate with community partners, such as interviewing, surveying, generative research methods, participatory design, and so forth. They learn writing processes, including invention, drafting, and revision, with the sponsor as the end audience who receives the proposal prior to students arriving. They must submit and have their methods approved by the university's Institutional Review Board (IRB). The two faculty advisors who will accompany the students meet weekly with teams during this preparatory term to guide them through problem statements, help them set agendas, and provide general advice on project management. Students earn full course credit for the prep course and half a course credit for other preparatory work in this term. Some centers require additional sessions on culture and/or language instruction, as relevant.

On-Site Project Work

On site, students confer weekly with advisors and sponsors, and they work with community collaborators for seven weeks as they further study the problem, identify resources, and evaluate and implement possible responses. They earn the equivalent of three courses of credit (a full term's worth at WPI) for on-site work. One required deliverable is a final, written report, typically 60–100 pages in length, which is uploaded to the university library's database and shared with the project sponsor and community stakeholders. The report provides both analysis and recommendations for the problem or opportunity addressed. Students also showcase their work in a community presentation.

Depending on the site, other deliverables may also be submitted or documented. For example, in Costa Rica, students worked with an environmental organization to design an interactive map that can document endangered sea turtle sightings and determine migration patterns along the coastal regions. Students at the India site conducted extensive meetings with migratory sheepherders and construction crews, producing a portable origami shelter prototype that can be used by these workers. Collaborating with an NGO and residents of an informal settlement, students in Cape Town produced computer-animated drawings for a dry sanitation facility now operating in an informal settlement. Projects have produced a wide range of deliverables—from a website for startup cottage industries looking to expand sales of handmade crafts to hydroponic gardens for inner-city food deserts.

Since new project teams travel to project sites each year, individual projects may be extended over the course of several years at a given project center, allowing deeper relationships to form with community groups, and allowing subsequent teams to follow through on work begun by earlier teams. The on-site phase of the projects is labor and time intensive, often requiring students to work on site for 40–50 hours per week. And students do, citing this project experience to be one of the most challenging and formative in their undergraduate tenure. In what follows, we summarize assessment data on student learning in the IQP as gleaned from their final reports and from interviews with alumni who have participated in the off-campus experience over the years. I then discuss the types of support that, in my experience, seem most essential for projects like this.

IQP ASSESSMENT

WPI conducts regular assessments to measure learning outcomes for its required projects. Every three years, for example, the Interdisciplinary and Global Studies Division (IGSD) conducts a blind review of recently completed IQP reports. Below, we summarize key findings from the 2013 review. Many of these findings are consistent with reviews conducted over the past two decades (Rissmiller). Moreover, WPI recently conducted an alumni survey, analyzing responses from over 2,500 WPI engineering alumni who answered questions about the long-term impact of their project work (Vaz and Quinn). Relevant findings from each of these studies are discussed.

Methods for the Report Review and Alumni Survey

In the most recent review of student reports, 10 faculty evaluated 150 randomly selected reports from a pool of 284 completed between 2012 and 2013. Of these, 95 were completed on campus and 55 were completed off campus at a project center.[2] The assessment instrument was comprised of 63 performance items, most of which reviewers scored using a five-point scale, 1 indicating poor/unacceptable performance, 2 indicating below-par/unacceptable performance, 3 indicating fair/acceptable performance, 4 indicating very good performance, and 5 indicating excellent performance. The option of "absent" was available to denote whether a particular item was missing in the report. Specific performance items addressed categories of information summarized in table 3.2, which correspond to the faculty-approved learning objectives for the IQP. Reviewers also gave each project a holistic quality score, using the same five-point scale. Faculty reviewers participated in two norming sessions prior to scoring the reports.

Table 3.2. Assessment categories for project reports

Reviewer scoring sheets asked for an overall project assessment score as well as scores for 62 specific items related to the following categories

Ability to communicate effectively in writing and with visuals

- Writing reflects an understanding of audience (tone, word choice, appropriate use of active and passive voice, appropriate use of first, second, and third person)
- Writing is globally and locally coherent
- Writing incorporates sources appropriately, and it critically engages with sources
- Document design is used rhetorically to visually and organizationally enhance writing

Ability to research and analyze problems

- Frame the problem (objectives, introduction, executive summary)
- Locate, critically evaluate, and use relevant sources of information
- Make and justify appropriate methodological choices, noting limitations
- Interpret and analyze data
- Make persuasive recommendations and conclusions based on analysis

Awareness of social and ethical dimensions of the problem-solving context

- Awareness of global issues
- Ability to discuss the impact of technology on society and vice versa
- Ability to articulate ethical issues/questions that arise when technology is integrated into society
- Awareness of the researcher's ethical responsibility in using data/sources and in working with others

As figure 3.2 indicates, much of the off-campus experience is assessed based on writing and communication, research and analytical thinking, and global and cross-cultural communicative competency, all central concerns in writing and rhetoric programs in the United States. Data on the long-term impact of IQP experience are also available through an alumni survey conducted by Vaz and Quinn, completed in 2013. They compared responses of alumni who attended WPI between 1974 and 2011, 42 percent of whom had completed at least one of their projects at an off-campus project center and 58 percent who had completed their required projects exclusively on campus. These alumni were asked to rate the impact of their project experience on their worldviews, on their personal development, and on their professional abilities, such as communication, teamwork, project management, and awareness of ethical responsibilities in professional work. A five-point Likert scale was used in the survey, with response options ranging from "not at all" to "very much," with a "not applicable" category as well.

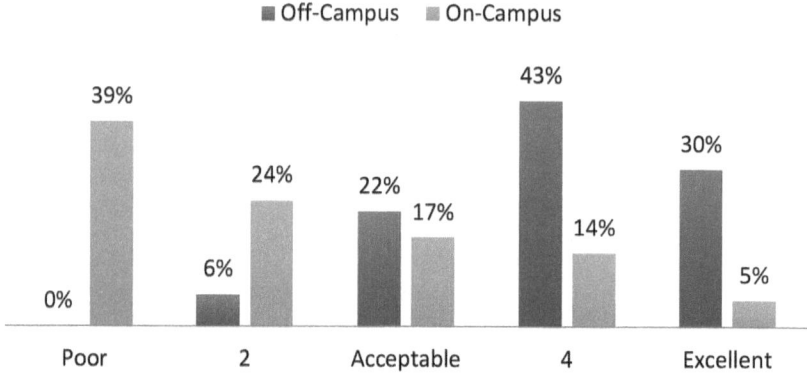

Figure 3.2. Holistic scores for on- and off-campus project reports

Assessment Findings

The recent review of student reports indicated that off-campus project reports were rated significantly higher for quality overall than on-campus reports (figure 3.3). Immediately apparent is that 73 percent of off-campus project reports were scored as very good or excellent, whereas only 19 percent of on-campus project reports were scored in this range.

Students whose projects were embedded in off-campus communities also received higher report ratings on most of the more specific assessment items, including those related to quality of writing, problem-driven research and analysis, and objectives related to social/ethical awareness. The challenge that on-campus IQPs faced could often be traced to the lack of a sponsor, which resulted in on-campus projects looking more like research papers than project reports—they tended to lack sophisticated social science methods that put them in touch with actual community stakeholders, especially any hands-on collaborative methods. In many ways, this merely echoes Miller's older argument that the student's audience is always fiction, a challenge that community sponsors help to overcome in many ways.

These numbers extended into the quality of the writing overall. Students who went to a project center had better quality of writing (mostly 4s and 5s) when compared to reports written on campus (see figure 3.4). This is probably linked to the fact that all off-campus project centers have two dedicated faculty advisors whose only teaching assignment at that time is advising and responding to student drafts, whereas on-campus projects tend to be advised by faculty in addition to their normally assigned workload.

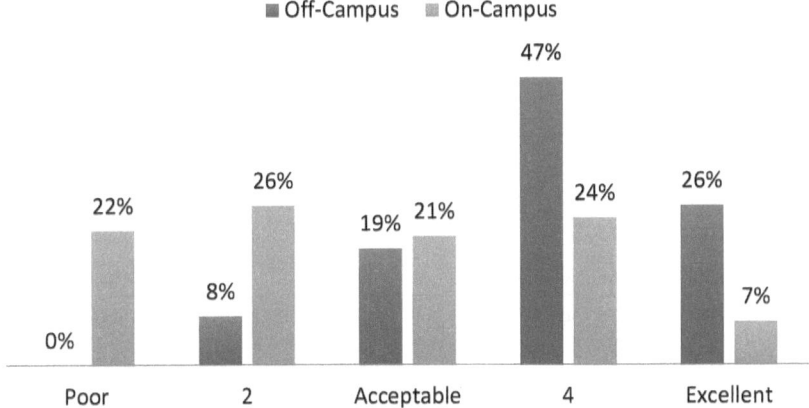

Figure 3.3. Scores on overall writing quality

The alumni survey data also suggest that off-campus projects might have a bigger impact on student communication than on-campus projects. When asked how much their project experience had expanded their abilities in writing, speaking, presentation, and visual communication, over 60 percent of the alumni who had off-campus experiences replied "much" or "very much" for each of these categories. In comparison, a significantly smaller percentage of those who had done on-campus projects responded "much" or "very much" (table 3.3).

Additionally, data concerning problem research and analysis indicated that 58 percent of off-campus project reports scored as "very good" or "excellent" in terms of locating, assessing, and using relevant literature, more than double the on-campus projects at 23 percent. Further, 61 percent scored above average for findings and analysis, as compared to the 21 percent above average scores for on-campus projects.[3] These scores are significant for writing instructors to consider because they point to an ability to define and scope community-based projects meaningfully.

The alumni survey attempted to rate the impact of on-campus and off-campus project work in several areas relevant to social and ethical awareness and behavior. The percentage of alumni in each group who responded with "much" or "very much" impact was again significantly higher for those who completed at least one project off campus. Table 3.4 summarizes those results; all reported percentage differences across the two groups except for "understanding connections between technology and society" are statistically significant ($p < 0.001$).

Table 3.3. Project Impact: Percentage of alumni groups indicating that project work impacted their communication abilities "much" or "very much"

Project Impact	Alumni with only on-campus project experience	Alumni with at least one off-campus project experience
Writing clearly, effectively	53%	63%
Speaking clearly, effectively	42%	61%
Delivering effective presentations	45%	64%
Communicating effectively with visuals	49%	62%

Note: All reported percentage differences between groups are statistically significant ($p < 0.001$)

Table 3.4. Percentage of alumni groups with on-campus versus off-campus project experience, reporting that project work had much or very much impact on areas related to their social/ethical awareness and practices (Vaz and Quinn)

Area of Impact	On-campus projects	At least one off-campus project
Viewing issues from multiple perspectives	55	62
Understanding people from other cultures	19	48
Understanding global issues	24	44
Understanding people of other races and ethnicities	22	41
Respect for cultures outside of your own	17	45
Ability to manage interpersonal dynamics	56	68
Ability to function as a team	65	75
Understanding ethical responsibilities as a professional	30	44
Understanding connections between technology and society	51	55

Table 3.4 speaks to a broadening of cultural awareness and global issues in addition to interpersonal communication or ethical responsibility. As is well documented in study abroad literature, doing work in another community or country increases a sense of understanding of people from other cultures or societies (Kitsantas; Anderson et al.; Clarke et al.).

DISCUSSION AND IMPLICATIONS

Multiple factors may account for the disparity in report scores in the off-campus and on-campus groups, but here, I discuss those components of the off-campus preparation and experience that may contribute the most to positive outcomes. These include engagement with community stakeholders throughout the problem-solving process, training in social science methodology, and ongoing feedback on presentations and writing as the project develops.

The Importance of Engagement with Local Communities
Off-campus students have frequent opportunities to work directly with local community stakeholders and sponsors, not simply as sources of information, but often as co-researchers and collaborators. Such a connection has already been found to improve both L1 and L2 writing in service-learning contexts (cf. House; Wurr; Deans; Wisla et al.). Most project sites involve weeks of fieldwork, which allows students to become familiar with community stakeholder needs, interests, and resources, as well as to involve stakeholders at every stage of problem solving, from understanding the source and consequences of a problem to finding available resources and obstacles to addressing it and to evaluating and testing alternative responses. Even after students retreat to their apartments or offices on site to finalize deliverables or write up ideas, they often return to the community to test those ideas in practice—or, in some cases, subsequent teams follow up, test, and refine those ideas further in the field, which is often impractical in the context of on-campus projects.

On-campus project students have fewer opportunities to interact with actual community members, particularly diverse stakeholders who may be affected by the problems they research. Without situated engagement, students address stakeholders they can only imagine; they do not have access to the breadth of perspectives often needed to understand and address complex socio-technical problems. Although library research (particularly local studies, when they exist) can provide some background, students who work on campus are somewhat limited by their isolation. It may even be true that the absence of sustained community engagement may have negative repercussions on students' methodological approach, their ability to communicate clearly and appropriately, and their ability to realize ethical responsibilities and social impacts in their work.

The Importance of Explicitly Teaching Methodology
Learning a range of methodological practices for working with and collecting data from community stakeholders is critical. Although students

who complete on-campus projects do work with a faculty advisor, they do not have the opportunity to take the social science methods course specially designed for their projects. The methodological preparation off-campus students receive prior to working at project centers *enables* them to gather more pertinent data and to interact with community members in a productive, ethical, and collaborative way. At the urging of advisors, these students continue to revise and add to their methods once on site and while interacting with community members and sponsors, who often work as co-researchers in addition to information sources.

Without the preparatory course, on-campus students are not exposed to a larger range of methodologies and the ethical and practical reasons for method selection. In the on-campus projects, students often explore problems through laboratory testing, library research, or if their explorations do involve other stakeholders, through online surveys that anticipate and contain responses to a drop-down menu of choices. These methodologies are amenable to what Sun has called a traditional "engineering approach," where developers predetermine the kind of (usually technological) solutions people need and the goals they should serve. In contrast, Sun advocates an emerging, humanistic approach to technology design where the lines between developers and users is blurred, and engineers, in tandem with communities, define needs and goals for new technologies and specific solutions that can meet those goals.

Although all students need more support in developing awareness of sociocultural and ethical dimensions of problem solving, program data show that the off-campus students show more indications of learning in this area. Again, this may be a result of exposure to actual communities and the different perspectives they encounter on site. In addition, the need to think critically about their methodological choices for exploring a particular problem in a particular context—and the effects those choices may have on stakeholders—becomes apparent as they address the IRB. Moreover, directors and advisors at specific sites emphasize to students that methods for working with marginalized and subordinated stakeholders can in fact be deliverables themselves, and as they find effective ways to partner with these communities, they should document the successes and failures in their process.

Importance of Feedback on Writing and Presentations

Differences in the quality of student writing and the content of their writing (in terms of their defined objectives, presentation and analysis of data, and arguments developed from their research) may be attributed to the feedback they receive in the process of drafting and discussing their ideas. Effective communication and writing are highly dependent on communicators' awareness of social contexts and audience/stakeholders, and we see here that the students are negotiating those relationships with traditional academic genres and projects to positive ends.

WPI offers training to faculty advising in these off-campus programs, administered through the Communication Across the Curriculum program (CXC). In this program, writing and non-writing faculty are trained to provide guiding holistic feedback on drafts for revision, focusing primarily on rhetorical purpose of the report, stakeholder analysis, information synthesis, and logic and organization of the materials. Off-campus students receive a great deal of initial feedback on their framing of the problem and objectives as well as their approach as early as the prep term—both from their social science instructor, who assigns drafts of the introduction, background, and methods chapters of their proposal, and from faculty advisors, who comment on students' weekly progress report presentations. This feedback loop continues on site, where students are asked to revise these materials and draft and revise new results and discussion chapters. They get feedback from sponsors at weekly meetings and from community partners, all of whom are engaged and invested audiences for their written reports and final presentations. Further, new advisors are paired with experienced advisors to learn effective feedback methods, and the director of the CXC revises educational materials for advisor retreats at least once a year based on current practice or needs.

Having real, identifiable audiences and purposes in a situation where the stakes are high and students feel personally accountable can be very motivating, as Vaz and Quinn point out. Moreover, some faculty advisors have developed forms of reflective, narrative writing to help students process their experience and reflect on their interactions with and interpretation of stakeholders from other cultures and backgrounds. There can also be moments to study and reflect upon how we imagine and write about others. However, personal experience narratives that document interactions in these cultural contact zones do not always result in productive reflection and can in some cases reinforce stereotypes and unequal power relations. Students can use journaling to complain and blame, to stigmatize others in moments of frustration and misunderstanding. And despite students' growing understanding of and dependence on the expertise of the stakeholders with whom they work, a dominant language of professional service (McKnight) can persist in students' writing, where they seem to claim ownership of positive project outcomes and disown any failures, projecting fault onto community partners. Students also tend to appropriate authoritative roles, referring to themselves as experts who fix, solve, educate, inform, or repair stakeholder communities they sometimes narrowly characterize as poor, broken, uninformed, or unable. Findings suggest, therefore, that it is critical for students to share and get feedback from advisors and teammates (and in some cases, trusted stakeholder collaborators or sponsors) who challenge them to consider "rival" interpretations as they document critical incidents they experience in the project centers and to prompt them to think critically about the default language of service when it emerges.

Ethical Engagement in Off-Campus Projects

Because students in off-campus projects often work very closely with community groups as they conduct research and enact change, they are required to file IRB applications. In the process, and in the social science methods course they take, they learn about ethical research practices. Nevertheless, the social and ethical awareness that we hope students develop in off-campus projects is more difficult to evaluate. For example, in response to a question on awareness of social ethics, or the extent to which discussion of the impact of technology on society reflected recognition of the social responsibilities of individuals, scientists, and/or engineers, evaluators reported in their comments that, in some cases, they couldn't tell. And this can be seen in figure 3.4.

It is difficult to account for the "absent" data points. In some cases, comments indicated weakness in the literature review for low numbers, while other comments differentiated topics that are inherently about social ethics from the reflection and engagement with social ethics. Of those reports in which social ethics is present and evaluated, we see again that the off-campus IQP projects engage with these questions in the acceptable to excellent range. Much of this can be attributed to the close working relationship that students have with communities, which increases an awareness of people and cultures in complex systems. In other words, as many reports confirm in their discussions and conclusions, there is not an easy technological fix to most challenges.

Nevertheless, we cannot ignore the lower scores found in our evaluation of ethics. Some of this might simply have to do with a problem of culture, something that Finelli et al. discuss in "An Assessment of Engineering Students' Curricular and Co-Curricular Experiences and Their Ethical Development": "engineering students' levels of ethical reasoning are lower than their peers in other fields. This is the first US assessment of engineering students' ethical reasoning, and these results,

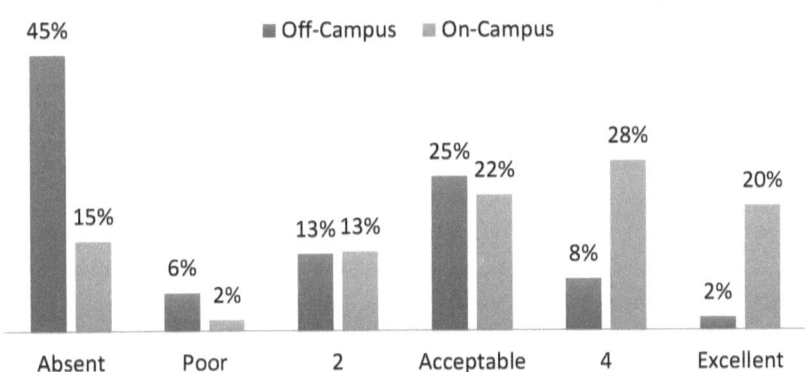

Figure 3.4. Demonstrated awareness of social ethics in on- and off-campus student reports

like those for the knowledge of ethics, suggest that there is significant room for improvement" (487). Yet this particular assessment comes from a survey of current college students. It might simply be that these early experiences can only be assessed in longitudinal studies post-graduation. With that in mind, and simultaneous to this IQP report assessment, WPI conducted a longitudinal study to evaluate the impact of the off-campus project experience with alumni. In this study, which surveyed 2,532 WPI alumni who graduated between 1974 and 2011, Vaz and Quinn found that students who completed project work at a project center rather than on campus indicated greater gains in the following areas: (1) expanded world views, including understanding and respecting others' cultures, and appreciating the complexity of global issues; (2) enhanced personal lives and a greater sense of self-efficacy and value; (3) improved communication skills in both written and verbal forms; and (4) enhanced interpersonal skills and a greater appreciation of ethical responsibilities (3–5). Indeed, the number of students who answered "much" or "very much" to the question of expanded ethical responsibilities was significantly higher (14%) in respondents who had at least one off-campus experience (44%, $n = 723$) than those who completed all their projects on campus (30%, $n = 941$).

These data indicate that students participating in these study-away service-learning projects self-report that they developed a sense of the ethical complexity of their work during their project and that they continue to develop and apply their ethical awareness throughout their professional and personal lives. One of the challenges that we face is that assessment focuses on the written document rather than all of the non-point-specific interactions that help students develop ethical and cultural awareness, which echoes Keith's assertion that service learning in an intercultural communication classroom or context decreases students' levels of ethnocentrism (178). The problem, of course, is that assessment mechanisms need an object to assess, and service learning is often messy and recursive. Much of the transformative work occurs during meetings, in-group collaborations, and in invisible changes to personal worldview. Nevertheless, the reports and the alumni survey do indicate that the off-campus, service-learning projects are engaging students in such a way that they achieve both academic and personal goals. Further, the off-campus work, in situated and active communities, asks students to think through what civic engagement is in a local context, and what their role in a global context should be.

CORE COMPONENTS FOR ESTABLISHING GLOBAL SERVICE-LEARNING CENTERS

Recent self-studies at WPI about the efficacy and value of the global project approach indicate that students working off campus with a sponsor in a targeted community is both transformative for the student and has real positive impact on student learning outcomes. The effect of this approach can be felt in the campus culture as students compete for international project centers where they feel that they can learn from and help communities for a focused period of time.

While this program is a signature program for WPI, such an approach is scalable to other institutions. WPI is on a seven-week term in which students on campus only take three classes for a full load. Thus, there is a roughly one-to-one equivalency for quarter-based institutions, although the three additional weeks do add to the operating cost on site. For semester systems, either summer study options or winter term intense options would enable the projects to be scaled for cost efficiency and learning objectives without detracting from the five- to six-course load typical in a semester system. Time consideration aside, for those interested in establishing similar service learning–based study-away options, the following lessons learned might prove valuable.

Project Center Director

These projects are time intensive, and project center directors are often called upon to visit the country to meet with sponsors off cycle. These meetings enable the director to identify and solidify new and existing sponsor relationships, negotiate the type and scope of a student project, and possibly collect sponsor fees. For some of our projects, we can solicit between $1,000–5,000 in fees in exchange for four undergraduate students working in a team with two faculty advisors on a sponsor priority. Setting up these relationships is time consuming and costly, so a faculty center director ensures stability and continuity. WPI recognizes the increased workload and compensates faculty with a course release for directing one of these programs.

Faculty Advisors

Faculty advisors are released from a term of teaching to accompany the students and teach the equivalent of three course credits. The ratio is typically twelve students to one faculty advisor with a project center running with two advisors and twenty-four students. WPI compensates faculty with airfare, hotel, and a living allowance that is based on a reduced amount of the State Department's Meals and Entertainment allowances. Faculty teaching in the summer are not released from a class but are instead paid summer salary.

Faculty advisors receive training on crisis response. In addition to this, they are trained in how to give writing feedback through constructive comments (in many ways, this works as an informal Writing Across the Curriculum program) and teach team dynamics and professional presentation styles.

Prior to departure, all faculty advisors meet weekly with each group for approximately 30–60 minutes. This only carries one credit value for the students, and the faculty do this in addition to their regular teaching load. The weekly meetings are driven by the students, who prepare agendas that outline their project goal, problem statement, research questions, and current preparatory activities. Faculty provide feedback in the meetings.

Methods Course

WPI established a formal social science methods course that students can take to fulfill one of their social science requirements if they are traveling to a project center. The course has a dedicated instructor who teaches this class in load. This course teaches students research methods, problem defining, social science methods that are appropriate to the task, and ethical research plans (enforced through participation with the IRB).

The faculty member who teaches this class is responsible for reading all drafts of the preparatory materials and helping students learn to work in groups. They also teach how literature reviews provide a foundation for approaching problems. In many ways, this class acts as a composition class, teaching skills in information literacy, invention, drafting and revision, and presentation. Additionally, students often learn an overview of the culture of the location they are about to visit, and in some cases, like Thailand, Japan, and Denmark, the course offers a language component.

Sponsor Selection

Sponsor selection is often one of the most difficult challenges we face in establishing a project center. First and foremost, sponsors need to speak English, which is not a problem in London or Melbourne but becomes a particular challenge in other locations. Further, like Einfeld and Collins, faculty at WPI believe that the "primary goal of higher education is to create responsible, moral, and productive citizens" (108), and that there is a connection between service learning, social justice, and multicultural competency. As such, sponsors need to provide the affordances for our students to engage in communities, often around issues of social and environmental justice, cultural and social preservation, and service to underrepresented or underprivileged communities. We typically target sponsors from the following categories:

- Community-serving NGOs
- Environmental agencies
- Regional development agencies
- Museums and cultural institutions
- Municipal governments
- Educational organizations

We look for sponsors who need to interface with local citizens for community improvement. As such, students have worked to develop educational material for museums, build sustainable infrastructure with communities (such as toilets or mobile STEM labs), develop policy plans with informal settlements, and so forth.

Sponsors also have to agree to a certain number of responsibilities for the seven weeks that students are on site, such as providing our students space to work (not required but desirable), meeting with our students and advisors at least once a week, providing feedback, and paying for supplies or project-based travel (our students have done everything from building hydroponic gardens to installing museum exhibits). Sponsors are also asked to meet with students, if they have the time, to answer questions during the week, and also to help organize a final presentation to their organization.

Oftentimes, when we ask sponsors informally about the impact of these projects, sponsors will point to the object that the students built or the report, but just as often, they discuss the ways that sponsoring projects helps to train up-and-coming managers and get the word out on what they are doing through WPI marketing, or how having an external group helps them move along projects that were languishing from lack of concentrated attention.

Faculty-Student Interaction

While at the project centers, the faculty attend weekly meetings at the sponsor site to listen to students present to and interact with their sponsors. This is important for the faculty to understand what the sponsor is saying; faculty advisors are then able to help students interpret feedback from the sponsors, meet sponsor goals, and sometimes push back against the sponsor to protect student time and scope. Additionally, faculty tend to meet with the students, either in a large group for a few hours once a week or individually with the teams. Again, this is important for getting updates from students, providing verbal advice and feedback, and doing a general well-being check-in. Finally, faculty receive weekly drafts of the project report and provide written feedback on student writing for revision.

Toward the end of the project, faculty and students work together to prepare for the formal presentations with the sponsors and stakeholders from the community. These presentations have been as small as an informal presentation with 1–3 people to three-hour formal presentations with intense question and answer sessions with upwards of sixty people in the audience. As such, students need to be prepared not only with their presentation materials but also with the knowledge needed to answer complex questions about the topic and its implications. To prepare for this, faculty often organize a series of practice presentations, advising students to create "answer slides" of additional data that might be needed during the question and answer time.

Finally, faculty are all given a budget to do cultural enrichment activities with students. These are typically low-stakes activities, such as taking students out to lunch or on a hike followed by lunch. However, in countries in which costs are lower, WPI often organized weekend or special trips with the students so they can see more of the country. These are important cultural excursions not just for the students' broad exposure to the hosting location, but also for the social connection developed among faculty, professional staff, and students as they work and learn alongside one another.

Opportunities for Further Development

While WPI has been doing this for just over forty years, WPI remains a small STEM-based university. More comprehensive universities would be better able to take advantage of certain opportunities that WPI does not have the capacity to, such as in-depth language instruction and reentry activities.

WPI only offers four languages at the beginning and lower intermediate levels—Spanish, German, Arabic, and Chinese—yet we have project centers in many more linguistically diverse locations. Universities with more robust language programs would be able to take advantage of area studies expertise in different geographical regions and send students to work more closely with partners who might not be proficient in English, thus widening the impact of the projects for both students and sponsors.

Additionally, research shows that reentry programs help students process their learning and synthesize their experiences with previous knowledges and suppositions (Arthur, "Preparing"; Arthur, "Re-Entry"; Gray and Savicki). However, at WPI, students tend to jump right back into their studies, and reentry programs tend to be unevenly subscribed to. Universities with international studies, area studies, or communication and writing studies would be able to incorporate reentry courses and activities into the major meaningfully, building on the study-away experience to generate new knowledge through reflection, synthesis, and additive research.

CONCLUSION

I write this conclusion with slightly more personal reflection. I have been the faculty advisor in Thailand, Morocco, Worcester, Boston, London, and Japan, leaving home for seven weeks (oftentimes taking my children with me) to work closely with another faculty advisor with whom I had previously had little to no interaction, overseeing student projects. And while the data above speak to student achievement within themes important to rhetoric and composition scholars interested in global civic engagement, I would like to speak informally in the conclusion about the personal and anecdotal benefits for individual faculty.

I love to travel and to spend meaningful time in new places, and these programs support that, and I am able to pass that benefit on to my family. Additionally, I now have excellent friends from across the university from different departments, made possible by the close bonds of seven weeks with a colleague who is, quite often, the only other person with whom I could work and socialize. And I am not alone in reporting this. In our annual retreat for our global projects program, faculty talk about this benefit repeatedly among one another and to new volunteers.

But here's what I love the most: Working with sponsors, whose expert knowledge differs so much from my own. First, sponsors belong to the communities into which our students are embedded, and as a result, we are given different access to that community, joining them in events, meeting sponsors socially, and engaging with really smart and motivated individuals. And second, to be a faculty member, to hold a PhD, is to have proceduralized approaches to expertise building. As such, when our students are tasked with creating middle school lesson plans for the Museum of Homelessness or building biogas digesters for rural schools in Southeast Asia or even helping iterate a robot design so that elderly patients will use technology intended for them, we as faculty are often starting from the same place as students. While we cannot necessarily pass content expertise on to students, we can teach students approaches for defining the problem, creating a plan, and developing the expertise necessary to complete the sponsor project. This is invigorating. When I write comments on student drafts, my question "What do you mean here?" is not asking for general clarification of a poorly integrated quotation; I am truly asking for help in developing my own understanding to then help students act on research and determine in the report what the sponsor needs. And then these experiences return to campus with me, providing examples and touchstones for in-class teaching while also (hopefully) inspiring students to apply for the project center. Global civic engagement, then, is as much about the transformation of the faculty as it is about the student, and as educational facilitators for civic education, this might sometimes be the more important outcome for these projects.

NOTES

1. I use international here as an acknowledgement that when our students join groups in other nations, the project is inherently international, asking both sides to navigate cultural and communication differences that are often dictated by geopolitical demarcations.

2. Although far more students participate in the off-campus option, off campus project teams are larger, meaning there are fewer total reports than in the on-campus sites, where teams sometimes consist of only two students.
3. The alumni survey did not directly ask about impact on problem solving and analytical skills.

WORKS CITED

Anderson, Philip H., et al. "Short-term Study Abroad and Intercultural Sensitivity: A Pilot Study." *International Journal of Intercultural Relations*, vol. 30, no. 4, 2006, pp. 457–469, doi.org/10.1016/j.ijintrel.2005.10.004.

Arthur, Nancy. "Preparing International Students for the Re-entry Transition." *Canadian Journal of Counselling*, vol. 37, no. 3, 2003, http://files.eric.ed.gov/fulltext/EJ672649.pdf. Accessed 12 Nov. 2017.

Arthur, Nancy. "Re-Entry Transition." *International and Cultural Psychology Counseling International Students*, 2004, pp. 51–63, doi:10.1007/978-1-4419-8919-2_4.

Chow, Patricia, and Rajika Bhandari, editors. *Open Doors 2009: Report on International Education Exchange*. Institute on International Education, 2009.

Clarke, Irvine, et al. "Student Intercultural Proficiency from Study Abroad Programs." *Journal of Marketing Education*, vol. 31, no. 2, 2009, pp. 173–181, doi.org/10.1177/0273475309335583.

Deans, Thomas. *Writing Partnerships: Service-Learning in Composition*. National Council of Teachers of English, 2000.

Dessoff, Alan. "Who's Not Going Abroad?" *International Educator NAFSA*, Mar./Apr. 2006, http://www.nafsa.org/uploadedFiles/NAFSA_Home/Resource_Library_Assets/Publications_Library/who_s_not_going_abroad.pdf?n=1479. Accessed 12 Nov. 2017.

Einfeld, Aaron, and Denise Collins. "The Relationships Between Service-Learning, Social Justice, Multicultural Competence, and Civic Engagement." *Journal of College Student Development*, vol. 49, no. 2, 2008, pp. 95–109, doi.org/10.1353/csd.2008.0017.

Farmer, Mark. "Trends in U.S. Study Abroad." *NAFSA: Association of International Educators*, 2016, http://www.nafsa.org/Policy_and_Advocacy/Policy_Resources/Policy_Trends_and_Data/Trends_in_U_S__Study_Abroad/.

Finelli, Cynthia J., et al. "An Assessment of Engineering Students' Curricular and Co-Curricular Experiences and Their Ethical Development." *Journal of Engineering Education*, vol. 101, no. 3, July 2012, pp. 469–494, doi.org/10.1002/j.2168-9830.2012.tb00058.x.

Gray, Kelsey, and Victor Savicki. "Study Abroad Reentry: Behavior, Affect, and Cultural Distance." *Frontiers: The Interdisciplinary Journal of Study Abroad*, vol. 26, Fall 2015, pp. 264–278, http://files.eric.ed.gov/fulltext/EJ1084430.pdf. Accessed 12 Nov. 2017.

House, Veronica. "Community Engagement in Writing Program Design and Administration." *Writing Program Administration*, vol. 39, no. 1, Fall 2015, pp. 54–71.

Johnson, James, et al. "Cross-Cultural Competence in International Business: Toward a Definition and a Model." *Journal of International Business Studies*, vol. 37, no. 4, pp. 525–543, July 2006, http://lib.cufe.edu.cn/upload_files/other/4_20140605102059_Cross-Cultural%20Competence%20in%20International%20Business%20Toward%20a%20Definition%20and%20a%20Model.pdf. Accessed 8 Oct. 2010.

Keith, Kenneth. "The Culture of Teaching and the Teaching of Culture." *Psychology Learning and Teaching*, vol. 11, no. 3, 2012, pp. 316–325, http://journals.sagepub.com/doi/pdf/10.2304/plat.2012.11.3.316.

Kitsantas, Anastasia. "Studying Abroad: The Role of College Students' Goals on the Development of Cross-Cultural Skills and Global Understanding." *College Student Journal*, vol. 38, no. 3, Sept. 2004, pp. 441–452, https://eric.ed.gov/?id=EJ706693.

McKnight, John. "Professionalized Service and Disabling Help." *Disabling Professions*, edited by Ivan Illich, Marion Boyars, 3rd ed., 2010, pp. 69–92.

Meldrim, Arthur, et al. "Helping WPI Students Make Better IQP Choices." *Worcester Polytechnic Institute*, https://web.wpi.edu/Pubs/E-project/Available/E-project-030211-142926/unrestricted/Helping_WPI_Students_Make_Better_IQP_Choices.pdf. Accessed 4 Mar. 2011.

Miller, Susan. "The Student's Reader Is Always Fiction." *Journal of Advanced Composition*, vol. 5, 1984, pp. 15–29, http://www.jstor.org/stable/20865557.

National Academy of Engineering. *Educating the Engineer of 2020: Adapting Engineering Education to the New Century*. United States, National Academies Press, 2005.

Riemer, Marc. "Communication Skills for the 21st Century Engineer." *Global J. of Engng. Educ*, vol. 11, no. 1, 2007, http://www.wiete.com.au/journals/GJEE/Publish/vol11no1/Riemer.pdf. Accessed 12 Nov. 2017.

Rissmiller, K. "Achievement of IQP Learning Outcomes as Indicated in 2013 IQP Review of Project Completed On Campus." Worcester Polytechnic Institute, 2014. Internal Report.

Sobania, Neal, and Larry Braskamp. "Study Abroad or Study Away: It's Not Merely Semantics." *Peer Review: Study Abroad and Global Learning*, vol. 11, no. 4, Fall 2009, https://www.aacu.org/publications-research/periodicals/study-abroad-or-study-away-its-not-merely-semantics.

Sun, Huatong. "Exploring Cultural Usability." *IEEE International Professional Communication Conference (IPCC), Portland, Oregon*, 2002, pp. 319–330, doi.org/10.1109/ipcc.2002.1049114.

Vaz, Richard, and Paula Quinn. "Long Term Impacts of Off-Campus Project Work on Student Learning and Development." *IEEE Frontiers in Education Conference, Madrid, Spain, Oct. 2014*, doi.org/10.1109/fie.2014.7044128.

Wisla, Heather, et al. "Service-Learning: Boldly Going Where EAL Students Have Not Gone Before." *BC TEAL Journal*, vol. 2, no. 1, 2017, pp. 1–13.

"WPI: 2014 Fact Book." 1 Oct. 2014, https://web.wpi.edu/Images/CMS/IRO/2014_Fact_Book_for_Web(2).pdf.

Wurr, Adrian J. "Service-Learning and Student Writing: An Investigation of Effects." *Service-Learning through a Multidisciplinary Lens*, edited by Shelley H. Billig and Andrew Furco, Information Age Publishing, 2002, pp. 103–122.

PART 2

US Students and International Experiences at Home and Abroad

4
THE USE OF WRITING FOR TRANSFER IN STUDY ABROAD

Kathryn Johnson Gindlesparger

This collection has argued that the continued pursuit of global learning within rhetoric and composition is dependent on global competencies of writing instructors. As such, faculty leading students on study abroad programs must be aware of the cultural contexts of the students participating in those programs so that they may more acutely support their students' abilities to transfer their experiences once they are back on campus. One such cultural context is the professional orientation of students. While study abroad has been identified as a "high impact practice" by the Association of American Colleges and Universities for its ability to encourage students to explore "worldviews different from their own" ("High Impact"), the writing and reflective practices often utilized while abroad are under-theorized in the role they play in exploring identity development in professionally oriented educational contexts. Professionally oriented students have been shown to be less likely to study abroad than traditional undergraduates in part because time studying abroad is perceived as a distraction from the professional track (Stroud). Research also suggests that professionally oriented students can become "stuck" in static understandings of their future professions, relying on inflexible and often inaccurate information (Brady and Schreiber), which can lead to damaging assumptions about the role global perspectives play, if at all, in a student's future profession. Using interviews with professionally oriented students who recently studied abroad as a case study, I suggest that flexible thinking about one's future professions allows students to transfer skills and strategies from the travel experience to their preprofessional training.

The students interviewed here perceived the skills learned abroad as professionally relevant when the written genres encountered abroad mirrored the genres of their future profession. That is, what they believed the work of their profession to be, which may not be as rich of a representation that someone currently working in the field could imagine. Licona et al., in this collection, argue that essentialist approaches to identity, including disciplinary identity, decrease the ability to "sustain ambiguities" and "understand contradictions as possibly generative" (2). Essentialist perceptions of a profession—for example, that engineers only use math—decrease a student's ability to navigate the cultural situatedness of a professional discourse community, which invariably includes ambiguities and contradictions. An intervention, then, is needed in how faculty position the study abroad experience as professionally relevant; reflection is one such strategy.

At the heart of student application of newly acquired professional skills is the importance of reflective writing to the transfer of knowledge. Reflective writing has become a well-used and valuable practice in writing assessment (Yancey; White) and teaching for transfer (TFT), an emerging area of pedagogical research within writing studies that aims to frame knowledge acquisition for future recall (Yancey et al.). The practice of reflection has also become popular in study abroad (Brockington and Weidenhoeft). But as Pagano and Roselle have pointed out, misguided or unintentional reflection can steer students away from global engagement. Leaning on Kathleen Yancey's maxim that "you can't reflect on what you don't know," study abroad reflection that encourages students to anchor their emerging professional identity in essentialist understandings of their future professions can be a threat to the continuation of professional students pursuing foreign study. In fact, the absence of professionally mindful reflection abroad may steer students away from ultimately acquiring the intercultural competencies that employers so desire.

CHANGING FACE OF STUDY ABROAD: ENCOURAGING MORE PROFESSIONALLY ORIENTED STUDENTS TO GO ABROAD

From a rhetorical perspective, professional education can be defined as students' enculturation to a discipline-specific discourse community. At professionally oriented institutions, this enculturation is encouraged early and often as a way to assimilate students to the standards of their future professions. This enculturation proliferates an "insider" perspective to academic success; to be outside of a discipline is to be, literally, undisciplined, or at risk of failure. At my own professionally oriented institution, for example, only 1 percent of students in the most recent institutional headcount list their major as undeclared, and 75 percent of students report that they are "quite" or "very" interested in "acquiring job or work-related knowledge and skills" (National Survey of Student Engagement). This urge to remain situated within a major and acquire discipline-oriented skills has ramifications for extracurricular activities that may be seen as obstacles rather than opportunities. In fact, students in professional majors like architecture and the health sciences are less likely to study abroad because the experience interrupts strictly sequenced courses and keeps students from the material conditions of taking required courses at their home campus such as labs or studios (Stroud 502).

This "insider" approach to disciplinarity poses problems for more complex approaches to professional education, as has been discussed in the literature on academic enculturation (Lu and Horner). They suggest working with students to "recognize the diverse, often competing economies and economic sectors in which they are involved" (118), with the understanding that disciplines themselves are economic sectors. Even while students aspire to be, say, an architect, with all the cultural capital that title invokes, they are constrained by a disciplinary production of knowledge that expects campus residency to participate in studio culture and the careful sequencing of skill-related courses. Thus, the accommodations made for professionally oriented students to participate in study abroad present both opportunities and constraints: while more diverse representation among students abroad is only a good thing, faculty are tasked with meeting the needs of these students, who may have different expectations about the relevance of what they learn while abroad.

At my own institution, improvements in the study abroad system have made foreign study more appealing to professionally oriented students. The study abroad industry, independent of any one institution, has also changed to attract and accommodate more students. The Institute for International Education (IIE)'s *Open Doors* report series estimates that all types of study abroad have "more than doubled" in the past fifteen years, with the vast majority of students (60%) in 2012–2013 participating in short-term study abroad, defined in the IIE's studies as "summer or 8 weeks or less." These short experiences are often referred to as "short courses." The long-term (academic year or longer) experience of years ago accounted for only 3 percent of students participating in study abroad during the same reporting period. Shorter periods of time abroad can be more cost-effective options for students—while also generating revenue for institutions and third-party conduits, such as the IIE itself—and provide students with more flexibility in scheduling work and family obligations.

My own institution has integrated short courses into the curriculum, particularly across the summer, spring, and winter breaks. To offset both student and institutional cost, faculty created a multi-course option, where students enroll in one course but travel as a group with the students and faculty in the other two courses. These short courses often cover more than one country, with the increased number of faculty working as both chaperones and instructors. The study abroad experience detailed here, "Nexus Abroad," is one such option. While the addition of faculty-led short courses has encouraged more students to study abroad, an additional hurdle is to help students transfer the experience to their professions.

CHANGING FACE OF PROFESSIONAL EDUCATION: WHAT EMPLOYERS WANT

Professions, particularly those responsible to accreditation and licensure requirements, have articulated employers' desire for intercultural and broad communication skills as a part of their work with undergraduate majors. One such example is ABET, the accrediting body for engineering programs, which articulates how employers want soft skills in addition to more technically oriented skills. It lists among its sample skills for engineering graduates:

- ability to communicate effectively
- ability to function on multidisciplinary teams
- the broad education necessary to understand the impact of engineering solutions in a global, economic, environmental, and societal context
- a recognition of the need for, and an ability to engage in, lifelong learning
- a knowledge of contemporary issues. ("Criteria")

These skills are not separated out from other more vocationally oriented skills; they are requirements included in the accreditation process.

Additionally, *Educating the Engineer of 2020: Adapting Engineering Education to the New Century*, published by the National Academy of Engineering, advocates for more interdisciplinary education, among other measures, to prepare future engineers for an increasingly diverse and global profession. The summary of recommendations highlights the importance of nontechnical skills as the profession grows and forecasts "a growing need for interdisciplinary and system-based approaches [and] demands for new paradigms of customization" (3). They predict that "the steady integration of technology in our public infrastructures and lives will call for more involvement by engineers in the setting of public policy and in participation in the civic arena" (3). These are not calls for more technical, skills-based education; instead, they are requests for engineers able to work with others, anticipate needs and opportunities, solve problems, and advocate for the greater good. Both the ABET criteria and *Educating the Engineer of 2020* show that even technically focused employers want to hire employees who are flexible, who can collaborate, and who can work in multidisciplinary teams. These skills and abilities contribute to a dynamic view of professions where disciplinary knowledge and job skills are continually evolving. These are all habits of mind and practices that can be acquired via study abroad.

While study abroad allows students to develop the flexible and interdisciplinary strategies mentioned above, students do not necessarily transfer the study abroad experience to their majors. This is due in part to the fluid nature in which professional identities are typically formed; it is difficult to transfer fluid skills to a fluid identity. In "Static to Dynamic: Professional Identity as Inventory, Invention, and Performance in Classrooms and Workplaces," Brady and Schreiber discuss how genre, perceived mastery of which is a common marker of professional identity development, is also fluid and contributes to individuals' performance of their profession. They note that "such performances are contextualized and fluid . . . and require 'expressive equipment,' such as appearance, verbal and physical expressions, bearing, and manner" (347). One complication in this process of professionalization is that students often inflexibly, or even incorrectly, imagine their disciplinary genres. Viewing the profession from the outside in, students may not see the richness of the genres, including how they work with other disciplinary genres and combine to make new genres. Their views of the profession are static rather than dynamic, resulting in a lack of knowledge transfer. This static view of the profession can be a challenge for professionally oriented students trying to reconcile their disciplinary ambitions with broad interdisciplinary experiences like study abroad, and faculty who teach professionally oriented students in study abroad courses.

WRITING FOR TRANSFER IN STUDY ABROAD

The concept of knowledge transfer is at the heart of connecting skills learned on study abroad to students' professions. As transfer has become a popular topic of conversation in higher education, it has given rise to the ubiquity of reflection as a tool to facilitate transfer. Yet the transfer of habits and skills encountered on study abroad has been an under-theorized area of exploration.

Elizabeth Wardle's work on transfer in first-year composition breaks theories of knowledge transfer down into three categories: those that perceive knowledge as task conceptions, or the "transition of knowledge used in one task to solve another task" (67); those involving individual conceptions, in which students "seek out and/or create situations in which what they have learned will transfer" (Tuomi-Gröhn and Engeström 24 qtd. in Wardle); and those from "context conceptions," which emphasize the social construction of tasks and de-emphasize the role of the individual learner (67). For the purposes of this essay, I rely on the first two: Transfer is the knowledge used in one task to solve another task, and students can use prior knowledge to create or seek out new situations where they can use that knowledge. Additionally, transfer is ongoing. In *Writing across Contexts*, Yancey et al. cite the National Research Council's *How People Learn*, which defines transfer as "an active, dynamic process rather than a passive end-product of a particular set of learning experiences" (53 qtd. in Yancey 104). In the literature on teaching for transfer, reflection and attention to genre are two areas that garner attention.

Reflective Writing

One reason students may have a hard time connecting their study abroad experiences to their emerging professional identities is that the reflection that they are asked to do while abroad prompts thinking about personal growth instead of professional growth (or instead of how the two might fit together). Yancey's 1998 *Reflection in the Writing Classroom* lists hallmark features of reflective writing; many of the features focus on the self within the context of the learning experience and seek to connect what is known to what is unknown. Though Yancey warns that prompts for reflection should themselves be rhetorical, she offers a basic reflective tool that can be iterated, based on Peter Elbow's *Embracing Contraries*. It proceeds as follows: *believe* that this is the best project/paper you have ever created, then *doubt* that it's worth anything at all, then *predict* what your audience will think of it, and *agree/disagree* with their judgment (32). Modified to prompt students to think about a particular learning experience, the heuristic can change to: "What have you learned? How does this connect with what you already knew/know? Is this what you expected to learn? Why or why not? What else do you need to learn? How will you go about learning it?" (61). The key to both of these sets of questions is context, which is what Yancey argues is the whole point of reflection anyway. Good reflection should connect contexts, in this case, study abroad and the profession. But Yancey warns, "*We cannot reflect upon what we do not know*" (27, italics in original). This is useful to remember any time reflection with knowledge transfer is an end goal, but particularly when both contexts the student is attempting to connect are unstable or unknown. In the case of study abroad and the professions, students may not feel like they "know" either context: They may have only been abroad for a short time, and they have not yet had legitimate experience in the profession.

Students who struggle to find connections between their majors and cocurricular activities may have a fixed understanding of what their future professions are (Brady and Schreiber). In other words, they do not *know* the dynamism of their profession. Reflective practices can even support these fixed—and incorrect—perceptions, especially in the case of portfolios or other "reflection-in-presentation" (Yancey) that is meant to showcase student learning for an audience.[1] Brady and Schreiber echo Yancey's concern about not being able to reflect on what you do not know when they admit that reflection, especially in this high-stakes reflection-in-presentation style, can sometimes (accidentally) reveal "what they do not know about their professional identities" (345). For students who have not yet entered their fields, a future professional identity can be understandably difficult to conceive. This may especially be the case at professionally oriented institutions where students enter a major to "be an architect" rather than "perform cultural practices that relate to architectural and industrial design."

Attention to Genre

As Schryer and Spoel suggest within the frame of healthcare professions, and which many others in genre theory have articulated, genres "articulate a framework that at once legitimates and constrains . . . professional practices" (267). Students who have trouble connecting the learning done on study abroad to their future professions may have inflexible perceptions of disciplinary genres in their field. Furthermore, students who are particularly guarded about boundaries surrounding previous knowledge may have a harder time transferring information than students who are less guarded about these boundaries. In *Writing across Contexts*, Yancey et al. differentiate between boundary-guarding and boundary-crossing students, with boundary-guarding students more interested in "problem solution than problem exploration, and whose use of prior knowledge [is characterized as] assemblage, where new learning about writing is grafted into an unchanged basic structure already defining writing." Boundary-crossing students, however, are "interested in problem exploration, [where] prior learning is integrated into new learning (remix) and . . . writing is often infused with individual values" (133).

Students who are inflexible about the boundaries around their previous knowledge may have a hard time connecting their study abroad experience to their professional identity formation.

The teaching for transfer (TFT) approach draws on recommendations made in *How People Learn*. Some recommendations for transferring knowledge include: (1) explicitly recognize what knowledge, assumptions, preconceptions students come in with; (2) organize learned facts in a way that facilitates retrieval; (3) define learning goals and let students chart their progress toward achieving those goals; and (4) integrate the metacognitive activities (i.e., reflection, charting of learning goals) into the content that is being taught (Yancey et al. 137). Because student thinking about what their professions will be—what they imagine themselves doing—may constrain their learning of related skills and behaviors, faculty taking professionally oriented students abroad must consider if and how those students are prompted to transfer the information from study abroad to performances of professional identity.

STUDENT VOICES: PERCEPTIONS OF PROFESSIONAL RELEVANCE OF THE STUDY ABROAD EXPERIENCE

Over the summer of 2016, I contacted forty-one students who previously participated in the Nexus Abroad courses. Sixteen students responded, and seven of these respondents and I were able to schedule interviews. While seven students is not a large enough group of students to make generalizations about how transfer happens on study abroad, the students' interviews provide insight into the gaps between professional identity formation and study abroad, and how writing may help or hinder that connection. I was particularly interested to hear whether students perceived their time on campus as disciplinary "insiders" and their time abroad as "outsiders," and if this shift in rhetorical perspective seemed useful to them, as emerging professionals. To understand how students valued their time abroad, I asked:

- Academically, what did you find most challenging about the study abroad experience? What was challenging about the experience that

was not academic? Did you reflect on these moments in any way while you were abroad?
- How might you use what you learned during the travel experience in your future profession?
- Did the writing you did during your travel experience help facilitate your understanding of your profession/major?

Students participated in the interviews at varying lengths of time after their study abroad experience. This variation in professional maturity is visible in their interviews, as Allison, who I interviewed five years after her study abroad experience, was able to connect the study abroad experience to her current professional context, noting that in her current job as an Air Force communications officer, she travels a lot, and the Nexus Abroad trip "jumpstarted me to know that I can travel by myself, I can do this." Students who had completed more major courses before studying abroad would ideally have a more nuanced understanding of the profession and would be more likely to reflect meaningfully on the experience because, to refer to Yancey's maxim, the profession is more "known."

Students who anticipated the dynamism of their future professions were able to more readily find professional relevance for their study abroad experience. While some students viewed their majors as being static, there was also evidence of an emerging understanding of the profession, as students also reported that they learned habits of mind related to their majors while abroad. Students who reported getting the most out of study abroad professionally were most able to see their future professions in a flexible way.

Interestingly, students reported that writing only tangentially helped them make the connection or did not help at all. In fact, it seemed like they made most of these realizations about what was professionally valuable to them in real time during our interview. Allison reflected: "I don't think I ever sat down and thought or wrote about this specifically, but definitely talking to you now makes me realize I'm a little more confident from that trip. Looking back, I can see how it shaped that skill in my life. But I don't think I necessarily sat down to think about it." The student interviews that follow point to a gap in study abroad pedagogy that can be filled with reflective writing practices that can help students connect their study abroad experience to their future profession. To support students more fully, I suggest that a more professionally minded approach to reflection might encourage students to consider their disciplines more broadly while doing metacognitive work.

Pre-Professional Education as Static and Fixed

Students reported that their majors, specifically course loads, scheduling, and social expectations, are static and fixed. Yet simultaneously, they had a more fluid understanding of the strategies and skills involved in being a professional, separate from their disciplinary expectations.

Chloe is a senior in engineering with a concentration in textiles. She went on Nexus Abroad in the summer of 2015 when she was a rising junior. When I interviewed Chloe, she said she had always wanted to do study abroad but had trouble figuring out how to balance her coursework and internship opportunities, which are highly valued in textile engineering, with a full semester away from campus. When the institution advertised the Nexus Abroad experience with the one general education course that she could take as an elective, Chloe jumped at the opportunity. For Chloe, the experience would add something "fun" to her engineering degree; the purpose was not to learn disciplinary knowledge while abroad:

> I wanted to study abroad a full semester but I was having trouble figuring out with the Engineering courses, what places to go and what courses would transfer. Being an engineering student you have a very specific course load. There's a prerequisite string for eight courses. So there's not much wiggle room for electives. I think that's one of the reasons I wanted to do something fun with this elective I have.

Chloe separates out her major coursework from "something fun." The separation reinforces the notion that engineering content is static; engineering is fixed while the world moves around it.

Paige, an interior design student, was also concerned about going abroad for a whole semester and took the Nexus Abroad course to satisfy a general education requirement that happened to be taught by an interior design faculty member. Her description of her time abroad shows how valued major coursework is to students, even when abroad, as she noted, "even though it was a gen ed, we still talked about a lot of stuff in our major."

Paige seems to have circumvented the perceived obstacle of study abroad to a professional orientation by staying intellectually close to faculty and other students in her major. Her major was static and unchanging, while the study abroad travel experience became the variable.

Students also perceived a one-to-one transfer of skills: that what students learned about their majors would only transfer to other discipline-oriented, yet international, contexts. Paige suggests this when she notes the difference in interior design working environments in the United States versus in Europe, but she dismisses the use of this knowledge in professional contexts that are not overtly international. She says: "We did learn a lot about how my major, interior design, works over there. I don't think I'll necessarily be working abroad, but it'll be good to know that things work differently here and there." Paige's view represents a static view of the profession because it assumes that international experience would only be useful professionally if she were working abroad.

Even though the three courses on Nexus Abroad are meant to be intimate and encourage cross-disciplinary communication among students and faculty while on the trip, the students did see disciplinary content as separate from the travel content. Chloe, the engineering student with the strict prerequisite schedule, makes the distinction between learning content related to her profession and content related to the professional world, joking, "I didn't learn any math when I was there. I think [the experience] would help me in the professional world, not my profession." Looking back to the ABET guidelines and the *Engineer of 2020* report discussed above, it is apparent that the accrediting body for engineering and the National Academy of Engineering might disagree, that the ability to work in a complex, global, and interdisciplinary setting is in fact now part of the profession. The perceived distinction between skills "for the professional world" and skills for "the profession" was replicated across the interviews.

"Soft" Skills as Relevant and Transferrable

Students reported that they learned soft skills that were relevant to broad professional behavior, but not necessarily disciplinary behavior. Paige, the interior design student, noted that the ability to adapt to different working environments and the expectations of various clients will help her in the future. She expands:

> If your ultimate goal is to design for hospitality, it's probably not always what you're going to be doing. You're going to have to adapt to design for healthcare, or for corporate offices. You're probably going to have to do a lot of different projects and you're also going to probably have a lot of different clients. And you'll have to adapt to how each client wants something done. Or if you're working with a different office, how they work.

She then credited traveling between different countries during the study abroad experience as one way she learned to adapt, noting, "I guess just kind of adapting to any situation [is a skill I learned]. It's not like we had to learn the language or anything but we had to learn how to fit in. We didn't want to stick out." What motivates Paige to adapt is not wanting to "stick out." This is an acute rhetorical understanding of both the travel experience and, ultimately, professions: to some extent, complying with cultural conventions is a marker of professionalism and disciplinarity. If Paige moves from one office to another, she'll need to blend in with the expectations of a new professional culture.

Katelyn, a graphic design communication major, stated at the beginning of the interview that "I don't really think that the experience fit directly with graphic design," yet she eventually admitted that confidence and perseverance, both habits she practiced on study abroad, are also pillars of graphic design. She says:

> If you're not confident in what you're doing, no one's going to hire you. No one's going to take you seriously if you don't have confidence as a designer; you're not going to be able to push yourself to keep going.... Perseverance. Just keep going. Because you have to produce something. You have to have something! You can't say, "I'm sorry but I couldn't come up with something."

She connects this to the travel component of the course, which was significant (booking tickets, finding hotels, securing tickets for museums, meal planning, and so forth—all of which were handled by the course faculty). She adds,

> I learned so much from that. I never would have been able to do any of that on my own. I think having been through that experience and seeing other people like [our teachers] get everything together, and show us the way ... I think I could go to Europe by myself and do the same thing. But I wouldn't have been able to do that had I not been on this trip.

To me, the unnamed ability she describes is confidence, one of the skills that Katelyn says is so essential in graphic design.

Allison, a rising junior when she went on the trip and an alumna when I spoke with her on the phone, said that she remembers confidence being the key skill that she learned on the trip. She says, "I used to be a very quiet person, so being thrown into those situations, and obviously the military, makes you come out of your shell and I think afterwards, at least when I was giving my speeches senior year and stuff, this trip gave me a little push out of my comfort zone."

Donna is an international business major; during her interview, she told me that she'd never been out of the country before this trip but that she'd always wanted to travel. For her, the price point of the short course was one of the factors that encouraged her to go. She imagined her professional life as a series of trips abroad to countries where she would need to navigate unfamiliar languages, currencies, and customs. She imagined,

A lot of business is done in China or other countries, new ones are coming up. You don't go into a meeting with someone in a different country and think that you're better than them. They have different views and so do you and you just have to work together and find compromises. . . . Not every country is fast paced. Some are going slower and making sure everything's done right. Not rushing through because that seems like you're too eager and not worried about the outcomes.

Donna had never been out of the country but was eager to learn. Yet as a first-year student, her understanding of international business was influenced by our culture's painting of that profession: characters on TV shows or suit-wearing models in waiting room magazines. In Donna's case, international business is imagined as a field wherein the same business practices—"going to meetings," "working together," "finding compromises"—replicate across cultures, yet those engaged in the field should be prepared to push against these practices.

Donna pointed to the study abroad trip as an opportunity to learn about how to adapt to these cultures; what she called being "culturally aware." She says, "When I am working with a company and we're working with outside clients, even if they live in this country but are from somewhere else or if they practice a different faith: I think [study abroad] will make me more open minded and down to earth and think about what they may need or [about] their differences." Donna mentioned the physical schlepping between cities and countries, changing money, using public transportation as areas of the study abroad trip that would help her be more open-minded with clients who do not share her cultural perspective: "How to get around a city very easily, really use hotel resources, the concierge. Really use them, that's what they're there for. 'What's the quickest way to get here?' We did our laundry and stuff and we didn't necessarily know where it was at." While she imagines international business as a steady stream of encountering "different faiths" and "differences," she simultaneously acknowledges the importance of being open-minded.

Chloe, the engineer, echoed the importance of collaborating across different cultural perspectives and expectations. She noted that engineering is a field with a particularly international workforce, and that even within engineering as a field, there are great differences between the various branches: "There are a lot of different backgrounds and cultures in engineering. . . . Even just from electrical engineering to mechanical engineering, you're going to be working together in some way or another." She adds that knowing how to work across these differences and identify common thinking is a trait that is professionally valuable: "Taking one engineer's idea and saying oh, I don't really know if I agree with that and talking to someone else. And trying to mesh things together to make sense for myself. Like my internship right now, many of those people have many different opinions and trying to sift through them all is . . . not trying to find the right one, but trying to find the best one to follow or merging them together."

The students are able to see that the practices they learn on study abroad are relevant to professional life, but not necessarily to their future discipline. They also rely on essentialist understandings of the profession to theorize how they might be more flexible given their recent study abroad experience. Given the obstacles of more students going abroad, and the opportunity reflective writing can present to student' transfer of knowledge, what can composition faculty do to better support professional students abroad, particularly as these students attempt to reconcile their learning abroad with their preprofessional cultures?

RECOMMENDATIONS: USES OF REFLECTIVE WRITING ABROAD

Perhaps the most interesting finding from this exploration was an unexpected one: the students did not find writing to be a meaningful contribution to their learning abroad, and most of them had not reflected on the value of the study abroad experience to their profession before our interview. In fact, our interview functioned much like a written reflective activity might have during the extended travel experience.

The potential role of reflective writing abroad emerges not in the students' reports of salient curricular features of their experience, but rather in the gaps: in the missed opportunity revealed in the interviews. When Chloe says that her study abroad experience would help her in "the professional world," but not in her profession, there is room to explore the difference between the two, especially in light of what Chloe, from her vantage point as an undergraduate, imagines to be "professionalism" (the ability to collaborate) and "the profession" (doing math). When Katelyn says that the study abroad experience didn't really "fit with graphic design," yet during the interview acknowledges that she learned the confidence necessary to succeed as a designer, it is apparent that the transfer of knowledge from study abroad to the profession is complex and could be facilitated more intentionally. And when Donna imagined that "a lot of business is done in China," there is room, as Yancey suggests, to enhance her reflection by reconsidering "what is known" about the sites of various corners of international business. The students' interviews, while not explicitly describing the writing process, instead call for writing; the missed opportunities to connect the study abroad experience to the preprofessional track all call for reflection.

One recommendation is to have professionally oriented students explicitly connect their experiences abroad to a dynamic conceptualization of their future profession. This might have helped Chloe, who noted that she "didn't do any math" abroad, imagine how her experiences might fit into an engineering context. During predeparture discussions, faculty may take up Amy Devitt's approach of teaching the fluidity of genre as a way of seeing professions as performative and flexible. Devitt suggests that each performance of a genre is unique, which may encourage students to expect that their professions will change over time and across geographic and cultural contexts. A predeparture discussion would prepare students to be flexible in thinking of how their experience will be relevant professionally.

A structure for integrating reflection into the study abroad courses themselves would also support faculty in encouraging students to write. My own institution has adopted a one-credit reflective writing course that can be taken by any student currently studying abroad (even at partner institutions). We have also adopted an electronic portfolio as a metacognitive tool in delivering the general education program (Schrand et al.), which can also be used as a familiar location and set of prompts for students to engage with while abroad. As more students go abroad, some with specific professional contexts and expectations, faculty who take those students abroad must be prepared to help them apply the experience to their preprofessional contexts.

NOTE

1. While Brady and Schreiber are describing technical communication students, it is safe to say that other disciplines likely have this same problem, as all professions evolve over time and are context dependent. That is, all professions are always changing and thus present the problem to students of assimilating into an ever-moving target.

WORKS CITED

Brady, M. Ann, and Joanna Schreiber. "Static to Dynamic: Professional Identity as Inventory, Invention, and Performance in Classrooms and Workplaces." *Technical Communication Quarterly*, vol. 22, no. 4, 2013, pp. 343–362, doi.org/10.1080/10572252.2013.794089.

Brockington, Joseph L., and Margaret D. Weidenhoeft. "The Liberal Arts and Global Citizenship: Fostering Intercultural Engagement through Integrative Experiences and

Structured Reflection." *The Handbook of Research and Practice in Study Abroad: Higher Education and the Quest for Global Citizenship*, edited by Ross Lewin, Routledge, 2010, pp. 117–132.

"Criteria for Accrediting Engineering Programs, 2018–2019: Student Outcomes." *ABET*. http://www.abet.org/accreditation/accreditation-criteria/criteria-for-accrediting-engineering-programs-2018-2019/#outcomes.

"High Impact Educational Practices." https://www.aacu.org/sites/default/files/files/LEAP/hip_tables.pdf.

Lu, Min-Zhan, and Bruce Horner. "Composing in a Global-Local Context: Careers, Mobility, Skills." *College English*, vol. 72, no. 2, 2009, pp. 113–133.

National Academy of Engineering. *Educating the Engineer of 2020: Adapting Engineering Education to the New Century*. Committee on the Engineer of 2020. National Academy of Engineering, 2005. www.nap.edu/catalog/11338/educating-the-engineer-of-2020-adapting-engineering-education-to-the.

National Survey of Student Engagement (NSSE). "Philadelphia University: Mean Comparisons." 2012. https://www2.philau.edu/ir/secure/NSSE/NSSE12%20Mean%20and%20Frequency%20Reports%20(PhilaU).pdf.

"Nexus Abroad." *PhilaU Study Away*. https://philau.studioabroad.com/index.cfm?FuseAction=Programs.ViewProgram&Program_ID=59634. Accessed 26 Jan. 2018.

"Open Doors 2014: A 15 Year Snapshot." Institute of International Education, 22 July 2015. www.iie.org/Research-and-Publications/Open-Doors.

Pagano, Monica, and Laura Roselle. "Beyond Reflection Through an Academic Lens: Refraction and International Experiential Education." *Frontiers: The Interdisciplinary Journal of Study Abroad*, vol. 18, Fall 2009, pp. 217–229, frontiersjournal.org/wp-content/uploads/2015/09/PAGANO-ROSELLE-FrontiersXVIII-BeyondReflection.pdf.

Schrand, Thomas, et al. "'Reflecting on Reflections': Curating ePortfolios for Integrative Learning and Identity Development in a General Education Senior Capstone." *International Journal of ePortfolio*, vol. 8, no. 1, 2018, pp. 1–12.

Schryer, Catherine F., and Phillippa Spoel. "Genre Theory, Health-Care Discourse, and Professional Identity Formation." *Journal of Business and Technical Communication*, vol.19, no. 3, 2005, pp. 249–273, doi.org/10.1177/1050651905275625.

Stroud, April H. "Who Plans (Not) to Study Abroad? An Examination of U.S. Student Intent." *Journal of Studies in International Education*, vol. 14, no. 5, 2010, pp. 491–507.

Wardle, Elizabeth. "Understanding 'Transfer' from FYC: Preliminary Results of a Longitudinal Study." *Writing Program Administration*, vol. 31, no. 1–2, 2007, pp. 65–85, writingaboutwriting.umassd.wikispaces.net/file/view/Wardle-+Transfer.pdf/278764734/Wardle-+Transfer.pdf.

White, Edward M. "The Scoring of Writing Portfolios: Phase 2." *College Composition and Communication*, vol. 56, no. 4, June 2005, pp. 581–599, www.jstor.org/stable/30037887.

Yancey, Kathleen Blake. *Reflection in the Writing Classroom*. Utah State University Press, 1998.

Yancey, Kathleen Blake, et al. *Writing across Contexts Transfer, Composition, and Sites of Writing*. Utah State University Press, 2014.

5
REFLECTIONS ON AN EMERGENT ENTREMUNDISTA PEDAGOGY
Teacher-Researchers in Engaged Transdisciplinary Public Scholarship

Adela C. Licona, Stephen T. Russell, and
The Crossroads Collaborative[1]

> *To contribute to social transformation, bricoleurs seek to better understand both the forces of domination that affect the lives of individuals from race, class, gender, sexual, ethnic, and religious backgrounds outside of dominant culture(s) and the worldviews of such diverse peoples. In this context, bricoleurs attempt to remove knowledge production and its benefits from the control of elite groups.—Kincheloe and McLaren, 423*

> *I am an entremundista, a traveler between worlds.—Licona*

How/Can multiple critical, investigative vantage points and critical perspectives be brought into conversation to create and promote public scholarship aimed at social transformation? How/Can such an approach be the pedagogy for preparing transdisciplinary scholars to re-vision and reconfigure the historically binary relationships and oppositional pairings of researcher/teacher, scholar/activist, quantitative/qualitative, university/community, adult/youth? Both quotations we use in the opening of this chapter, one by Kinchelow and McLaren and the other by Licona, speak to a call for transformative power of people and groups moving within and between boundaries and communities. In this chapter we share the story of an action-oriented teaching, research, writing, and outreach collaborative, the Crossroads Collaborative, designed to inquire into and address youth sexualities, health, and rights (YSHR). Begun at a moment when YSHR were explicitly contested, we committed to a practice of cultivation and reflection that we identify and will elaborate on in this chapter as an *entremundista pedagogy*. We focus first on the origins of our collaboration as situated in its historical time and in its transnational borderlands place. We then describe our approach to transdisciplinary preparation in a transnational context that served as the foundation for a critical mixed-methods approach to research, teaching, and writing practices. We then turn our attention to collaborative arts-based inquiries with young people, as these offer particularly rich examples of the messiness of critical and creative inquiry and of what emerged as an entremundista pedagogy.

An *entremundista pedagogy* is change-oriented, community informed but globally aware, and engaged in contested knowledges; contextual and aware of possible connections across contexts; intersectional and interdisciplinary; able to sustain ambiguities; and understanding of contradictions as always possibly generative. We, therefore, moved beyond a traditional understanding of the researcher as being exclusively an inquirer. Instead, we consider our community research contexts as also always being opportunities for us to teach, and—following our commitment to feminist pedagogy and the principles of action-oriented research—as also always being opportunities to learn. Given our distinct disciplinary locations in the social sciences and humanities and our inclusion of community members as co-researchers, our goal was to question, as well as to attempt, qualitative and quantitative inquiry that might bring stories and numbers together in new ways. We drew inspiration from Morse and Niehaus's notion of a mixed-methods design as a "design [that] is a scientifically rigorous *research project*, driven by the inductive [and/or] deductive *theoretical drive*, and comprised of a qualitative [and/or] quantitative *core component* with qualitative [and/or] quantitative *supplementary component(s)*" (14, emphasis in the original). The vision we had was at once qualitative and quantitative as well as creative and critical. We were prepared for open-endedness and aimed to develop and remain critically aware of power and power differentials. The social scientists were sometimes challenged by what they perceived as needlessly dense theoretical discourses and the humanists were sometimes challenged by what they perceived as reductive implications in quantitative approaches to the complexities of human sexuality. By moving beyond either/or sexual essentialisms and their implications for static and prescribed notions of sexuality, an entremundista pedagogy helped us consider the rhetorical function and force of social discourses (local, state, national, and transnational). It was also helpful in demonstrating how theory, methods, and methodologies can come together in productive and interesting cross-disciplinary ways to prepare teacher-researchers to move beyond limiting essentialisms (including disciplinary essentialism) in order to engage the cultural and structural dimensions as well as the lived complexities of sexual subjectivities.

As university colleagues from distinct personal, disciplinary, and epistemological backgrounds, we share an interest in social justice and transdisciplinarity and began discussion about the possibility for a deliberate move to experimental approaches to co-teaching, co-research, and co-writing.[2] By transdisciplinarity we mean reconsidering and unsettling epistemological assumptions from our distinct disciplinary locations to inform innovations in collaborative scholarship to include research, writing, and teaching practices. We imagined that such emergent scholarship practices might, in turn, inform and be informed by each of our disciplinary locations as well as by the local communities and community contexts with which we are connected and the worlds within which we were situated. We were deliberate in the multi-method approaches to our teaching and research and learned more than we might have imagined about our own assumptions as well as those of some of our students and community participants. We committed ourselves to read broadly and, following Denzin and Lincoln, to work "between and within competing and overlapping perspectives and paradigms" (5).

We began our collaboration at an extraordinary moment: Arizona's 49th legislature introduced regressive, nationalist legislation and associated public rhetorics that launched a hostile climate that reached across national borders and threatened as well as criminalized the non-normative—especially im/migrants (through the infamous SB 1070), but also LGBTQ people and young people. This historic moment was characterized by a building sense of (legislative and legislated) panic—one that a group of six United Nations human rights experts referred to as a "disturbing pattern of legislative activity hostile to ethnic minorities and immigrants."[3] Following Susan Finley, we recognized that a "new kind of research pedagogy is needed in such a panicked context of diminishing democracy" (446). We were teaching and researching—living—in a moment of "diminishing democracy," particularly evident in the production of moral, social, and sexual panics (Herdt; Wieringa; Hall et al.). Arizona's moral and sexual panic manifested itself in the legislation of surveillance of particular bodies and bodies of knowledge. Recognizing and understanding this state of panic, and the borderlands surveillances it instituted, was crucial for our project, our students, and the youth and community organization leaders with whom we were working. We felt a responsibility to expose these social panics for what they are: instruments of nativism, homophobia, and xenophobia in the service of particular power constellations. Discursive strategies that were deployed in and by the state both informed and were informed by nationalist discourses that worked in tandem to pathologize and criminalize immigrants and non-dominant Others that set the tone and culminated in the passage of regressive legislative measures. This panic is informed by the ideological construction of immigrant and "reasonably suspicious others" as (economic) threats to the state, as violent and pathological criminals, and—in proposed (but not passed) legislation—as hypersexual.

As teacher-researchers in Arizona, situated along the Mexico–United States border in Tohono O'odham territory, we recognized the need for transnational awareness and for deep reflections on our differently privileged positions and the responsibility we had to teach and research in ways that not only did not inadvertently or explicitly fuel hateful rhetorics but rejected the premises upon which they were built. Following Yvonna Lincoln's discussion of bricoleurs, our entremundista pedagogy is also committed "methodological eclecticism [that permits] the scene and circumstance and presence or absence of co-researchers to dictate method" (694). Thus, our collaboration became necessarily informed by place-based pedagogy, critical localism,[4] and related understandings of bricolage,[5] especially as these are expressed and experienced in the classroom and applied to borderlands research contexts.

We had to think about our inquiries as being place-based and consider how our borderlands location could be always explicit in our teaching, inquiries, and community relationships. Gloria Anzaldúa's influential work on borderlands moved us to reconsider the power and purpose of borders imposed upon geographies, bodies, sex, gender, class, psyches, and the imagination. Her work, especially, materialized the concept as well as the practice and potential of an entremundista pedagogy. The term entremundista[6] is one inspired by Chicana scholars including Anzaldúa. It is a spatialized concept that denotes a conscious navigation of distinct geographies and their multiple histories, including erasures, contestations, and evacuations. An entremundista conceptual approach aligns meaningfully for us with our historic, geographic, and cultural transnational contexts in the state of Arizona during a time of heightened xenophobia, transphobia, and related social and sexual panics that focus on the (imagined) undocumented im/migrant with significant implication for youth and migrant youth in particular. *Entremundista pedagogy*, therefore, is one that flouts disciplinary boundaries and the knowledge domains they contain (are contained by) in search of new understandings, practices, and knowledges. Understanding youth as problematically positioned in dominant discourses between the statuses of child and adult became an especially productive boundary-flouting approach to engage a more complex understanding of youth as always multiply situated (see also Russell, "Social Justice"). As a boundary-transgressing approach, entremundista pedagogy is interested in social change and in the potentials for engaging contested histories to produce new guiding myths for our time, as called for by Anzaldúa. It is, for us, also committed to engaging (in) queer world-making practices, as considered by José Esteban Muñoz as well as Laura Gutiérrez. The entremundista engages in a both/and (rather than an either/or) approach to the production of knowledge, pedagogy, place, and people; it is a term of third-space.[7] The entremundista, or the one "between worlds," is always *both* teacher *and* inquiring student; a teacher-researcher.

THE CROSSROADS COLLABORATIVE: YOUTH, SEXUALITY, HEALTH, AND RIGHTS

Deeper understandings of ourselves as teacher-researchers emerged during our cross-disciplinary conversations about the function of community knowledges in classrooms and research contexts. We were also driven by the urgent political context; we wanted our work to recognize and reject the deficit-driven mis/understandings and mis/characterizations of youth, particularly youth of color, that were prevailing in and beyond Arizona. Our state's legislative measures were, and remain, what American Indian Studies scholar Tsianina Lomawaima referred to as a "regressive suite of legislation." Informed by a neoliberal emphasis on individualism, and fueled by nationalist and xenophobic sentiments, this suite was epitomized by Arizona Senate Bill (SB) 1070. While the practical details of the bill are crucial, it is the intent of the law that has profound implications for the continued cultivation of fear and panic among—and with regard to—documented and undocumented youth and youth of mixed family immigration status in Arizona. We felt it was crucial to attend to the implied intent of the law—namely, attrition through enforcement, a climate in which persons who are undocumented, or those who are related to undocumented persons, are treated and understood as "reasonably suspicious" and both symbolically and practically invited to leave the state.[8] In other words, while the law was characterized as a crackdown on undocumented immigration, the broad invitation to leave was not limited to the undocumented. Rather, a criminalizing climate of ubiquitous suspicion and implicit guilt proved productive of new vulnerabilities as well as particularly threatening to those persons who appeared to be migrants (including, of course, youth of color). SB1070 was only one of many legislative acts that established the regressive political climate that had specific implications for youth. These included Arizona House Bill (HB) 2281, banning ethnic studies curricula.[9] Passage of this bill inspired student protests that were taken up by state politicians and often the media to fuel local panics about youth and particularly youth of color in Tucson. These youth were described by a state education official as "uncivil," "rude," and "hostile" in their responses to a climate of restricted knowledges, dehumanizing discourses, escalating hostilities, and increased surveillance (Martin 18; Horne 2).

Contemporaneous with both SB 1070 and HB 2281, Arizona Senate Bill (SB) 1266 created a criminal category for "sexting," effectively transforming what had been treated as a school behavior problem[10] into a legally punishable misdemeanor. This bill passed at a time of growing national awareness of the criminalizing consequences of exclusionary discipline policies—including zero-tolerance policies in schools, whose punitive effects were imposed disproportionately on students of color, poor and disabled students, and LGBTQ and gender nonconforming students (see Burdge et al., "Gender" and "LGBTQ"). A "parents' bill of rights" (SB 1309) also passed at this time and required parents to sign an "opt-in" form for any school-based discussion of sex, sexuality, or sexual health. The parents' bill of rights is a sweeping law that applies to all aspects of health and education of minors, placing decision-making authority squarely in the hands of parents (including but not limited to access to sexuality education as well as health care, including sexual health care). Additionally, SB 1188 gives preference to heterosexual married couples in adoptions. We mean for this sketch of legislation, and its neoliberal imperatives, to illuminate the sociopolitical climate in Arizona as particularly productive of new vulnerabilities that were reflective of an increasingly globalized world with implications for local and transnational contexts and populations. Such a political climate that presaged a rise in the authoritarian and heteropatriarchal regimes of the Global Right demanded a critical and creative approach to teaching, research, and writing, especially when working with local communities who were bearing the brunt of these consequential hostilities. In the face of dehumanizing discourses prevailing in Arizona, with implications throughout and beyond the United States, we were called to consider the role of the humanities and to interrogate constructed notions of the human/e and the in/human/e as well as to imagine new ways of understanding the human at the limits of what we can know, what we can hear, what we can see, and what we can sense. We recognize the need to explicitly contend with the dehumanizing effects of the 49th legislative session in Arizona. The ways in which we thought and taught, and even how we inquired about YSHR, could not be extracted from the racist, classed, gendered, and anti-immigrant policies and hostile as well as hateful rhetorics that were being continually generated across and beyond the state.

Following Finley's ideas that the "fulfillment of a resistance politics in research requires new urgency, requires renewed commitment, and calls for continuing development of research methodologies to support interpretive studies that extend democracy, freedom, and political voice into the everyday lives of politically oppressed people" (436), our course content and ideas for research projects were informed by a growing emphasis on the arts and on artivists[11] by our community partners and shifted to not only include but focus on feminist and critical arts-based inquiry. We understand feminist pedagogy as "marked by the development of non-hierarchical relationships among teachers and students, and reflexivity about power relations, not only in society, but in the classroom" (Crabtree et al. 8) as containing the potential to link "classroom-based teaching with opportunities for application in communities through social action using strategies such as service-learning, feminist-action research, and other methods of engaged and community-based learning" (9). We confronted the politics of knowledge and knowledge production and worked from an understanding that the university students, community youth, and adult allies with whom we were working were also and simultaneously positioned as teacher-researchers and therefore also with something to teach and something to learn. The understanding of these multiply situated positionings is important to an entremundista pedagogy that recognizes movement in and through different subject positions.

AN ENTREMUNDISTA APPROACH TO ACTION-ORIENTED AND RELATIONAL RESEARCH: ATTEMPTING INNOVATIONS IN CO-TEACHING, CO-RESEARCH, AND CO-WRITING FOR SOCIAL CHANGE

We developed a three-semester graduate seminar to serve as the genesis of the Crossroads Collaborative. Sixteen graduate students from distinct disciplinary locations enrolled in our first seminar on YSHR. Six of those students were selected as funded Crossroads scholars who continued as graduate participants for the next two semesters; the group sustained itself over the following two-and-a-half years. The lab concept was meant to encourage innovations in action-oriented research design and writing. The first-semester seminar addressed action-oriented research; collaboration; mixed and multiple methods; approaches to and production of new and social justice multimodal media; feminist and queer theory and queer-of-color critique; professional development, with attention to the role of funding in applied scholarship; applied developmental science; and strategic communications regarding research findings and their policy implications with an emphasis on collaborative writing for distinct audiences. We were each committed to a meaningful role for community members in community research design and practice. We committed ourselves and asked our students to similarly commit to being open to shifts in perspectives and practices that the dynamism of transdisciplinarity implied. We encouraged innovations in thinking and practice. Throughout, we worked to enhance understandings of the philosophical, historical, theoretical, creative, and methodological dimensions of YSHR scholarship.

In preparing for the first part of the seminar, and in order to pursue the innovations to which we had committed ourselves as collaborators, we wanted to understand, interrogate, and move beyond an exclusive focus on positivist and even post-positivist approaches to both qualitative and quantitative research. We wanted our students to draw insights from both of our disciplinary locations in the humanities and social sciences in order to engage in cross-disciplinary discussions through which we could begin to imagine, articulate, and ultimately enact transdisciplinary practices. Such a transdisciplinary approach required from us a kind of radical openness that we have come to understand is encoded in an entremundista pedagogy—that is, a willingness to be prepared to travel across disciplinary knowledge domains, to have our taken-for-granted assumptions unsettled, and for the notion of secure disciplinary knowledges to be challenged and even reconfigured. Our primary goal was to participate in work that could shift academic thinking and local practices and discourses about YSHR that are static and oppressive. To prepare graduate students for asset-informed research with respect, action-oriented research, practice, and policy-relevant work, we began selecting texts that would allow us to consider the power of discourses around dominant/nondominant and normative/nonnormative identity formations. We considered local, national, and transnational contexts that produced climates similar to the one in which we found ourselves in Arizona. We called on a range of texts that engaged the theoretical dimensions of youth and sexuality through multiple dimensions, while retaining the understanding that "youth sexuality" is both an embodied and a discursive construct.

We began with readings that set the context and framed the goals for the course and the research collaborative and that moved students to situate our local reality within broader, transnational contexts and conversations. *Sexuality Research in the United States* (di Mauro) provides a lens for understanding key advances and limitations in sexuality research in the latter half of the twentieth century as research that has remained largely defined by the culture and goals of the academy rather than responsive to community and policy exigencies. Additional readings focused on understandings of adolescence, sexuality (Russell, "Conceptualizing"; Tolman and McClelland), and agency (Herndl and Licona), which helped students think through both constraints and possibilities in action-oriented collaborations. Remaining texts provided a critical approach to action-oriented research and the broad theme of YSHR. We believed these texts could move students to reflect on the political implications of research, the power dynamics and geometries within the contexts of their eventual inquiries, and to inspire them to consider how structures of power delimit comprehensive and progressive approaches to sex and sexualities—particularly youth sexualities. Even more important is that these texts address the relationship between YSHR and the production of social and moral panics. They were therefore well suited, too, to the development of an entremundista pedagogy.

Sexuality, Health and Human Rights, offering a range of disciplinary perspectives and insights from the "global South and North," approaches sexual health and healthy sexuality as human rights while also attending to the limits of a human rights approach by moving toward understandings of "erotic justice" as a demonstrated understanding of the need "to approach both research and intervention in relation to sexuality as extension of broader struggles," including those regarding citizenship status, rights, and justice (Corrêa et al. 3). Such an approach was particularly relevant to our time and place. The editors acknowledged what we believed our context was revealing—that sex "is not only about bodies and desires but also the economies, systems of governance, cultural and religious norms, kinship structures, and power dynamics of all of these issues." This book demonstrated for us and for our students the possibility of bringing queer theory together with policy-oriented work in ways that did not subordinate the discursive and/or material realities of the body; the role of pleasure in sexual health, sexuality, and sex; and the pursuit of social change within a social justice framework. It was particularly helpful to us as we worked to understand and enact the role of an entremundista pedagogy for the development of teacher-researchers and as a model for simultaneous engagement with cross-disciplinary, embodied, and lived theory, practice, and method.[12]

In *Moral Panics, Sex Panics: Fear and the Fight over Sexual Rights*, Gil Herdt asks if people "speak out against the violations of rights and citizenship especially at the beginning of a moral panic?" He answers, "Sometimes, . . . [but] when fears are heightened, as with parents who feel 'weird' if they defend sex education against its fanatical enemies, the answer is no" (10). Herdt points out that sexual panic (defined in the book as "public arguments about sexual citizenship") dehumanizes and always targets vulnerable populations; moral panics enable a "sexual sanitation"—in which police undertake a "cleansing" of the social body hinged on the concept of sexual deviancy. Herdt goes on to note that targeted undesirables are chased out or scapegoated, and new controls are implemented to regulate and control these populations. These insights helped promote students' awareness that state-level regressive legislation threatened the most vulnerable, and that the work we were embarking on had real material consequences. Jasbir Puar's book *Terrorist Assemblages: Homonationalism in Queer Times* was equally apt for the Arizona context at the time of our course. Arizona's governor, Jan Brewer, had claimed that terrorist-style beheadings were being conducted by immigrants in the Arizona desert (see Licona on regime of distortion). Governor Brewer was unable to corroborate this patently fictional claim (see Milbank). Puar's work is concerned with the optic through which perverse populations are called into nominalization for control (xiii). Such concepts were particularly relevant to our course emphasis on the traveling force and function of public rhetorics: what produces and is produced by dehumanizing discourses of devaluation and visual misrepresentations. Rather than focus only on the resistant or oppositional, Puar purposefully considers the "convivial relations between queerness and militarism, securitization, war, terrorism, surveillance technologies, empire, torture, nationalism, globalization, fundamentalism, secularism, incarceration, detention, deportation, and neoliberalism" (xiv); she speaks of historicizing the biopolitics of the now. With theories of intersectionality and assemblage in mind, we worked to consider the dynamic relationships between Arizona's legislative measures (what they obscured and what they produced) and embodied and fluid subjectivities in Arizona.

Yolanda Chávez Leyva's work addressing Chicana/o histories moved us to consider the pain and the healing potential in facing and acknowledging erased and evaporating histories to confront and work from multiple historic truths. This work was especially relevant as young people in Arizona were witnessing and experiencing obstacles to and devaluing of particular knowledges. Saskia Eleonora Wieringa's "Postcolonial Amnesia: Sexual Moral Panics, Memory and Imperial Power" offered us a postcolonial perspective and helped us to further consider historic erasures and the ways in which "sexual moral panics were an important motor for the establishment of imperial power" (205). We used Wieringa's text to witness the power of imperialism to frame entire populations as deficient and to consolidate power through potent erasures of the non-normative and of panic-inflected rhetorics. This was especially important as our teaching, research, and emergent community relations were taking place on the traditional and occupied lands of the Tohono O'odham. We also read Linda Tuhiwai Smith's work, *Decolonizing Methodologies: Research and Indigenous Peoples,* which informed our practice to teach ways of engaging in research that understand and treat local knowledges and histories as informative and as vital to local needs, interests, and desires. Finally, as we moved from theory to praxis and community collaboration, Jeff Duncan-Andrade's *Urban Youth, Media Literacy, and Increased Critical Civic Participation* helped us to confront youth-held knowledges, examine urban social inequalities, and become better positioned to see and understand youth literacies and civic engagements as well as to witness their development. Duncan-Andrade's work also moved us to conversations about youth as producers of valuable knowledges and helped us to consider the relationship of these knowledges with youth literacy(ies) and civic potential. In this way, Duncan-Andrade's text intervened in the notion of youth as always learners, rather than knowledge producers, and subjects needing to be saved by authorized knowledges and practices. Such understandings were particularly relevant to an entremundista pedagogy that understands learners as dynamic and multiply situated.

Together, course readings helped prepare students for inquiries and community relations informed by work that engaged meaningfully with local and transgressive knowledges. Students could better consider the productive force and function of hostile, criminalizing, dehumanizing rhetorics and the role of sex panics and moral panics in re/producing structural violence and devaluation with transnational implications. In our historical context, we witnessed the formation of "inferior" citizenships, as well as alien "others" and used our readings and our relationships to identify and better understand consequences and needs before initiating our community engagements. Class discussions of the texts we assembled moved students to better understand how assumptions embedded in discourses of inquiry can shape research outcomes and conclusions.

ACTION-ORIENTED RESEARCH, RELATIONAL LITERACIES, AND THE POSSIBILITIES FOR RECIPROCITY: ENTREMUNDISTA PEDAGOGY AS ENGAGED PRACTICE

Our approach to teaching and researching informed our community research contexts and how we worked to be integrated there so that teaching, research, and writing were consciously and simultaneously engaged for their relational and reciprocal potential. As Kincheloe et al. note, critical theory and critical pedagogy can "challenge regularly employed and obsessive approaches to research," especially when they make explicit efforts to eschew "positivist approaches to both qualitative and quantitative research and refus[e] to cocoon research within the pod of unimethodological approaches" (Kincheloe, McLaren, and Steinberg 173). As teacher-researchers, we were committed to drawing from texts from across disciplines and from community contexts and knowledges, particularly those that were being threatened, delegitimated, and/or eliminated by legislative measures and by the sociopolitical climate in the state. Our commitment extended to experimenting with collaborative writing practices to include community writers and new ways of naming authorships.

As we prepared to enter our community contexts, we turned our attention to the role of the local in the production of knowledge/s, and to the question of whose knowledges, needs, and desires count in research design as well as whose knowledges were accessible and to whom, which we knew was a necessary function of our goal of transdisciplinarity. We started to consider what is understood and what can be imagined as data and how bringing qualitative and quantitative work—"stories and numbers"—together can attend to the complexities of distinct contexts and interlocking practices. We approached, for example, youth poetry, performance, and video productions as theoretical productions and as data, and thereby instructed students to identify and approach data in new ways and as always potentially poetic, performative, and interventionist. We discussed how to develop relationships in these community contexts across lines of our differing privileges. Literatures and practices built upon action-oriented and decolonizing research informed our efforts as teacher-researchers planning community work that did not exclusively include predetermined research agendas. We sought to make room for thoughtful exchange between teacher-researchers in academic and community contexts. These kinds of knowledge exchanges contributed, in turn, to a research design that considered the powerful forms of youth-produced knowledges and their literary activism as both critical and creative productions of knowledge in the forms of spoken word poetry, creative writing, and new media productions. As Finley notes, "in critical arts-based inquiry, arts are both a mode of inquiry and a methodology for performing social activism" (436). Such inquiry seemed particularly compelling given both our explicit aim to shift public discourse, practices, and policies around YSHR and the existence of youth movements in our community powered, in part, by artivists. Through this design, we were able to approach critical and creative youth productions as expressions of transnational civics that demonstrated experiential and borderlands awareness of complex histories, complicated geographies, and geopolitical as well as economic injustices that resulted in restrictions and surveillances on particular bodies and bodies of knowledge.

We utilized a research pedagogy that promoted the development of respectful relationships with youth participants and with adult allies in youth-serving organizations—all of whom we approached as community teacher-researchers. Working toward these relational and reciprocal engagements became an essential component of our entremundista pedagogy. Understanding ourselves as teacher-researchers also gave us the opportunity to participate in community literacies and to inform and be informed by such everyday knowledges (Licona). We have come to understand these as relational literacies[13] undertaken sometimes by youth as tactics that make them intelligible and, therefore, potentially recognizable and knowable—legible—to one another and perhaps to others. We believe that the knowledges revealed through these relational literacies should inform local practice and related policies as well as research writings (on relational literacies, see Martin; Licona and Chávez; Martin and Licona).

In our efforts to prepare teacher-researchers, we worked in accordance with what Finley considers to be the practice of a people's pedagogy research. Specifically, she notes that "[i]n practice of a people's pedagogy research can become a tool for advancing critical race theory and opening space for an aesthetic of artist-researchers and participant-observers belonging to oppressed groups and to individuals traditionally excluded from research locations" (Finley 446). Finley's characterization of arts-based inquiry as a particularly strategic approach in the face of neo-cultural politics also inspired our cross-disciplinary interest in local literary activism. A few Crossroads scholars were quickly involved as collaborators in community arts projects involving youth and regional YSHR studies. As a result, several developed their own youth-informed, action-oriented projects: four dissertations and one master's thesis have been completed through the Crossroads Collaborative (Martin; Tilley; Vinson; Watson; Fields). Innovative approaches emerged about the idea of poetry as data to include discussions of emergent themes in youth poetry as well as about the frequency (and implications of the frequency) of those themes. Qualitative approaches, informed by close readings, rhetorical analyses, critical race theory, LatCrit, and funds of knowledge research, emphasized themes, while quantitative approaches, informed by probability theory that included multivariate analysis and factor analysis, emphasized patterns (Fields et al., "Youth Voices"). While these distinct approaches produced results that were differently interpreted across disciplinary boundaries, they worked together to more fully illuminate the fact that young people are interested in and knowledgeable about their communities and community histories, and that their slam poetry and performances are expressions of their civic engagement that address issues of their consistent and informed concern.

TEACHER-RESEARCHERS AND ENTREMUNDISTA PRACTICES, PROJECTS, AND PEDAGOGY: ESTABLISHING A "THINK-AND-ACT" COLLABORATIVE FOR TEACHING, RESEARCH, AND WRITING

Following the first semester of the graduate seminar, in weekly meetings we discussed collaborative research design challenges and triumphs, prepared community-oriented and academic collaborative writings, hosted community members for discussions about our shared goals and ideas, and discussed strategic communication plans for public circulation of collaboratively written results and implications. Together we collaborated as teacher-researchers in several youth-driven civic and community projects; we highlight several below.

Nuestra Voz: Stephen has long been involved in research on bullying. In partnership with Nuestra Voz, a YWCA racial justice program in Tucson, the Crossroads Collaborative worked to learn and teach about bullying and to intervene in bullying. To understand students' experiences of bullying, racism, and in/justice, school climate surveys were co-developed with community members, including youth, and distributed to students throughout Tucson. Two youth programs (*Let's Get Real* and *Youth. Art. Activism. Summer Camp*) were implemented under the direction of social justice educator J. Sarah Gonzales. These projects were designed to elicit knowledge from youth as well as to educate and inform them about bullying, in addition to providing tools for youth to learn about how to intervene in bullying in their communities.

Crossroads Collaborative members collaborated in the Nuestra Voz summer camp, exploring participants' interests at the intersections of racial, economic, educational, sexual, gendered, immigrant/immigration, and economic justice. In one camp workshop, Adela and Londie Martin provided a Matsuda[14] guide to youth participants that moved them to consider intersectional systems of oppression to better understand youths' intersectional experiences with transnational implications across differences of race, class, gender, sexuality, immigration, and education status.

For one camp installation we created "toolboxes" filled with information and resources from distinct local youth-serving organizations regarding youth justice, as well as media and art supplies that youth could use to create their responses to the themes they co-identified for the camp: (1) youth, sexuality, health, and rights; (2) the school-to-prison pipeline; and (3) the (right to) ethnic studies. The "youth, sexuality, health, and rights" toolboxes, for instance, were filled with resources (collected by Zami Hyemingway from the local Eon Youth Lounge) for healthy sexuality and sexual health. Eon, the local queer youth–serving organization, provided materials for the "sex ed" toolbox that included condoms, dental dams, information about safe and pleasurable sex, and community health resources. Crossroads scholars provided information about the new "parents' bill of rights" and its provision for parents to opt students out of (already limited) sexuality education classes.

While working with this toolbox, two camp participants, Enrique Garcia and Alexia Vazquez, discussed how their schools had not provided sexual education. They connected this restriction of sexuality knowledge to the banning of ethnic studies: Before then, they had not made the connection between human rights, educational rights, and sexual rights. In this way the summer camp provided a space for youth to begin exploring intersectional considerations and coalitional possibilities around shared understandings of social justice. Garcia and Vazquez were inspired to co-write *No More Ignorant Love*, a slam poem performed by Garcia at the camp's culmination.[15] Through their poem, we learned how the concept of intersectionality was taken up, understood, and deployed in the service of a call for knowledge and in the development of a politics of refusal to be informed by xeno- and homophobic state agendas, and a refusal to be silenced or shamed. In other words, their poem became data for our research on youth needs, interests, knowledges, and desires and, in expressing experiential knowledges, they became pedagogical resources to us and to the adults we worked with from youth-serving organizations.

Kore Press Grrls Literary Activism (GLA): Kore Press, one of the last remaining feminist presses in the United States, regularly hosts Grrls Literary Activism workshops designed for girls and transgender youth interested in developing the use of their individual and collective creative voices and visions in the pursuit of progressive social change. Adela made several presentations to GLA youth and adults about issues identified by youth, including legislation that limited youth access to knowledge and information about healthy sexualities and sexual health. The Crossroads supported local filmmaker Jamie A. Lee, artists as community educators, and youth to develop creative media productions as opportunities to voice youths' interests and concerns about YSHR. Adela and Londie prepared and delivered a new media presentation for youth and adults from GLA that addressed media literacy. Grrls used poetry, collage, creative writing, oral history-like interviews, and video for their social activism. The GLA produced a twelve-minute documentary, "Works in Progress or How I Stopped Worrying and Learned to Love . . . ," about sex, gender, the body, double standards, and media mis/representations. The film opened for the Tucson debut of *Miss Representation*, a film directed by Jennifer Siebel Newsom and Kimberlee Acquaro and introduced by Jean Kilbourne, to a full house at Tucson's independent movie theater in October 2011.

Tucson Youth Poetry Slam (TYPS): Continuing with our interest in public rhetorics and as our engagement with youth literary activism projects intensified, we needed to more seriously consider the role of and for emergent creative voice and performance relevant to YSHR. We understand youth slam poetry to be producing and responding to public discourses, dialogues, and issues relevant to community and civic contexts. With the Tucson Youth Poetry Slam (TYPS) organizers and participants, the Crossroads Collaborative attended local slams and international competitions. We analyzed youth poetry and slam performances as youth creatively confronted the social and cross-border implications and injustices of Arizona's regressive legislation. Crossroads scholar Amanda Fields worked with TYPS as an action-oriented researcher and wrote her dissertation in rhetoric with TYPS as its focus. The youth who established and now lead TYPS, primarily youth of color and LGBTQ youth, are those who participated in the Nuestra Voz Racial Justice summer camp. TYPS provides local and larger possibilities for understanding youth civic involvement and for youth intervention in and disruption of deficit-driven assumptions about youth and youth knowledge, particularly at the intersections of education, race, economic status, immigration justice, gender, sexuality, and health (see Fields et al., "Youth Voices").

Our presence at local slams gave us the opportunity to see and experience these events as generative spaces that can forge coalitions, build community, and create possibilities that engage and extend beyond counter-narratives (for more on counter-rhetorics and coalition see Licona and Chávez). Following Adela's work in *Zines in Third Space*, we recognize poetry slams as events and, much like feminist and queer zines of color, as creative acts and performances of critical discursive in/ter/vention that can begin to delineate a space of urgency, community-building, grassroots and relational community-literacies, and opportunity for coalitional action by and for misrepresented youth in Tucson. An entremundista pedagogy recognizes these spaces and practices as vital. It allowed us to approach the practice of spitting poetry at the mic as a knowledge that TYPS slam poets were producing to address topics ranging from immigrant rights and contested knowledges to the local ban on ethnic studies. Led by Amanda Fields, TYPS youth were engaged in the process of inquiry by being asked to respond to themes we identified in their poetry so that their voices and visions informed how we understood and made meaning of their poetry. This work produced collaboratively written articles reflecting a mixed-methods approach to inquiry (Fields et al., "Youth Voices"; Fields et al., "Performing Urgency").

EPILOGUE

We began our collaboration with a shared commitment to transdisciplinary and experimental approaches to co-teaching, co-research, and co-writing. Our goal was to engage meaningfully with multiply situated subjects in our classroom and in research contexts. Framed by an entremundista pedagogy, our work continues to be attentive to the current xenophobic and transphobic context in Arizona as well as informed by literatures of YSHR, by critical, feminist, queer, decolonial, and increasingly trans perspectives, by the limitations and possibilities of the teacher-researcher, and by community-based participatory action scholarship and praxis.

Our graduate seminar grounded us in the epistemological, methodological, and practical limitations and potentials of the multiple fields of knowledge that have informed contemporary thinking, practice, and policies related to YSHR. From this, our collaborative developed as a *think-and-do* collective for cultivating the practices and pedagogy of the entremundista in transdisciplinary academic and (transnational) community collaborative inquiries, analyses, and dialogues. These inquiries, analyses, and dialogues, in turn, served as the pedagogical framework for collaborations in writing and action with community organizations and with youth. In keeping with our goal to write and circulate research findings for both academic and local communities about issues pertaining to YSHR, more fully participating in a much-needed shift in YSHR public discourses and policies, we co-produced a series of research briefs titled "Crossroads Connections."[16] These briefs provided opportunities for Crossroads Scholars to write collaboratively with one another and with community members (including youth). They served as instantiations of an entremundista pedagogy, to translate research projects and findings across distinct platforms for diverse academic and non-academic constituencies. All briefs have primary authors and all are co-authored with the Crossroads Collaborative as a collective.

It is through reflection that we have come to understand the researcher-teacher role as the pedagogical work of the entremundista—operating in ways that are place-based; transnationally aware; cognizant of distinct and competing worldviews and the productions of (new) vulnerabilities; transdisciplinary; equally responsive to "expert" and everyday knowledges, to the creative and the critical, and to the dynamics of shifting subject positionings; and, therefore, willing to value knowledge production in both academic and non-academic contexts, while simultaneously considering the inquiries and contributions of researchers and research participants in their roles as teacher-researchers.

NOTES

1. Members of the Crossroads Collaborative whose work has informed this article include Amanda Fields, J. J. Sarah Gonzales, Londie T. Martin, Shannon Snapp, Leah Stauber,; Sally Stevens, Elizabeth H. Tilley, Jenna Vinson, and Ryan Watson.
2. We met at a social gathering hosted by a friend and colleague who wanted to bring gay/queer families together for an afternoon meal and games. We were with our partners and children and realized over the course of the afternoon that we had some overlapping interests. Stephen was particularly interested in Adela's research into the rhetorical functions of queer and queer-people-of-color zines, and Adela was especially interested in Stephen's advocacy research undertaken to shift in-school practices and policies in order to promote comprehensive sexual education and healthy sexualities for young people.
3. "Arizona: UN experts warn against 'a disturbing legal pattern hostile to ethnic minorities and immigrants.'" http://www.ohchr.org/en/NewsEvents/Pages/DisplayNews.aspx?NewsID=10035&LangID=E.
4. My (Adela's) teaching is informed by critical localism, a concept to which I was first introduced in the work of Stephen Goldzwig. The values of critical localism call us

to place-based curricular inclusions. Such an approach seems especially appropriate given the goals of critical and feminist pedagogy—to bring awareness to and ultimately shift the dynamics of power and powerlessness; for knowledge to be understood as relevant and meaningful to social action; to raise consciousness and to address social responsibility; to be broadly informed by always engaging localized knowledges, histories, and practices.

5. Our understanding of the concept and practice of teacher-researcher is informed by the concepts of bricolage and bricoleur, particularly as Joe Kincheloe, Peter McLaren, and Shirley Steinberg engage them. We understand the history of these terms as they are connected to cultural studies as well as to educational theory and especially to the multiperspectival and multimethodological approaches conceptualized by both Denzin and Kincheloe.

6. Entremundista, a traveler between worlds, is a term inspired by the works of Gloria Anzaldúa and especially her treatment of the Nahuatl term *nepantla*, which signifies the liminality and the state of being in-between. It is the title of a zine Adela wrote while working on *Zines in Third Space: Radical Cooperation and Borderlands Rhetoric*, 2012.

7. On third-space and third-space pedagogies, see Anzaldúa, Sandoval, Ali Black et al.; Janice Kathleen Jones; Licona.

8. SB1070 and the localized concept and practice of attrition through enforcement is related to de Genova's *regime of deportability*, which function to create a real material threat of deportation and thereby a pervasive climate of social panic and intolerance.

9. State of Arizona, House of Representatives, Forty-ninth Legislature, Second Regular Session, 2010, House Bill 2281, Section 15–11, Declaration of policy. HB2281 specifically targeted the Tucson Unified School District's Mexican American Studies Department; the curriculum in Tucson Magnet High School, one block from our university, was the focal point of the legislation.

10. Prior to this law, as was the case in many states, the only legal categories to interpret sexting were felony statutes related to the distribution of child pornography. The new law creates the possibility and mechanism for schools to turn over the management of the burgeoning complaints about sexting to law enforcement.

11. Artivist is a neologism that considers the roles and relationship of art, artist, activism, and activist in social change. Some trace its emergence to anti-globalization efforts. See Sandoval and Latorre, 2008, on Chicana/o artivism.

12. We extended these discussions with readings on sexualities and rights specific to the experiences of youth: Russell, "Conceptualizing"; Tolman and McClelland; Russell, "Queer"; Self.

13. Relational literacies is a concept named and taken up explicitly in Londie Martin's 2013 dissertation titled "The Spatiality of Queer Youth Activism: Sexuality and the Performance of Relational Literacies through Multimodal Play."

14. In "Beside My Sister, Facing My Enemy: Legal Theory out of Coalition" (1990), Mari Matsuda searches for the interconnections and relationships between all forms of subordination stating that "The way I try to understand the interconnection of all forms of subordination is through a method I call 'ask the other question.'" When I see something that looks racist, I ask, "Where is the patriarchy in this?" When I see something that looks sexist, I ask, "Where is the heterosexism in this?" When I see something that looks homophobic, I ask, "Where are the class interests in this?" Working in coalition forces us to look for both the obvious and non-obvious relationships of domination, helping us to realize that no form of subordination ever stands alone. If this is true, we've asked each other, then isn't it also true that dismantling any one form of subordination is impossible without dismantling every

other? And more and more, particularly in the women of color movement, the answer is that "no person is free until the last and least of us is free."

15. *No More Ignorant Love*
   We the youth believe abstinence-only is not acceptable.
   Comprehensive sex education is not promoting sex, but knowledge.
   It's better to be aware, informed, and prepared instead of ignorant and fearful.
   We are a new generation. We are change,
   tolerance, and understanding.
   No longer streets gathered of polychromatic lowriders and the competition of Macho Men stuck through cities and cries of 'no homo.'
   We need purified love, acceptance, forgiveness, understanding,
   and bravery for change
   We the youth want love,
   no more ignorant love.

16. Research briefs available at http://mcclellandinstitute.arizona.edu/crossroads/researchconnections.

WORKS CITED

Anzaldúa, Gloria. *Borderlands/La Frontera.* Aunt Lute, 1999.

Arizona House of Representatives. House Bill 2281. 49th Legislature, 2nd reg. sess. 2010, http://www.azleg.gov/legtext/49leg/2r/bills/hb2281s.pdf.

Arizona Senate. Support Our Law Enforcement and Safe Neighborhoods Act. 49th Legislature, 2nd reg. sess. 2010, http://www.azleg.gov/legtext/49leg/2r/bills/sb1070s.pdf.

Burdge, Hilary, et al. *Gender NonConforming Youth: Gender Disparities, School Push Out, and the School-to-Prison Pipeline.* Gay-Straight Alliance Network, 2014.

Burdge, Hilary, et al. *LGBTQ Youth of Color: Gender Disparities, School Push Out, and the School-to-Prison Pipeline.* Gay-Straight Alliance Network, 2014.

Corrêa, Sonia, Rosalind Petchesky, and Richard Parker. *Sexuality, Health and Human Rights.* Routledge, 2008.

Crabtree, Robbin D., David Alan Sapp, and Adela C. Licona. *Feminist Pedagogy: Looking Back to Move Forward (A Feminist Formations Reader).* Illustrated, Johns Hopkins University Press, 2009.

Denzin, Norman K., and Yvonna S. Lincoln. *The Sage Handbook of Qualitative Research.* Sage, 2011.

di Mauro, D. *Sexuality Research in the United States: An Assessment of the Social and Behavioral Sciences.* The Social Science Research Council, 1995.

Duncan-Andrade, J. "Urban Youth, Media Literacy, and Increased Critical Civic Participation." *Beyond Resistance! Youth Activism and Community Change: New Democratic Possibilities for Practice and Policy for America's Youth,* edited by P. Noguera et al., Routledge, 2006.

Fields, Amanda. *Critical Lattice: The Coalitional Practices and Potentialities of the Tucson Youth Poetry Slam.* PhD dissertation, The University of Arizona, 2015.

Fields, Amanda, et al. "Performing Urgency: Slamming and Spitting as Critical and Creative Response to State Crisis." *Kairos: A Journal of Rhetoric, Technology, and Pedagogy,* vol. 20, no. 1, 2015. https://kairos.technorhetoric.net/20.1/topoi/fields-et-al/index.html.

Fields, Amanda, et al. "Youth Voices and Knowledges: Slam Poetry Speaks to Social Policies." *Sexuality Research and Social Policy,* vol. 11, no. 4, 2014, pp. 310–321, doi:10.1007/s13178-014-0154-9.

Finley, Susan. "Critical Arts-Based Inquiry: The Pedagogy and Performance of a Radical Ethical Aesthetic." *The SAGE Handbook of Qualitative Research,* 4th ed., edited by Norman K. Denzin and Yvonna S. Lincoln, Sage, 2011, pp. 435–450.

Gutiérrez, Laura G. *Performing Mexicanidad: Vendidas y Cabareteras on the Transnational Stage.* University of Texas Press, 2010.
Herdt, Gilbert. *Moral Panics, Sex Panics: Fear and the Fight over Sexual Rights (Intersections, 8).* New York University Press, 2009.
Herndl, C., and A. C. Licona. "Shifting Agency: Agency, Kairos, and the Possibilities of Social Action." *The Cultural Turn: Perspectives on Communicative Practices in Workplaces and Professions,* edited by M. Zachery and C. Thralls, Baywood Publishing, 2007.
Horne, Tom. "An Open Letter to the Citizens of Tucson." 11 June 2007.
Kincheloe, Joe L., and Peter McLaren. "Rethinking Critical Theory and Qualitative Research." *The Landscape of Qualitative Research,* 3rd ed., edited by Norman K. Denzin and Yvonna S. Lincoln, Sage, 2008, pp. 403–456.
Kincheloe, Joe L., Peter McLaren, and Shirley R. Steinberg. "Critical Pedagogy and Qualitative Research: Moving to the Bricolage." *The Sage Handbook of Qualitative Research,* edited by Norman K. Denzin and Yvonna S. Lincoln, Sage, 2011.
Leyva, Yolanda Chávez. "The Revisioning of History Es Una Gran Limpia: Teaching and Historical Trauma in Chicana/o History, Part II." *La Voz de Esperanza,* Oct. 2002.
Licona, Adela C. *Zines in Third Space: Radical Cooperation and Borderlands Rhetorics.* SUNY Press, 2012.
Licona, Adela C., and Karma R. Chávez. "Relational Literacies and their Coalitional Possibilities." *Peitho,* vol. 18, no. 1, 1 Nov. 2015.
Lincoln, Yvonna S. "An Emerging New Bricoleur: Promises and Possibilities—A Reaction to Joe Kincheloe's 'Describing the Bricoleur.'" *Qualitative Inquiry,* vol. 7, no. 6, Dec. 2001, pp. 693–696.
Lomawaima, Tsianina. "Arizona at the Crossroads 2010." Presentation sponsored by the University of Arizona's Faculty Governance and President's Office, University of Arizona, 10 Sept. 2010.
Martin, Londie Theresa. *The Spatiality of Queer Youth Activism: Sexuality and the Performance of Relational Literacies through Multimodal Play.* PhD dissertation, University of Arizona, 2013.
Martin, Londie T., and Adela C. Licona. "Remix as Unruly Play and Participatory Method for Im/possible Queer World-Making." *Unruly Rhetorics: Protest, Persuasion, and Politics* edited by Jonathan Alexander, Susan C. Jarratt, and Nancy Welch, University of Pittsburgh Press, 2018.
Matsuda, Mari J. 1991. "Beside My Sister, Facing the Enemy: Legal Theory Out of Coalition." *Stanford Law Review,* vol. 43, no. 6, 1991, pp. 1183–1192.
Milbank, Dana. "Headless bodies and other immigration tall tales in Arizona." *Washington Post,* 11 July 2010.
Morse, Janice M., and Linda Niehaus. *Mixed Method Design: Principles and Procedures.* United Kingdom, Left Coast Press, 2009.
Muñoz, José Esteban. *Disidentifications: Queers of Color and the Performance of Politics.* University of Minnesota Press, 1999.
Puar, Jasbir. *Terrorist Assemblages: Homonationalism in Queer Times* (Next Wave: New Directions in Women's Studies). Illustrated, Duke University Press Books, 2007.
Russell, S. T. "Conceptualizing Positive Adolescent Sexuality Development." *Sexuality Research and Social Policy,* vol. 2, no. 3, 2005, pp. 4–12.
Russell, S. T. "Queer in America: Sexual Minority Youth and Citizenship." *Applied Developmental Science,* vol. 6, no. 4, 2002, pp. 258–263.
Russell, S. T. (2016). "Social Justice, Research, and Adolescence." *Journal of Research on Adolescence,* vol. 26, no. 1, 2016, pp. 4–15, doi: 10.1111/jora.12249.
Sandoval, Chela, and Guisela Latorre. "Chicana/o Artivism: Judy Baca's Digital Work with Youth of Color." *Learning Race and Ethnicity: Youth and Digital Media,* edited by Anna Everett. The John D. and Catherine T. MacArthur Foundation Series on Digital Media and Learning, The MIT Press, 2008, pp. 81–108, doi: 0.1162/dmal.9780262550673.081.

Self, Hinda. "'Wise Up!': Undocumented Latino Youth, Mexican-American Legislators, and the Struggle for Higher Education Access." *Latino Studies*, vol. 2, 2004, pp. 210–230.

Tilley, Elizabeth H. *Bridging the Gap: Fertility Timing in the United States, Theoretical Vantage Points, Effective Public Policy, and Prevention Design*. PhD dissertation, The University of Arizona, 2012.

Tolman, D., et al. "There Is More to the Story: The Place of Qualitative Research on Female Adolescent Sexuality in Policy Making." *Sexuality Research and Social Policy*, vol. 2, no. 4, 2005, pp. 4–17.

Tolman, D. L., and S. I. McClelland. "Normative Sexuality Development in Adolescence: A Decade in Review 2000–2009." *Journal of Research on Adolescence*, vol. 21, no. 1, 2011, pp. 242–255.

Smith, Linda Tuhiwai. "Research Through Imperial Eyes." *Decolonizing Methodologies: Research and Indigenous Peoples*, Zed Books, 1999.

Vinson, Jenna. *Teenage Mothers as Rhetors and Rhetoric: An Analysis of Embodied Exigence and Constrained Agency*. PhD dissertation. The University of Arizona, 2013.

Watson, Ryan. *Inquiries into Sexual Minority Youth and Young Adults Over Time and Across Cultures*. PhD dissertation, The University of Arizona, 2014.

Wieringa, Saskia Eleonora. "Postcolonial Amnesia: Sexual Moral Panics, Memory, and Imperial Power." *Moral Panics, Sex Panics*, edited by Gilbert Herdt, New York University Press, 2009, pp. 205–233.

6

SERVICE LEARNING AS AN AGENT OF LOCAL AND GLOBAL SOCIAL CHANGE

Building Civic Engagement in Central America through Literacy and Sustainability

Patricia M. Dyer and Tara E. Friedman

The Spanish *el sembrador*, which may be translated to "seed thrower" in English, provides an image that illustrates the focus on environmental and social sustainability at our university. As English faculty at a small comprehensive university near Philadelphia with approximately 3,500 undergraduates, we provide opportunities to share this concept with our students as we connect content with the realities of literacy and food security concerns facing our neighbors locally in Pennsylvania and globally in Honduras. We make this connection through a credit-bearing Academic Service-Learning course, which includes a week in Honduras during spring break. Our goals for our students in Academic Service-Learning classes are:

- to foster inquiry with the use of reflection and to create interdisciplinary connections through co-curricular and curricular experiences
- to encourage our students to see themselves as active participants in sustainability efforts with community and global partners
- to provide opportunities for students to establish and develop sustainable friendships and professional contacts

Academic Service-Learning courses with a focus on sustainability assist students in finding meaningful opportunities to contribute to solving literacy and food-security concerns both locally and globally; understanding their own reasons for pursuing such opportunities in the communities and workplaces they encounter in their years of undergraduate study and the ones that lie ahead of them; and using their writing experiences and skills to respond to local and global sustainability needs, taking action as socially responsible citizens.

The theme of our Academic Service-Learning course (Honduras: Languages and Cultures—with spring break in Honduras) incorporates a focus on literacy and sustainability, both locally and globally. Two Widener University humanities faculty take up to ten students for spring break and complete the class when we return. Depending on their research interests, other faculty opt to join us. Over the past five years, our thirty-nine students have come from a variety of majors and minors: political science, biology, anthropology, psychology, hospitality management, business, social work, nursing, engineering, gender and women's studies, and English, to name a few. At the interest sessions prior to the trip, students find out from the faculty and, most significantly, from students who have taken the class and have gone on the Honduras trip in previous years, that they will learn about poverty locally, especially hunger-related issues, both on campus and in the community, and efforts to respond to these hunger problems, including assistance to college students and school children alike. Our students develop cultural competence by examining their own values and principles, as noted by Kleinhesselink et al. (9–10), as well as those communities in Pennsylvania and Honduras. For example, new students learn about hungry students on our own campus, and they read about how widespread this hunger problem is on US campuses and how it is being addressed (Kolowich 7). They learn that our previous students raised money to purchase a small freezer, requested by a nearby church to whom we regularly donate food pantry items. The new students hear that they will learn about poverty globally, especially hunger issues in what is known as the dry corridor: Honduras, Guatemala, and El Salvador. On site at Zamorano, Escuela Agricola Panamericana in Tegucigalpa, Honduras, students participate in English classes by collecting proverbs from the Zamorano students. Faculty from both institutions collaborated on the design of this project. In teams, students analyze the data collected as preparation for the individual research assignment. They volunteer in the bilingual elementary school on campus and also at an orphanage near the university. Our purpose here is to describe how commitment to and active participation in our local and global communities honor the social and environmental responsibilities of *el sembrador*—one we continue to foster and sustain through high-impact practices (HIP) in our classes.

PREPARING THE SOIL

As faculty fellows in a two-semester Academic Service-Learning Fellows Seminar on our campus, we learned that building engagement begins with partners listening to each other—brainstorming about needs, wants, and dreams—imagining. We focus on an assets-based approach when working with community partners and together build student engagement throughout the semester and beyond (Kleinhesselink et al. 25). Our efforts to build and maintain engagement with a small agricultural college in Central America with students representing twenty countries in Latin America began ten years ago with plans by one English department faculty member to participate in a study trip to the 1,200-member campus in Honduras, where the pedagogy centers on Learning by Doing. The one-week visit by an established group, called International Friends, included several of their board members, longtime financial supporters of the institution, administrators of the institution, a retired principal of an international secondary school in Mexico City, and a US college professor. The group heard presentations on recent innovations on the campus and plans for the future. For the second part of the visit, the group flew to Panama to meet with graduates of the college to experience firsthand their prosperous coffee plantations in different regions of the country. This experience provided the participants with clear examples of the impact of Learning-by-Doing education on their graduates, as evidenced by their professional lives in Latin America after college as farm owner/managers and as employees of such organizations as the USDA and the World Bank.

The most intriguing part of this orientation to the college was a detailed explanation of *Aprender Hacienco*, Learning by Doing, the academic foundation of Zamorano, Escuela Agricola Panamericana, our partner college in Honduras. This philosophy harkens back to the work of Dewey and Montessori, among others. Our group saw the students working in the fields, tending the livestock, working on environmental projects, and managing the grocery store on campus. The grocery store stocked and sold fresh produce that students had grown, meats they had butchered, yogurt they had processed, and jams and salsa they had made. All of this practical experience has faculty supervision. For the second part of their day, these students are in their classrooms and labs, learning about the theories that support their work in the fields from integrated pest management to irrigation. This version of experiential learning was important to see because our own institution had been heading in a similar direction through our focus on civic engagement, experiential learning, leadership, sustainability, and HIP.

Subsequent visits to the Honduran campus resulted in one of us taking a sabbatical semester there to conduct classroom research on teaching technical writing using a problem-solving approach. As partners, we addressed the development of a faculty partnership; addition of a member of their English department to our professional presentations on such topics as critical thinking, pedagogy, and academic and professional writing; presentations with their English faculty at Teachers of English to Speakers of Other Languages (TESOL) conferences both in Honduras and the United States; joint efforts to arrange an internship at our campus for one of their students; and planning a spring semester course on our campus incorporating a spring break study trip for our students to their campus to include our students volunteering to work on projects with their students in their High Beginner English classes, volunteering at the bilingual elementary school on their campus, and volunteering at a nearby orphanage.

SOWING THE SEEDS

In the Humanities Service Learning course, we begin with two questions: What is the face of hunger in Pennsylvania, and what is the face of hunger in Honduras? When we interview our students after they apply for the trip in the fall semester, we describe the commitment involved. We ask directly if the interviewees are willing to take part in ongoing local efforts to combat hunger, such as volunteering at a small housing authority community farm nearby; collecting and delivering canned goods for local food pantries; attending assigned campus events, specifically, taking part in a hunger banquet; participating in a poverty simulation; and attending various documentary films. With respect to promoting literacy, we ask the students to assist with book drives for the children, both in the communities surrounding our campus in Pennsylvania and in the bilingual school on the Honduran campus, as well as for the children at the orphanage. This involves collecting, sorting, repairing, and delivering books. Locally, the books go to the Boys and Girls Club, the local farm, and five smaller organizations. These efforts are spearheaded by the student-run Presidents United to Solve Hunger (PUSH) Committee of Nineteen, which includes faculty from several disciplines, staff, and, among others, all of the students who have been or will go on the Honduras trip, even those who have graduated. The PUSH committee sets membership as a three-year commitment and keeps in touch with graduates by email and Facebook. Evidence of involvement of our graduates with the Honduras project is seen in the participation of an alumna, this year participating in her second trip with our group, as well as Facebook encouragement from two participants now in graduate school in Pennsylvania and one two-time participant now in graduate school in China. In all, seven students have taken the trip twice—with different but related assignments focused on sustainability; two others returned to the campus in Honduras in the summer to work on a different research project with one of our science professors.

AN INTERNATIONAL HARVEST: GROWING WITH PROVERBS

Students enter the course having experienced different cultures in a variety of ways: through our study abroad trips, cultural immersion trips in the United States, and family excursions; through readings and discussion in classes and clubs; and by developing friendships with international students. In the classes during the seven weeks prior to the trip to Honduras, our students read about and discussed proverbs from a variety of cultures, a precursor to their assignment to collect proverbs in the Honduras classroom as a vehicle for gaining cultural understanding. The students reviewed "Mexican Dichos: Lessons Through Language," in which Roy describes Mexican *dichos* (proverbs) as "pithy condensations of wisdom gained through centuries of experience" (289). With the readings as background, the students set out to collect proverbs in the English classes in Honduras, a collaborative effort of negotiating meaning with the Spanish-speaking students to learn what this special form of language reveals about cultures. Mastrangelo and Tischio refer to such interactions as active reciprocity (32); they note the value of interdisciplinary efforts and the opportunity to see the interaction of knowledge gained from reading assignments with writing assignments in another social context (33), in our case, in classrooms in another country. According to one of our students:

> In hindsight, if I could not have gone on this trip it would have been one of the biggest mistakes in my college career. The experience and interactions I was fortunate to have, taught me so much about the Honduran cultures, world issues, and life in general. The dichos or proverbs we collected from the elementary and college students had themes of hard work, family, destiny, and perseverance, and have definitely resonated with me.

She noted that many proverbs present universal truths: respect for authority, judicious use of time, and respect for others. This student's reflection is supportive of Charry Roje's position in chapter 8 that such reflections provide important insight into student perceptions of projects.

One student wrote that proverbs like *Cameron que se durerme lo lleva lo corriente* ("The shrimp that sleeps gets carried away with the current," or "If you aren't waking up, you won't achieve your goals") and *El que madruga dios le ayuda* ("If you have something important, don't wait; do it first thing in the morning"), and *No dejes lo de hoy para mañana* ("Don't leave for tomorrow what you could do today") exemplify Honduran respect for time. Our student also posited that the focus on time might have been a result of asking for proverbs in a school setting, where time is important. Her research suggested that, ideally, proverbs should be collected in ordinary settings without a prompt (Miedler and Holmes 92). In addition to the obvious cultural purpose of studying proverbs and the language stimulation of moving between languages, the collaboration in the classroom gave the students a chance to function as American students with an assignment getting help from Latin American students using first Spanish and then English. Another student offered the following assessment of her classroom experience with the Latin American college students:

> Every single student had potential and although some were shy, by the end of the week they were coming out of their shells. They benefitted because they practiced their English with someone who spoke fluently, and I benefitted by learning how to handle a group of foreign speakers as well as learning a few more words in Spanish. I noticed the parallels in Spanish proverbs and English proverbs. The students would try to explain them to me and once I figured out what they were trying to convey to me, we all had an "A-ha" moment and I knew how to relate it to proverbs in English. This really showed me how no culture is in a bubble, each culture borrows from one another, shares ideas and principles, and crosses over into the other.

These face-to-face dialogues provide all students the opportunity to develop cross-cultural awareness and begin to build knowledge across cultures (McDaniel and Samovar). Students learn that proverbs are both universal and specific. More important, they learn the value of working together to decode and recode language as they communicate hidden meanings and concepts.

Peer mentorship, in conjunction with high-impact practices, is an integral part of the course. Returnees who participated in previous trips report to the new group on their experiences volunteering in the college English classes in Honduras, at the elementary school on their campus, and at the orphanage nearby, sharing photos and describing the events behind the HIP poster presentations given to our Board of Trustees. These presentations are sponsored by a faculty committee that has been studying the high-impact educational practices supported by the Association of American Colleges and Universities (AACU) and include "first-year seminars, academic learning communities, writing-intensive courses, active and collaborative learning, undergraduate research, study abroad, service learning, internships, and capstone courses/experiences" (Kilgo et al. 509). Of these, our own student poster presentations feature study abroad, service learning, active and collaborative learning, and undergraduate research, all in one course and on one poster. Upon returning to our campus, students write a variety of reflective assignments in which they analyze their experiential learning. One returnee wrote about the challenge of being out of her comfort zone: "Exposure to a variety of activities took me out of my element, but that is why this trip was so beneficial to me." Another student, speaking about volunteering at the orphanage, commented: "We all agree that you have never really lived until you have done something for somebody who can never repay you." Students understand their affective responses through weekly reflective journal assignments and as part of the longer written assignments. By the end of the semester, the group addresses the questions of who, how, and why change occurs. Further, they consider their student roles in effecting change regarding literacy and food security both locally and globally, and they continue to plan actions they can take immediately in the summer and later on campus and in their personal lives as part of their commitment to social responsibility.

At the end of the semester, all of the students on the trip participate in a slide presentation on Student Project Day in which they individually explain what they learned on a surface level and also present deeper meaning they acquired. One insight that appeared in this presentation was also recorded in a written reflection:

> Just being among children that seemingly wanted no more out of life than to have fun and be loved slowly affected and inspired me to notice and enjoy the simple pleasure and details right in front of me. Moreover, by actively searching for ways to communicate with them without English, with nothing more than my gestures and my actions, I found genuine human ways to connect, and their passion and joy about life empowered me.

The student spoke about confusion about his complicated college life that had left him empty and confused, noting that at that time a few orphans from Honduras taught him valuable lessons in humility and being present in the moment.

> The challenges I faced in my service learning required me to look beyond the haze of my own emotions and focus on the most important aspects of human life: a sense and vision for community, a lifestyle of active responsive communication, and finding the common ground to make a

nonverbal, organic connection.... Who would have thought that a Latin American elementary school playground could teach me foundational values for my life?

In the final class discussion on effecting change, this student joined the others in a plan to provide local children with summer reading circles at a park next to campus and to continue to support a local food drop program for students, together with researching a similar program at another university in our region. These current projects and future initiatives demonstrate the vitality of global and local thinking for students, faculty, and community partners in Academic Service-Learning courses; Gindlesparger makes similar observations in her chapter of this collection. This mode of thinking challenges all to examine their own assumptions of other cultures, belief systems, and local and global concerns. As the relationships grow, so does the student engagement.

WRITING FOR SEED MONEY, FIGURATIVELY AND LITERALLY

As presented above, our students write for both academic and nonacademic purposes. They proudly point to their successful effort to write a grant proposal for the local community farm to provide $1,000 for the farm manager to create a beneficial habitat to support environmentally valuable insects. The money has been used to plant wildflowers and herbs to reduce pests and encourage pollination. With success comes confidence. The students have vowed to write for this grant every year, and they are totally committed to the farm, having volunteered there regularly in the fall and spring semesters. Unfortunately, their most recent proposal was not funded—not for a lack of quality but because the farm abruptly changed management and focus. This was a shock to the writers and a learning experience for our earnest students who were so dedicated to volunteering at the farm. The previous year, the students successfully wrote a piece for a larger grant proposal written by an outside group; for this request, they pledged over $26,000 worth of volunteer time at the farm over the next three years. The outside group's grant proposal, with our student writers' contribution, was successful. A different writing opportunity occurred when one of our seniors, at the request of her hometown newspaper, wrote about the insights she gained from the trip. Our returnees also tell the new group about writing directed journals in class each week, in addition to writing reflections upon their return from the spring break trip and a final research paper incorporating and analyzing the proverbs they collected from the college students in Honduras. These specific and focused writings allow for application of course materials as well as time for reflection, two key components in community-based learning through high impact practices (Kuh 11).

Each year when returnees explain that the new group of students will make a campus presentation about the Honduras experience on Student Project Day, a bond begins to form between returnees and the new group. In the final part of the Student Project Day presentation, the students explain how this cultural experience impacted them and what plans they will make as a result. One student referenced a proverb provided by one of the International Friends of the institution: "The fastest way to find a helping hand is to look to the end of your own arm." The student began: "This summarizes the entire trip." He added that the students at the Honduran college "embody that belief wholeheartedly, as evidenced by [a graduate] moving his life to and sharing his education with [the children at the orphanage and their farm]" for half a year. This reflection demonstrates how course writing assignments involve both writing to think about course content (understanding cultures) and writing to think about related social issues (poverty, hunger, literacy). More than that, however, as noted by Barrett in discussing grant writing, students in such situations learn why Academic Service Learning propels them into purposeful writing that addresses social needs, seeking action in response, and intersects with their writing in quest of professional development as well (76). With all of this writing experience, our students are prepared and encouraged to write reports to sponsors and pieces for public relations publications. Writing to thank a leadership sponsor who contributed to the student's expenses, one student recalled:

> Through the semester our class and others donated supplies to bring to the children in Honduras. Through all the donations and a grant we were able to bring over 350 pounds of arts and crafts supplies [and children's books] to help entertain the children. Through fundraising efforts such as bake sales we were able to raise $600 to donate to the orphanage to help pay for an additional part [a pipe] for the irrigation system for their farm. [The previous year] we were able to donate $1,000 for the [control system for the] pump, and we strive to aid the farm by offering any financial support we can.

As a result of reading her report, the donor doubled his contribution, sponsoring partial assistance for two students for the next year's trip. Here, a student writing with passion about the impact of the trip reached the reader such that he took action to provide that opportunity for future students.

At home, student writers had worked together to write a persuasive flyer soliciting donations on campus for the irrigation circuit board. They titled the flyer "Change an Orphanage Forever, Change a Life Together," and they included photos of a barren field on the orphanage property. A year later, the Honduran professor in charge of coordinating their students' efforts at the orphanage farm turned on the pump for our group: Water spouted from a hose in the well and a cheer burst out from our students. This enthusiasm reached campus when we returned; several bake sales followed as the students enlisted campus support for the lengthy pipe needed to make it easier to transport the water down the hill to the farm. In creating the flyer, the students learned how to persuade readers to act by donating to the irrigation project.

For the students, a valuable connection between academic writing and personal writing for professional purposes has recently surfaced. In writing graduate school, job, and honors applications, several students have included their analyses of what they learned on the Honduras trip. Wearing our other hats as Writing Center professors, we have had the opportunity to read drafts of these applications. Here we have observed a kind of synergy between classroom writing assignments and community writing assignments and, more important, between responding to community needs by strengthening engagement. This is capped off when students assign themselves the task of making the meaning of their trip clear to readers of applications when they present themselves for new opportunities. Thus, the reflective process used in their classroom assignments becomes part of their writing process in making the case that they have maturity in their intercultural communicative competence as well as an enduring commitment to global engagement.

SPREADING SEEDS THROUGH SOCIAL MEDIA

As our exchange has progressed, our Honduran faculty partner has identified several new directions. About a year ago, as chair of the English Department at our partner institution in Honduras, she asked us to be part of a Skype and Facebook project with their students. One element of the project involves Facebook postings on a closed Facebook page, just for the English class, responding to topics developed by two of their faculty that include family, home, school, food, customs, country and city life, national parks, environment, and sustainability. Working in groups, the students in Honduras research a topic, write about it, and post their reports. Our students read the posts and prepare some notes for a Skype conference with their partner groups in Honduras. On our side, this volunteer project was managed by a senior who elected to write her research paper for a methods class, Teaching English Language Learners, about technology and TESOL instruction. Thus, she was involved in both theory and practice. By coincidence, this student, an English education major, was doing volunteer work across the street from our university at an elementary school; she and the fourth graders built a garden as part of the Chef to Table program that focuses on growing, preparing, and serving healthy food. This student posted a photo of the fourth graders' raised-bed garden, prompting animated Facebook responses from the agriculture students in Honduras. Like many of her classmates, the student is interested in defeating hunger and promoting healthy food, concerns shared by our partners. In one of her reports, she explained that ten of our education majors were participating in the Skype project, while eleven of their students were participating. The students were from Nicaragua, Honduras, Ecuador, and Panama. She noted that the interactions varied:

> A majority of the groups use Skype or some other form of video chatting to communicate once or twice a week with each other. The groups also message back and forth on Facebook. Every participant also writes on the Facebook group page dedicated to this project. On the group page there have been pictures of projects that the students are working on together. . . . I have noticed a variety of levels that the students are at. If they mess up they are eager to ask if we understand or if we could clarify for them. As a leader I think that this project is going very well. This is a volunteer project from both schools and it is evidence that students are willing to take the next step in enhancing their education.

This senior, who would be doing student teaching two months later, exhibits a mature view of college students and offers a refreshing opinion of what college students—volunteers, in this instance—are willing to do in shepherding their own learning. In this Skype project, the participation of nine students from a Methods of Teaching English Language Learners class, plus one other who went on the trip twice, indicates that through the partnership of the members of the two English departments, a new project easily spread to involve our students from other classes and not just the group going to Honduras. This venture is clear evidence of students learning from informal transnational classroom exchange using the latest technology (Mendoza et al.).

Ten weeks into the Skype and Facebook project, the student leader noted that she enjoyed communicating weekly with the students from Honduras:

I also am Facebook friends with most of them, so it is interesting to see what they post. I have learned a lot from speaking with these students, such as patience. At some points, it is hard to understand exactly what they mean, but with patience and asking more questions, what they are trying to say becomes clearer. They seem to always be enjoying themselves because they are laughing a majority of the time.

The student noted that the partner students were curious about the daily lives of our students. The partners had to write summaries of the conversations. For example, one partner wrote that the US students said that "they don't have a traditional food . . . they eat fast food like hamburgers and pizza. One student prefers fried potatoes, pizza, and hamburgers. If they use the stove in their suite, they usually cook chicken or meat." A US student said she felt that the topics were aimed at making both groups of students think about cultural differences. Similarly, in analyzing student posts in a short story forum, Myers and Eberfors state that "the pedagogical intent is the self-examination or reflection on one's own cultural values, beliefs and practices" (155). Our student went on to say that the US students were able to "learn about a country and its culture through a person that lives there and not through a textbook or online article." This statement highlights this future teacher's awareness that learning can come from many sources; in this case, from a form of participatory learning—engaging with the students from Latin America in lessons mediated by social media. Another student mentioned that the students in the Honduran college's English class "love when I compliment their English. They also liked talking on Skype with my parents. They saw our house and yard and commented that it was different from what they are used to." A third student recalled a face-to-face meeting with her partner when our spring break group arrived at the other campus. She emphasized that this was especially meaningful to her: "It was such a great experience being able to finally meet in person after messaging each other for four months. We spent two hours just getting to know each other. We talked about our college experience and compared the two colleges. Being able to contact with my partner on a personal level while in Honduras was one of the most memorable moments I have from my trip." This student, unlike the other American students Skyping with their partners, went to Honduras and met the person she Skyped; she continues to communicate with him on Facebook. Neither Skype nor Facebook was available to the first few groups of students in the Honduras program. In fact, Internet connectivity and availability was limited, so students kept in touch only sporadically. Thus, taking advantage of advancements in technology has enhanced the communication opportunities for students from both campuses.

Most notably, in reflecting on the Skype Project, one of the Latin American partners said, "The best conclusion we catch in this Skype conference is that we learn a lot of the life routine of another person, what he does in another part of the world, also the characteristics of his city. [It is] wonderful that we can imagine being in [Honduras] sharing this kind of information; we can learn about the different culture of another person using the technology, in this case Skype." In assessing the project, one professor from the Honduran college mentioned a huge improvement in the speaking ability of one of her students: "One English Language Learner began the Skype project by memorizing what he would say while Skyping. By the end of the project he simply spoke to his Skype partner." This indicates a major change in both the student's fluency and his confidence. Overall, professors at both schools see this as a successful project. We think our partner students have developed their skills in speaking and writing, gained a multicultural perspective, and learned about foods, customs, families, sustainability, and geography. Months later, the students are messaging each other outside the parameters of the project, sending photos, sharing news, building their new transnational friendships.

COLLABORATIONS: SHARING OUR SEEDS

Our project led to a TESOL presentation with Honduran professor Grazzia Maria Mendoza, held in their Electronic Village, "Enhancing Speaking and Listening through Skype and Facebook: A Multicultural Experience." This also led to a publication in *Global Neighbors*, the newsletter of the English as a Foreign Language Interest Section of TESOL. Professional development for the English faculty at the Honduran college was one of the goals of our partner English Department. Keeping that in mind, a few years ago we presented jointly at the College Conference on Composition and Communication (CCCC), and for the past few years, we three professors have presented at TESOL. Further, we have taken advantage of other professional opportunities by presenting at Honduran TESOL (HELTA). Returning to PUSH, faculty at both institutions have promoted leadership opportunities for our students by getting them sponsorship to attend the Universities Fighting World Hunger and PUSH conferences. One of the authors' strongest memories, recorded in a photo, is of the two of us joining two students, one from the agricultural college and one from our university, in a food packing event during a PUSH conference in Missouri. Upon returning to their home institutions, each student wrote articles for campus publications. Clearly, these students will benefit from the experience of writing promotional pieces, an important aspect of engagement and useful in their future lives.

ACADEMIC IMPACT OF SOWING SEEDS

In the last decade or so, a new mindset has developed on our campus. Faculty have begun to focus on developing several cultures: a culture of writing, a culture of civic engagement, a culture of critical thinking, a culture of service and Academic Service-Learning courses, a culture of leadership, and, most recently, a culture of sustainability. These cultures and others have been proposed and/or championed by writing professors. Typically, we put these themes directly into our courses, train and encourage other faculty and staff, and write for grants, just as our colleagues in other disciplines do. We are very interested in actively engaging our students. Student engagement is a term that has expanded its meaning over time. Weimer refers to its "four dimensions—behavior, cognition, emotion, and conation (the will to succeed)" (8). For our purposes, engagement incorporates these dimensions as is clarified by students writing reflections; reading and talking about sustainability, literacy, and food security; and active involvement with these issues, both locally and globally.

For us, civic engagement is connecting assigned texts and videos to local and global contexts—for example, *The Last Hunger Season* by Roger Thurow and *YouTube* videos and documentaries, such as *A Place at the Table*, which has a local connection; working on proverbs and skits in the English classroom in Honduras; and creating art and music with the children at the bilingual school and at the orphanage. Engagement is also having weekly Skype sessions with high beginner–English students, which connects students in Pennsylvania with students in Honduras. Engagement is championing one member of our group as she established a birthday book project for the orphans, and chatting on Facebook just for the fun of it. Engagement is reporting back to campus, sharing photos in classes, recruiting (and training) the next student group, and, for some, returning with the group a second time, as seven students have done. Engagement includes seeing the connection locally and globally, working at the farm in our small city in Pennsylvania, and raising money for the farm at the orphanage—all of these building our reputation for high-impact practices in our classes. Engagement means responding to change when it happens. For example, when the local farm changed management, our students began to explore options at other community farms. Also, when we saw that the farm at the orphanage had fallen on hard times, our students spoke with their student partners, and together we revitalized our literacy focus by bringing reading circles and new songs, games, and pre-reading activities to the orphanage. Engagement means committing to long-term interaction with the Honduran people we meet using Skype and Facebook as well as in person, and committing to long-term interaction with the community members we work with in person in Pennsylvania throughout the academic year. Engagement means making volunteering a way of life. One student expressed her commitment this way: "The twelve days that we were [in Honduras] went by so fast, but we felt like we had been there all of our lives. Our group got so immersed with the students and the culture itself that now we have lifelong friends."

LIFELONG SUSTAINABILITY

One student's reflection was organized around values presented in the proverbs: trust, leadership, character, family, and God's will. In writing about leadership, she said:

> Accordingly, finding the leader in oneself is an important goal that should be discovered within everyone. The Spanish "Lo cortes no quita lo valiente" means that "Courtesy does not exclude courage," respect and politeness should not prevent standing up for one's self-respect. Leadership embodies standing up for the belief system of oneself and others. Courageous acts develop a stronger leader and will not restrain kindness, "errando se aprende a herrar," by making mistakes. In other words, this proverb, meaning trial by error, is similar to the US proverb, "if at first you don't succeed, try again." Leaders make mistakes all of the time; whether it is a bad business decision or an error on a project, mistakes happen. However, an effective leader will learn from their mistakes and try again until they get it right. . . . Leaders always stand behind their values; in fact, leadership distinguishes someone of good character.

Our students frequently talked about aspects of leadership and considered how they could bring a more enriched leadership to our campus as a result of the trip.

In the spirit of *el sembrador*, the seed thrower, both groups of students spread the seeds of new projects: At the host institution, a group of students formed a club to bring English literacy to the children at the orphanage. Through the auspices of their club, Sharing Knowledge through English, these students go to the orphanage regularly to teach

English, covering everything from pre-reading activities with the younger children to read-alouds with the older children. For our part, Widener students donated twenty-four white boards, many packs of markers, and fifty gently used books to support their effort. This club's activity complements the tutoring—which occurs in Spanish—at the orphanage, a service project that is provided by another group from their college. Also focusing on reading, our own students put into operation the birthday book project with the goal of every child receiving a book on his or her birthday. The Sharing Knowledge group delivers the books together with photo birthday cards created by our students. We get the books to the college any way we can, and the partners keep track of celebrating the birthdays at the orphanage. In the works is a project for our students to help the children make signs for the garden beds at the orphanage, similar to signs they noticed at the farm in Pennsylvania. The next group of students that goes to Honduras will bring the little wooden signs; they will paint the bilingual signs with the children, along the way learning the Spanish words for a variety of vegetables. Working together with the students in Honduras benefits our students as they apply this knowledge locally when they return. This connects nicely with Joyce Meier's work in chapter 7 on the benefits of Service-Learning projects, specifically in nurturing global voices. As our many examples suggest, students at both institutions are testaments to the impact of civic education, which "has the potential to help students acquire the necessary knowledge, skills, values, and motivation to take action in their communities as thoughtful, engaged, and socially responsible citizens" (Liss and Liazos 50). Together, these engaged students and citizens will help to solidify the lifelong sustainability of each community.

LEARNING FROM THE HARVEST

What do our students take away from the Honduras trip and their participation in sustainability and literacy activities locally and globally? In addition to developing travel skills, they gain confidence in problem solving, tolerance of ambiguity, increasing their flexibility, developing skills in risk-taking (in our case, managing rough mountain trails on our two-hour hike), and expanding their social media opportunities for long-term connections. They develop writing skills for academic purposes, for public writing needs, for championing causes, and for personal enjoyment. They extend their social consciousness as they apply firsthand knowledge of food security, literacy needs, and environmental challenges both in Pennsylvania and Honduras. For example, in Honduras, faculty and students climbed the nearby mountain maintained by the campus, returning with a love of the cloud forest and a determination to join the efforts of the host institution to care for the mountain. Students at both institutions have gained the confidence to create new initiatives in coping with sustainability concerns locally and globally. Among the impacts that our students shared on Student Project Day was the sense of accomplishment in dealing with our environmental and social sustainability goals; the feeling that they were empowering the children at the orphanage to learn and try new things; the certainty that they had gained great respect for Learning by Doing, plus the realization that they, themselves, were learning by doing; and the awareness that they had developed the habit of writing, whether for themselves in their personal journals, with Facebook partners, for assignments, for the public, or as a vehicle for advocacy.

CONCLUSIONS: REFLECTING AND PROJECTING ABOUT THE SEEDS OF ENGAGEMENT

In considering student engagement within a local and global engagement project, we have learned that faculty need to begin with the intent to sustain the relationship with the partner, have a simple goal (for example, an international experience for students that is suitable for both campuses), and be flexible to the needs of the host institution. From the Academic Service-Learning perspective, we can verify that it is essential to listen to the voices of the host institution and learn their wants and needs, as well as the new directions appropriate for them (Kleinhesselink et al. 22). From the perspective of directing writing to serve the group's needs, we learned that first-time grant writers and fundraising writers can be successful. More important, the students now feel empowered to use writing to achieve their goals related to social responsibility. Our engagement began as faculty-to-faculty, helping the English Department, and grew to be faculty and students helping others with English. In our case, with the surfacing of the poignant service project of getting water to the orphanage farm, the engagement includes many more participants: recent alumni keeping interest alive by sending emails; parents now making donations; faculty members contributing money, soccer balls, volleyballs, sewing equipment, and rolls of lab paper; community members like the dentist donating toothbrushes and toothpaste for fifty children every year; and others, including two US children using their gift cards to purchase and donate crayons, construction paper, markers, and other items for children who do not have them. Our project is surely enriched by expanding from student engagement to student engagement with family, faculty, friends, and communities united in a common purpose of helping others.

Our sustained, long-term commitment to engagement has always focused on knowing about and living with social responsibility as a guide and goal. We have worked to create a mindset centered on concern for others and opportunities for action. Our first group of students would hardly recognize the program we have today with Honduras. Students and faculty encountered challenges and discovered opportunities together as they contributed to the evolving nature of the program. We have "evolved into evolving"—a favorite saying of ours—and grown as the needs and opportunities reveal themselves globally and locally. For example, our Honduran student partners have maintained and improved our literacy project at the orphanage. As others have noted, including Bowman in chapter 11, global engagement must be ongoing and long-term. At our institution, our growth is tangible through our new programs and internships at several local farms, increased participation in both Food Day and Sustainability Showcase days, the ongoing collection and delivery of books to local programs, and, with the appointment of a chief sustainability officer, the subsequent establishment of several new sustainability committees on campus. As *el sembrador* reminds us, sowing, nurturing, and harvesting the seeds as the seasons require is a lifelong engagement.

WORKS CITED

Barrett, Kenna. "Where Professional Writing Meets Social Change: The Grant Proposal as a Site of Hospitality." *Composition Studies*, vol. 41, no. 1, 2013, pp. 70–83, eric.ed.gov/?id=EJ1005673.

Kilgo, Cindy, et al. "The Link between High-Impact Practices and Student Learning: Some Longitudinal Evidence." *Higher Education*, vol. 69, no. 4, 2015, pp. 509–525, doi.org/10.1007/s10734-014-9788-z.

Kleinhesselink, Katie, et al., editors. *Engaged Faculty Institute Curriculum*. Community-Campus Partnerships for Health, 2015.

Kolowich, Steve. "How Many College Students are Going Hungry?" *Chronicle of Higher Education*, 3 Nov. 2015, www.chronicle.com/article/How-Many-College-Students-Are/234033.

Kuh, George D. *High-Impact Educational Practices: What They Are, Who Has Access to Them, and Why They Matter*. AACU, 2008.

Liss, Jan R., and Arriane Liazos. "Incorporating Education for Civic and Social Responsibility into the Undergraduate Curriculum." *Change*, vol. 42, no. 1, 2010, pp. 45–50, doi.org/10.1080/00091380903449128.

Mastrangelo, Lisa S., and Victoria Tischio. "Integrating Writing, Academic Discourses, and Service Learning: Project Renaissance and School/College Literacy Collaborations." *Composition Studies*, vol. 33, no. 1, Spring 2005, pp. 31–53, eric.ed.gov/?id=EJ846367.

McDaniel, Edwin R., and Larry A. Samovar. "Understanding and Applying Intercultural Communication in the Global Community: The Fundamentals." *Intercultural Communication: A Reader*, edited by Larry A. Samovar et al., Cengage Learning, 2015, pp. 5–15.

Mendoza, Grazzia Maria, et al. "Skype and Facebook: A Multicultural Experience." *Global Neighbors*, June 2016, newsmanager.commpartners.com/tesoleflis/textonly/printall.php?id=tesoleflis20160613.

Mieder, Wolfgang, and Deborah Holmes. "'Children and Proverbs Speak the Truth': Teaching Proverbial Wisdom to Fourth Graders." Supplement series of *Proverbium*. University of Vermont, 2000.

Myers, Jamie, and Fredrik Eberfors. "Globalizing English through Intercultural Critical Literacy." *English Education*, vol. 42, no. 2, 2010, pp. 148–170, www.jstor.org/stable/40607959.

A Place at the Table. Directed by Kristi Jacobson and Lori Silverbush, produced by Participant Media, distributed by Magnolia Pictures, 2012.

Roy, Carolyn. "Mexican Dichos: Lessons Through Language." *Intercultural Communication: A Reader*. 13th ed., edited by Larry Samovar et al., 2012, pp. 288–292.

Thurow, Roger. *The Last Hunger Season: A Year in an African Farm Community on the Brink of Change*. PublicAffairs, Perseus Books Group, 2012.

Weimer, Maryellen. "Student Engagement: What Is It?" *Recruitment and Retention in Higher Education*, vol. 27, 2013, p. 8, www.magnapubs.com/newsletter/recruitment-retention/114/student_engagement_what_is_it-10794-1.html.

7
INTERCULTURAL COMPLICATIONS IN A "GLOCAL" COMMUNITY PROJECT

Joyce Meier

In this chapter, I examine global civic engagement by analyzing a community-based project involving international students in a basic writing course at a major US university. A dramatic rise in the number of our institution's international students—particularly from China—significantly affected the community projects I facilitated in spring and fall of 2014, when my mostly international students visited a nearby low-income school. There, 90 percent of the children were free-lunch recipients, and my college students shared their languages and cultures with two third-grade classrooms. Analyzing this project in terms of my students' reflective writings as well as my own field observations, I examine how this intersection of the global and local represents international service learning that simultaneously reflected *and* resisted neoliberal notions of global citizenship. In fact, given the effects of worldwide mobility that we increasingly see in US classrooms, I would argue for the affordances of a new frame for service learning that highlights its global implications considering local participants' cultures, languages, and identities. In other words, I ask that service learning take on a "glocal" perspective that attends to the global as enacted through local participants and their ongoing, complex negotiations of languages, cultures, attitudes, and experiences—both present and past.

Such a framework de-centers American exceptionalism and neoliberal theories that emphasize service learning within a context of distinctly US ideals: equality, democracy, individual development, and participatory citizenship. Instead, community projects that involve international students in US settings are by nature jagged and complicated by uneven axes of power. Like others in this collection (Aksakalova; Bowman; Austin), I am struck by the often surprising and unexpected ways that geoglobal trends and events impact local projects.

DOI: 10.7330/9781646421237.c007

These disparities call for a response that is both nuanced and "nimble" (to use Bowman's word): one that queries any easy valorizing or critique of home or host culture. Experiential learning that aims to forward global citizenship needs to draw on the rich diversity of all participants and to shape projects that are characterized by ongoing inquiries into the complexities of sameness and difference. In order to reflect the increasing diversity of US classrooms and communities, community projects must pay heed to the unequal, globally inflected power dynamics that manifest themselves through local interactions and relationships.

"INTERNATIONAL" SERVICE LEARNING IN THE UNITED STATES—INHERENTLY COMPLEX

Community projects that engage international students in US settings are distinct. They are not quite like many academic service-learning projects that take place in the United States, where US students work with or on behalf of low-income or otherwise de-privileged populations (US and otherwise); nor are they quite like international service-learning projects where US (or other privileged) citizens provide services to those construed as "less so" in other countries. Analyzing the discourse of globalization, Roman criticizes educators and learners who behave as intellectual tourists and voyeurs, as agents of civility and democratic nation-builders, and as multicultural consumers of ethnic, racial, and (inter)national difference (270). Blum seconds this critique in her discussion of international service-learning programs in which the "server" takes on the role of a "temporary volunteer, of a somewhat informed traveler," and so equates the encounters of visitors with the "other" (543). But the international students in my class were hardly "servers" in this sense. Instead, they came closer to Blum's alternate model of reciprocity, interdependence, and interaction. Educators and students need to pay historical attention to, in Roman's words, the "uneven, contradictory, and often conflicting interests of power in the social relations that define the stakes in and boundaries of belonging to particular communities," and to call into question "how communities, interests, and voices are constituted, and, in whose name" (283). In my case, the community project reflected the *entremundista* pedagogy that Licona describes in this collection as: "change-oriented, community informed but globally aware, and engaged in contested knowledges; contextual and aware of possible connections across contexts; intersectional and interdisciplinary; able to *sustain ambiguities; and understanding of contradictions* as always possibly generative" (emphasis mine). Such was the nature of the project outlined in this study, which engaged uneven and contradictory axes of power from the start. The project I describe here was strongly impacted by the experiences and attitudes of the international students on our university campus, including how these students had been viewed and treated by others (US students, faculty, and administration). While many US-based notions of community projects stress the ways in which power dynamics engage across forms of identity—such as class, race, gender, and so on—a project like mine reiterates the extent to which complex and even competing *national* identities, beliefs, and attitudes may also be very much in play.

INSTITUTIONAL CONTEXT AND PROJECT

In order to discuss the community projects in my bridge writing course, it is first necessary to connect the local with the larger economic, social, and political contexts that impacted them. In our case, the university had nearly 7,600 international students (out of more than 50,000 students total) enrolled in fall 2015; over 5,000 of these international students (or one in thirteen) were undergraduates; international student enrollment increased by nearly 30 percent over the past five years ("Statistical Report"). This trend is reflected nationally, as now almost a million international students enroll in US higher education, with students from China accounting for over 30 percent of that number ("Project Atlas"). Clearly, as technological advances bring about increased mobility among and thus contact between populations from different countries, these trends will continue. Keith, for example, describes the "time-space compression" that "enables the hyper-mobility of all kinds of goods and capital—human, informational, financial" (10)—circumstances that in her view have the potential to transform people's experiences of their physical and emotional spaces, their senses of community, and of themselves. The time-space compression Keith describes has made it all the more likely that people of distinctly different cultures and nation-states will not only develop and maintain relationships across distance but in actual space as well—certainly true of the project I describe here.

In our university community, the dramatic rise in international students has been fraught. While the international students provide valuable income—a pattern typical of other US communities (Sovic and Blythman)—the international students complain about the cost of tuition, which is nearly twice as high as that required of in-state students, and nearly $1,500 per year more than what our out-of-state students pay.

Tuition for fifteen credits costs in-state first-year students approximately $14,000 per academic year (a fall and spring semester), while out-of-state students pay almost $38,000 and international students pay slightly over $39,442 ("Detailed Costs"). Often the contrast between what the international students pay to attend our institution and their specific economic circumstances is striking, as a single Chinese student can represent three generations of his or her hard-working family's earnings. Another paradox is that our international students come with the desire to acquire English as a *lingua franca* and avenue to social mobility and economic success, yet their developing skills are often read as deficient in the eyes of many US students and faculty, who complain of how the course material must "slow down" as a result. Finally, for many of our international students, this is the first time they have been this far away from their home and family. Many experience acute homesickness, and even though their purpose of studying here is to practice their English, they often end up meeting and staying within groups of students from their home country. Thus, while the international students on our campus often cite the desire to make American friends, they instead find themselves segregated in dorm life, classrooms, and cafeteria, excluded by language, custom, and to some extent, prejudice.

These experiences are identified and highlighted in the Preparation for College Writing (PCW) class, a bridge that leads to our regular first-year writing class. PCW now has only a handful of domestic students, placed there on the basis of their ACT or SAT scores,[1] with the rest being international. In fact, even though housed within the university's writing program, the PCW course closely resembles our university's ESL writing courses that approximately 60 percent of the PCW students are required to complete before they are eligible for PCW. The other 40 percent of the international students in PCW place there directly based on their TOEFL scores and other assessment measures. Regardless of how they arrive, most of PCW's international students are from China, though others come from Africa, the Middle East, South America, and other Asian countries. In 2014, the year in which the two community projects described here took place, my spring course consisted of nineteen Chinese students (albeit from different parts of China), in addition to one Thai, one Korean, one Saudi Arabian, and one American (an older student who had served in the military, and thus had travelled or lived in many parts of the world). My fall 2014 course had two US citizens, one Mexican American, and the rest were international (one Venezuelan, Brazilian, Saudi Arabian, and Taiwanese, plus thirteen Chinese).

In terms of the community project itself, each semester we visited a local, low-income school for approximately an hour and a half. This school was chosen based on a long-standing professional relationship that had developed between a local third-grade teacher and myself; in the past, I had partnered with this teacher when I had the (mostly US) students in a Writing and Public Life in America course facilitate writing exercises with local third graders at the school where he then taught. When budget cuts ended in the closing of that school (at tremendous loss to the local community), and this teacher moved to another nearby school, I continued to explore ways to partner with him, even though I was now teaching PCW with its preponderance of international students. In so doing, I wished to continue supporting the local, low-income schools in my area—schools that are strikingly depressed economically. Like many academic communities, ours is shaped by a town-gown divide that plays out economically, and to some extent racially, in the local community. For example, while the elementary schools closest to the university and in its adjoining suburban community tend to benefit from superior or above average resources, the schools just five miles from campus exist in an urban desert that has been ravaged by the decline of the auto industry and subsequent job losses. At both schools where the third-grade teacher worked, over 90 percent of the children were on the federal free-lunch program. When my own teaching assignment shifted and I found myself more connected with the bridge writing course and its increasingly international student population, new and exploratory conversations with my school partner took place. Over time, the project described here emerged, as the third-grade teacher and I reasoned that it would not only serve the third-grade social studies curriculum but also give my international students the opportunity to share aspects of their languages and cultures with an audience outside of the university.

As constructed, then, the project complicated the model we often think of when we conceive of community projects: that is, mostly US (and white) students privileged by economic background worked with children at a school less privileged, with mostly US, non-white students. In fact, the school had its own linguistic, cultural, and even transnational complexities. There, nearly half (44%) of the students were African American; roughly 20 percent were Hispanic, another 22 percent were white, and finally, 13 percent were of two or more races ("Public School Review"). Moreover, as high as 20 percent of the students were bilingual, with Spanish being the most common language. Overall, as many as 20 percent of students in the school district in which this school exists are bilingual, with Spanish being their second language. During the two semesters described here, the third-graders with whom my international students worked appeared fluent in English, and indeed, were positioned as the experts on local American culture—a phenomenon mirroring the project described in Roje's study in this collection, in which local community members were positioned as experts and "service providers," so that the students involved in this community project had the experience of both serving and being served by others. Similar to our case, the children and university students had the experience of being *both* beneficiaries *and* givers of service. That is, my international students provided information about their languages and cultures in an entertaining, multimodal format, and the children provided a most appreciative audience as well as a window into US culture outside of the university. Still, a more nuanced study of the impact of the unique and varied diversities within the third grade classrooms, and in relationship to my international students, would be a rich subject for future study.

During the project, and as many service-learning scholar-teachers do (Ash and Clayton; Eyler et al.), I invited my PCW students to extensively reflect on their community experience in both writing and class discussion. For example, I had my students "pre-flect" before going to the school (What did they anticipate would happen there? What were they excited about? What did they fear?), and I adapted a form of Ash and Clayton's DEAL model for my students' post-school reflection. Ash and Clayton define this model as having three constitutive parts:

- a more-or-less objective **D**escription of the community experience(s);
- the students' **E**xamination of those experiences; and
- an **A**rticulation of the students' **L**earning, which includes goals for future action (41).

Where Ash and Clayton had their students analyze their experiences in light of specific learning goals or objectives, however, I chose to use a more open-ended approach, as I wanted to see what the students, unprompted by a specific goal, would identify as aspects of their learning. In addition to making my questions more open-ended than Ash and Clayton's, I extended the number of post-visit questions to five because I was teaching a course that aimed to help develop writing fluency in my international students. Essentially, my modified version consisted of having the students respond to the following:

- What did I do and observe [at the school]?
- What did I learn [there]?
- How did I learn it?

- Why does this learning matter?
- How might I use this learning in the future?

The students' responses to these questions form much of the basis of my analysis below, along with the brief surveys students completed after their experiences at the school.

DISCUSSION

Learning to Communicate: A Neoliberal Goal, and Then Some . . .

Overall, the international students' reflections indicate that one positive quality they took away from the community project was an enhancement of their communication skills, as they recognized that this experience allowed them to practice their developing language skills in an authentic context. In their end-of-term surveys, and in response to what they had learned from the project, PCW students cited communication skills (such as "how to explain knowledge" and "how to communicate" when the children asked questions, and to "follow their topics"). One student wrote, "It help me, an international student to overcome language barrier in some way." At the school, the international students found they were "*forced* to interact" (my emphasis), as one of my students put it. The communicative exigencies created by the school situation created an opportunity for my students to practice a form of active language-learning cited by scholars such as Beck and Simpson; Eyring; Fried-Booth; and Barreneche.

The project was successful in forwarding the international students' own goals of improving their English. The challenge, however, is that this goal unreflectively serves a neoliberal agenda as these international students' very motive for studying in the United States is to develop their English language skills, which reflects their understanding of the worldwide dominance of English as the language of social mobility and access to a better life (Joseph and Ramini; Munck; Pennycook). Yet the emphasis the students placed on the advantages of their visit to the school also involved a more socially responsible attitude—one that moved beyond individual self-development. One student, for example, wrote that this kind of intercultural learning was important more broadly because "we are different cultures and have many things are different. Then when we talked about each culture, we can learn about unsimilar things." Ultimately, according to the students' reflections, the learning of *English* did not seem to be the experience that mattered most in this project but rather the intercultural exchanges that ensued. Even the student who emphasized the active learning engendered in the project also emphasized intercultural learning, writing: "it's a great way for internationals that are shy to understand American culture." Such observations are compatible with what other researchers have found: Crossman and Kite cite the enhanced cultural sensitivity expressed by their ESL students involved in community projects; Hummel; Steinke; and Elwell and Bean all analyze the increased knowledge of local communities that their international students gain through service-learning. Even the students who tended to emphasize the *practical* advantages of the experience spoke more broadly of its long-term intercultural advantages: "I think I will have opportunity to use this learning in the future because I gonna need other people who are not from my country." Another student expressed his response to this intercultural experience in especially affective, altruistic ways: "Because children are human's hope, we should put more care to them, and teach them go to a right way to grow up." His comments suggest a model of global citizenship defined in terms of shared responsibility rather than individual self-advancement.

Ironically, while our university claims "cultural understanding" and "effective citizenship" as key learning goals for its students, it often repackages, as do many universities, "global citizenship not just as an ethical-moral orientation, but as a marketable set of skills and certifications" (Lewison). While community projects more broadly provide the opportunity for students to learn from one another and their community partners in ways that enhance intercultural understanding, this may be especially so when the projects involve international students who otherwise may experience isolation from the local communities they inhabit. As Singh and Sproats argue, we need to continue to "develop local/global pedagogies that bring students together to learn from and through each other" (64);[2] through our visit to the school, I extended this learning to include communities outside our classroom. My international students' intercultural learning was deepened at the community school, which opened up an experience of "real life" that had seemed unavailable to them on our US university campus. As one PCW student put it, "We don't have chance to touch normal American life, when we in college." This response suggests the limits of international students' experiences at US universities, where they can become— not entirely by choice, like Ogden's "colonial student"—isolated from local cultures. The children thus became what deWinter, in this collection, describes as "real, identifiable audiences" for my students' stories, histories, and experiences. While classrooms like PCW can provide distinct opportunities for these students to explore transnational commonalities and differences, bringing international students into US community settings also suggests the affordances of experiential learning—especially when that experience is framed by an approach that centers the students' languages and cultures as resources and complicates their initial perceptions of community partners.

Affordances of Centering Students' Languages and Cultures

Several years ago, responding to the increased number of international students in our courses, our PCW instructors began to examine the implications of translingual, asset-based pedagogies for our PCW classrooms. In so doing, we drew on Ladson-Billings's, González et al.'s, and Paris's argument for "culturally sustaining" pedagogies that, in Paris's words, support "young people in sustaining the cultural and linguistic competence of their communities while simultaneously offering access to dominant cultural competence" (95). Also influential were calls for a translingual/multilingual approach, which Lu and Horner claim expresses a "willingness to explore with students what they care to advance about people, language and cultures in which they are identified and may identify, and how and why and when to do it" (600). Eventually, we have incorporated these perspectives into our developing draft of PCW learning goals, which assert students' languages, cultures, and experiences as assets, sites of inquiry, and resources for learning. Specifically, our program now characterizes the PCW course as having two central "moves": the drawing upon students' languages and cultures as sites of inquiry and resources for learning, and the students' introduction to, and integration into, academic cultures.

In my course and in the PCW courses of my colleagues, a translingual approach took several forms. Emphasizing international students' languages and cultures as resources, PCW frequently incorporates an activity we call "Culture Circles," in which students are invited to discuss, interview one another, and write about one another's local cultures, exemplified through the sharing of multimodal works (cultural objects, neighborhood maps, drawings and video images, etc.) that represent their ideas of "home." Class activities such as these not only build community within the transnational classroom but respect the distinct local (and self-defined) histories, cultures, and experiences of each student; the maps, drawings, and objects also help make aspects of home cultures (and often differences) visible to others.

In still another typical PCW unit, students are asked to share, analyze, and compare jokes, idioms, and cultural sayings from their home cultures/languages, much as Dyer and Friedman (this collection) describe their Honduran and English students doing. Still another course exercise, which leads to a major writing project, involves the students translating a cultural song or story into a form that others in the class can understand. Next, the students compare their translations (noting similarities and differences), and then reflect in writing on what they learned about the process of translating, incorporating examples from their home languages—for example, of the challenges of finding the right English word for a Mandarin phrase of compressed meaning, or of explaining a highly inflected phrase from a rap song written in African-American Vernacular English (for a more detailed analysis of how this assignment works, see Kiernan et al.). The students thus produce highly analytical papers that draw from (and incorporate) their own expert knowledge of home languages and cultures. Finally, most of the assigned projects ask students to integrate multimodal work into their coursework, while still one other project explicitly asks them to remix a prior project into a new form (such as a video, poster, jigsaw puzzle, etc.). Such projects reflect Canagarajah's notion that the "'trans' in translingual . . . perceives communication as going beyond words and accommodating other semiotic systems (such as sound, visuals, body, and ecology) in creating meaning" ("First-Person Singular" 450).

In our ongoing work in creating learning outcomes for the PCW course, my colleagues and I implicitly recognize that PCW is already an "intercultural contact zone," which Pratt defines as a space where "cultures meet, clash, and grapple with each other often in contexts of highly asymmetrical relations of power" (34). But we also view the course as an opportunity to make these unequal relations more visible and to create an opportunity for intercultural understanding. Our students struggle to explain aspects of their languages and cultures to one another. Through Culture Circles and in-class ethnographic interviews, for example, US students learn of the numerous dialects and minority groups in China for whom Mandarin was not the first language (so much so that one of the Chinese students from inner Mongolia expressed difficulty understanding the Mandarin of some of her PCW classmates from South China). In turn, the US students, with their own histories of being marginalized by race and class, can become valuable resources and class leaders on subjects related to American culture. Because of this intercultural sharing, class discussions in PCW can also be difficult; in one case, when a Chinese female student introduced her "cultural artifact" of the parasol, which was designed to protect her "white" skin from the sun, a Dominican Republic student who had lived in Detroit asked, "Are there no dark people in China then?" provoking a discussion among the class about the differences and similarities in how race was constructed transnationally.

The degree to which individual and national identities, experiences, and interests can collide in a course like PCW was also apparent in the international students' initial response to the community project as many expressed strong anxiety about working with *children*—with whom, they admitted, they had little experience. Within the international cohort, many of my students, especially those from China, had no siblings. Yet this very challenge provided an opportunity to de-center the power dynamics in this class. Using a version of Minor's pairing of more English language–advanced students with those less so at a community site, I created small groups in which each had a self-identified "child expert." That is, students with strong prior experience working with children (through babysitting or family relations) were paired with the students with less experience. Shaped by formative reflective assessment, these groupings shifted existing class power dynamics by allowing PCW students, such as the Arabic, American, and Mexican-American students, to step up and take on leadership roles in a class where Chinese students—and their interests and concerns—tended to dominate, if only by sheer number.

De-Centering

The decision to work with children ended up contributing to the project's success. Despite initial misgivings, most of the ELLs expressed pleasure in finding such a receptive and curious audience in the children. Typical reflective responses included genuine surprise at the level of the children's interest and curiosity: "all the kids were excited," "many children have much curiosity," "they [small children] are interested in everything bout you . . . and also give you a chance speak English." The children ended up being a low-stakes, non-judgmental, and receptive audience for the international students—an observation that corroborates Hummel's contention that "interacting with children in elementary and high schools may have been particularly well suited to allowing [ESL] participants to use their L2 in nonthreatening circumstances" (83). Still, the fact that anxiety about working with children came up in the first place suggests the extent to which the facilitator of an international service-learning project needs to be responsive to her participants' particular experiences and fears, rooted as they are in home cultures, traditions, and experiences.

The other anxiety expressed about the school visit centered around the international students' fears about language inability and cultural difference. As one student wrote: "Honestly, in my first mind, I was planning to never show up on that day because I thought that I didn't have any courage and energy to deal with American kids due to the difference of cultures and languages." This anxiety resembles Arca's description of the students in her basic writing class; they arrive, she argues, "with a diminished view of themselves and of the power they have to effect change," including expression in discussion and written text (133). While my students differed from Arca's in that they had the mobility to travel and study in a major US research institution, they too were in a "basic" writing class and tentative about their communicative abilities and hence what they might contribute to a community project. Indeed, both the international students in my class *and* the low-income US third graders we visited at the school were disempowered and in distinctly different ways.

According to Keith, neoliberalism takes the tenets of free market economics and makes them into general principles for creating the good life and a good society; it views people as rational choosers who maximize their self-interest and supports market competition over the role of the state as protector of the public good. Globally, this translates into notions of a world economy in which the players are free economic agents, working for their economic advantage. But such a view also ignores the specificity of political and social disparity. While Munck; Roman; and Joseph and Ramini all acknowledge the concept of "glocalization"—that is, the interrelatedness of the local and global—they also critique a particular blindness that refuses to see how much the integration of these two may be based on their political inequality The local and global are not equal, Auerbach argues. Enacted through the local, a community project is always complicated by the exigencies of specific circumstance, individuals, and relationships. Today's transnational classroom and corresponding community projects require an asset-based, student-centered pedagogy that shares with translingualism the positing of the teacher as fellow learner in the classroom (Canagarajah, "World Englishes"). It calls for an agility of response and a stance of ongoing intercultural inquiry about the complex spaces where the local and global meet, as well as the histories and contexts that inform them.

Here, a translingual pedagogy helped me position my students' languages and cultures as assets, not deficits. To help prepare my PCW students for their school visits, I drew on a first-day classroom activity: a name exercise where the students write their first name in their home language, and then in English, on colored sheets of paper. When the PCW students visited the school, this became their first, introductory move. For other course assignments, the PCW students had brought in and explained "cultural artifacts" from their "home" cultures (Chinese yuan bill, a Thai amulet, an Arabic head scarf); when they went to the school, these "home" artifacts also came along.[3] The final school activity derived from our class reading of *My Place* (Wheatley and Rawlins), an award-winning children's book from Australia. In this book, a succession of child characters takes turns introducing families, holidays, and neighborhoods, vis-à-vis stories, drawings, and maps. Using this book as their model, my PCW students drew and shared with one another maps and stories of their own childhood homes, customs, families, and neighborhoods. In turn, we took these illustrated stories with us into the school, where the PCW students in teams worked with smaller groups of the schoolchildren—writing, sharing, and drawing their "home cultures" with them (and the children wrote and drew back).

Thus, the PCW students shared in the third-grade classroom a number of the asset-based, experiential activities they had done in the PCW class, which meant that when they presented information to the children, they had prepared in advance, which helped alleviate initial performance anxiety. Moreover, all three of these activities not only featured the rich variety of my students' languages and cultures, but they *embodied* them for the children. The multimodal aspects of this project afforded the international students with alternative ways of communicating with the children, rather than just through spoken language. For example, when my students shared their drawings with the children, the children would "draw back," a back-and-forth, multimodal process that greatly enhanced intercultural understanding. Reflections written after the visit included observations such as: "I *see* people's family, their life" and "I learned their family, their neighborhood *by their drawing*" (emphasis mine). Because conversations revolved around visual artifacts, both parties could draw on these resources to communicate their experiences and cultures to one another. Scholars have written about the affordances of multimodal work for international students as it can give them the opportunity to be successful in an area other than alphabetic English text (Van Rensburg; Warschauer and Cook). Also, the project's alternate "languages" of artifact, map, and drawing de-centered an emphasis on English as the sole lingua franca or mode of communication as the children not only "drew back" but demanded that their names and other words be written in Chinese, Korean, and the other home languages of their partners.

Relying on the multimodal tools they had, and emerging from their own languages and cultures, this community project helped position my

PCW students as givers rather than receivers of service—a position that uniquely empowered them in ways that the international students in my university are not. This is a paradoxical reversal of the ways in which traditional US service learning is often construed: with more privileged "providers" serving others who are less so. In the case of my international students, and given what they perceived as their English language deficiency and a distinct lack of experience working with children, many were initially anxious about the school visit and wondered what they might offer the children there (concerns that were identified in their pre-visit writing and class discussion). Yet the project ended up enhancing the students' feelings of empowerment; they indeed had something important to share. Thus, this project resonates with what Shah defines as an intentional realignment of power dynamics or with Arca's study of a community project whereby "basic" (US) writers become "authorities." Yet in our project, both parties were experts *and* learners, as the international students were as eager to learn about US culture from the third graders as the children were to learn from them.

The sense that my international students found themselves distinctly, and unexpectedly, empowered by the school visit was perhaps most apparent in my Taiwanese student's response. Initially, this young man had found himself marginalized within my class—at least in terms of how the (mostly Chinese) students responded to him. For example, when the Taiwanese student who had been part of a Culture Panel in class and the US students (and I) asked questions about the differences between Taiwan and China, the other Chinese students grew silent. This student's situation demonstrates the extent to which resistances can emerge *within* classrooms and national groups, not just between classroom and community (the more traditional theoretical construct in US-centered service learning).[4] In his response to the school visit, this student indicated how much he had enjoyed sharing with the third graders his stories about Taiwanese culture: the "difference between Taiwan and China . . . how unique Taiwan is, including food, tradition, holidays, and tribes." He went on to reflect that, "Interacting with American children is already one of my best learning experiences in my whole life." Clearly, this student's "culture stories" found a more receptive audience in the third-grade classroom than he had found in PCW. Thus, the community project created a kind of "third space" (Gutiérrez), where he too could draw upon and happily share his own cultural and linguistic resources. Examples like this Taiwanese student underscore the ongoing challenges of global citizenship and international service learning. Despite a current and prevalent rhetoric of isolationism (in the US, in Europe), the effects of national and international policies *do* emerge in our everyday lives; international encounters highlight this fact by calling upon the power of nationalist discourses and motivations. In fact, as in the case of my Taiwanese student, it is often impossible to totally isolate the two as the national/international continues to express itself in local experiences and interactions—something we need to be mindful of as we in the United States engage in community work involving non-US students.

Complicating the Obvious

One of the key dangers of any transnational community project is the tendency of one or the other party to stereotype, to make hypotheses on the basis of initial observations or interactions with the host culture. Take, for example, the Chinese student who compared the more formal style of Chinese schooling to the freedom he had noted in the American class: "I see the children in America are permeated with happy and positive feeling" whereas in China, his "nephew . . . keep a straight face and seems feel tired. I did not [know] huge pressure can make a 10 years old child lose happy in his childhood." A second student wrote that: "The education in America is more creative," while a third said: "The work in primary school in US is much easier than in China." Still another student compared the more "colorful" American classroom to his "orderly and dull" Chinese classroom back home.

This is not to say that these positive observations of US education were necessarily wrong—Chinese education may indeed be stricter that US systems, at least given the communities my students came from—rather, I wanted to complicate my students' initial impressions. In both semesters, I purposefully gave a post-visit mini-lecture with statistics on the social and economic inequality that plagues the US system of education (that is, the number of children who live below the poverty line, how poverty affects education, how US education is funded). This discussion complicated some of the students' earlier impressions of schooling in the United States. Incorporating Herzberg's concept of critical teaching, the mini-lecture was purposefully designed to challenge the PCW students' positive views of US education and to provide contextual information about the underlying political and economic inequalities that continue to shape US education. Along with the class discussion that followed, this lecture led students to make new intercultural comparisons in the reflections they subsequently wrote. For instance, one student commented: "There are lots places in China that still has no school or children have to spend more than 2 hours to go to school." A number of PCW students also expressed surprise that the system of education in the United States could be so flawed. One wrote, "It makes me think that every country has poor people, and they deserve to study in school, but they can't, they are too poor."

Such reflections respond to Blum's call for a critical approach to international service learning: one that involves authentic relationships and work that "does not tell, direct, fix . . . community, but that is about being *with* community and knowing that in the 'being with' that the work is always partial, never complete" (Anders and Lester 239, emphasis mine). Otherwise, Blum asserts, an international service-learning program runs the risk of perpetuating distorted, simplistic understandings of social problems (Ver Beek). Once more, though, the particularity of any given project and the experiences and identities of those involved must be taken into account. At the same time, students need to be aware that such relationships are always partial, impressionistic, and imperfectly made, tied to shifting past/present experiences and ideas about languages and cultures: our own and those of others. Ongoing inquiry into what is similar and different, and why, thus becomes key. Engendered by such projects, transnational "contact zones" require agility and an openness to others—in other words, the kind of "flexible thinking" that will be increasingly desirable in the professions our students will someday enter, as Gindlesparger points out in this collection.

Taking Time

As Deans argues from his fifteen years of experience in teaching service-learning courses, success in community projects is intrinsically linked to the "quality of the relationship students develop with their community partners" (229)—a view with which Crabtree concurs. One other lesson I would draw from this experiment in intercultural learning and global citizenship would be to find more ways to build on the positive, mutually affirming, and questioning relationships that started in those third-grade classrooms. This project was only a first step and would have been greatly enhanced had we returned to the school again, after our initial visit, in the interest of deeper learning on the part of both sets of students. The project also suggests that as a university, we are remiss in our responsibilities to the international students we bring to campus, who end up isolated within their own groups. Our classes can be missed opportunities for the development of intercultural understanding as a form of global citizenship as we, both US and non-US citizens, have so much to learn from one another. Global problems require nuanced solutions; how can my institution claim that it strives for global citizenship for *all* of our students—US and non-US—if we do not make space for examining the rich diversity of their experiences, languages, cultures, and ideas *within* our own classrooms as well as outside them?

CONCLUSION

Ultimately, it may not be possible to totally separate neoliberalism and the kind of engaged community connection and outreach described in this article because the project did forward a neoliberal agenda in the sense that the opportunity it created for my students to practice their English could be seen as their developing "marketable skills" that will help them in the global economy. This project was also limited by its single visit each term, the somewhat superficial impressions of my students, and the constraints of the participants' own sociopolitical views and biases (for example, my students' "read" of the US classroom as creative, or even, a third grader's almost visceral response of "Ewww! That stinks!" to the smell of the hot sauce brought by one of my Chinese students). Yet the project resisted a neoliberal agenda as well because it provided a window in terms of the opportunity for intercultural learning and listening on the parts of both my students and their third-grade partners. Overall, it affirmed my students' heritage languages and cultures (something not always found on our university campus), and it gave the third graders the opportunity to talk with people from halfway around the world (again, something that, according to their teacher, would also not be available to them, even though our campus, with all its international students, is a mere five miles away from the school).

Most of all, the project foregrounded the complexities that emerge in community projects that are already increasingly internationalized and, thus, intercultural and will continue to be so in the future. In highlighting the increasing diversity of students in US universities, Hall argues that the college writing classroom is one of those locations where the "local" needs to be negotiated with the "global," as these spaces represent an "intersection, a place where collisions and near-collisions occur"—where, as he puts it, the "multicultural, multilingual, multifaceted identities of our students meet the equally varied and complex academic discourses, which are themselves implicated in global dialogues, which are products of multinational conversation and cooperation and conflict" ("WAC/WID" 38). Given the striking, layered complexities of the local and global in any project, Hall then wonders how we can catch up to the future that is already upon us, in terms of the internationalized changes taking place in our classrooms and our communities. To paraphrase Hall's question, how can we best leverage what he calls the "multicompetent experiences" of our multilingual students? ("Multilinguality" 43). In fact, how can we engage our students' rich languages and cultures in the work of global citizenship, encountered through and situated in the specific circumstances of the local? Community projects in US settings would benefit from a translingual approach that recognizes and draws upon the languages, cultures, and experiences of multilingual, non-US students, and shapes community projects around cultural relativism and openness to the non-US cultures increasingly evident in our classrooms. At the same time, this model of civic engagement requires sensitivity to the multiple and ongoing complexities of the intercultural "contact zones" that will thus arise—and are often impossible to anticipate, as was the case with my Taiwanese student.

This relational complexity—this complex intermingling of the local and global—means that sometimes community work can be felt as unsatisfactory. Learning may cause discomfort as new information may contradict that which is formerly known; students may find themselves scrambling to "make sense of it all" (as indeed was the case for my students as they found themselves questioning their earlier assumptions of Taiwan or of the US educational system in general). It is especially important, then, that what happens in the contact zone is treated as a site of inquiry and reflection so that students have the opportunity to think through the differently (and complexly) inflected power dynamics of global economies and international politics as manifested through local interactions and relationships. Students require space to think through the implications (What have I just heard/seen/experienced? What did I thus learn? Why does this matter? What is the "so what?" here? How might this learning be useful in the future?). At the same time, if there is anything I could add to this list of reflective questions, I would include: "How does what I learned or experienced [at the school] contradict what I previously thought or expected?" In other words, a project like this should invite ample opportunity for students to self-consciously reflect on possible changes in their viewpoints or attitudes, both local and global, and as engendered by the school visit and/or in and through classroom discussion. That is why providing ongoing writing and discussion opportunities—and even having students compare their pre-visit reflections to what they write afterward—can be most helpful as the reflections serve as temporary markers of the students' shifting negotiations of new knowledge placed in relationship to the old.

Moreover, what is good for these (mostly international) students may be good for all. Here, I echo Zamel's assertion that good pedagogy for multilinguals—that is, one that engages participants' heritage languages and cultures—is good pedagogy for everyone, including the many monolingual students at our institution who may (but do not always) come from more homogenous backgrounds and often resist integration and interaction with the non-US students. Providing ample space for these students to reflect in the moment is key too, especially as they engage with the international students (and their thoughts, attitudes, and histories) in the classroom.

In summary, a translingual approach such as that described by Canagarajah ("Toward a Writing Pedagogy"; "Translingual Practice") accounts for the internationalization of all community projects (and classrooms), as it underscores the intercultural relationships that already exist within our universities as well as in community projects where classroom and community participants converge. What a translingual framework contributes to community projects is an accounting for the "glocal" (both local and global) in human interaction, as it highlights how human beings experience endlessly shifting loci of power as they negotiate both communicative practices and their own and others' understandings of sameness and difference—what they know, and what they learn. A translingual community project that is glocally framed entails risks *and* rewards and attests to the learning that is possible when people from different parts of the world come together, share, and listen to their respective stories, cultures, and languages.

Let me close by describing a class activity I borrowed from a colleague for use in my own PCW class. Now integrated in my own teaching, the exercise begins with my students responding to the following prompt: "When I see ___ is from ___, I think s/he is ___." Then they write a response to: "When people see I am from ___, they think I am ___." Subsequently, a class discussion of their responses helps the students see how easy it is to make superficial assumptions about others while also recognizing how they in turn can be misread. Finally, when I ask, "And what might change these initial impressions?" the answer is invariably something like getting to know others more deeply. That is the kind of intercultural understanding I want my students to have: that getting to know others who come from a different place or group is always an impartial and incomplete process, tied to one's own cultural perspective, and that such relationships take time and a certain tempering of judgment, a nuancing of understanding, based more on questions than on answers. It also takes a willingness to "rhetorically listen": reversing the concept of "understanding" to "standing under," Ratcliffe defines this listening as "letting discourses wash over, through, and around us and then letting them lie there to inform our politics and ethics" (28). The need for such listening is never more apparent, as problems both local and global require an understanding of others who differ from us. Paying heed to the languages and cultures of the international students in our classes and weaving their experiences into the very fabric of the community projects we facilitate is central to the practice of fostering global citizenship, especially as the intercultural contact zones of US classrooms make such transnational learning not only possible but more likely.

NOTES

1. When I first taught PCW five years ago, only a third of its students were international. Now the international students constitute most of the class.
2. For a pedagogical example of this framing, see Matsuda and Silva.
3. Because there was insufficient time to introduce all of my students' artifacts to the third graders, we voted as a class to choose just three, and the students whose artifacts were voted upon agreed to introduce them at the school.
4. Similar (albeit different) complexities resided in the third-grade classroom as well, as in one semester, we learned that as many as ten of the children had learning disabilities. Unaware of this fact, my students that semester admitted to the special communicative challenges entailed in the school visit; for example, having to repeat ideas and the need to practice patience and good listening skills.

WORKS CITED

Anders, Allison Daniel, and Jessica Nina Lester. "Living in Riverhill: A Postcritical Challenge to the Production of a Neoliberal Success Story." *Critical Service Learning as Revolutionary Pedagogy: A Project of Student Agency in Action*, edited by Brad J. Porfilio and Heather Hickman, Information Age Publishing, 2011, pp. 223–249.

Arca, Rosemary L. "Systems Thinking, Symbiosis, and Service: the Road to Authority for Basic Writers." *Writing the Community: Concepts and Models for Service-Learning in Composition*, edited by Linda Adler-Kassner et al., American Association for Higher Education, 1997, pp. 133–142.

Ash, Sarah L., and Patti H. Clayton. "Generating, Deepening, and Documenting Learning: The Power of Critical Reflection in Applied Learning." *Journal of Applied Learning in Higher Education*, vol. 1, Fall 2009, pp. 25–28, community.vcu.edu/media/community-engagement/pdfs/AshandClayton.pdf.

Auerbach, Elsa Roberts. "Re-Examining English Only in the ESL Classroom." *TESOL Quarterly*, vol. 21, no. 1, Spring 1993, pp. 9–32, doi.org/10.2307/3586949.

Barreneche, Gabriel Ignacio. "Language Learners as Teachers: Integrating Service-Learning and the Advanced Language Course." *Hispania*, vol. 94, no. 1, March 2011, pp. 103–120, /www.jstor.org/stable/23032088.

Blum, Denise. "Critical Race Pedagogy and Teaching English in Mexico." *Learning the Language of Global Citizenship: Strengthening Service-Learning in TESOL*, edited by James M. Perren and Adrian J. Wurr, Common Ground Publishing, 2015, pp. 541–568.

Canagarajah, A. Suresh. "First-Person Singular: Crossing Borders, Addressing Diversity." *Language Teaching*, vol. 49, no. 3, 2016, pp. 438–454, doi.org/10.1017/S0261444816 000069.

Canagarajah, A. Suresh. "Toward a Writing Pedagogy of Shuttling between Languages: Learning from Multilingual Writers." *College English*, vol. 68, no. 6, July 2006, pp. 589–604, doi.org/10.2307/25472177.

Canagarajah, A. Suresh. *Translingual Practice: Global Englishes and Cosmopolitan Relations*. Routledge, 2013.

Canagarajah, A. Suresh. "World Englishes as Code Meshing." *Code Meshing as World English, Pedagogy, Policy, Performance*, edited by Vershawn Ashanti Young and Aja Y. Martinez, NCTE, 2011, pp. 273–281.

Crabtree, Robbin D. "Theoretical Foundations for International Service-Learning." *Michigan Journal of Community Service Learning*, vol. 15, no. 1, Fall 2008, pp. 18–36, hdl.handle.net/2027/spo.3239521.0015.102.

Crossman, Joanne M., and Stacey L. Kite. "Their Perspectives: ESL Students' Reflections on Collaborative Service Learning." *Business Communication Quarterly*, vol. 70, no. 2, 2007, pp. 147–165, dx.doi.org/10.1177/1080569907301776.

Deans, Thomas. "Community Writing Pedagogies in the Spirit of the New Mestiza." *Service-Learning and Writing: Paving the Way for Literacy(ies) through Community Engagement*, edited by Isabel Baca, Brill, 2012, pp. 227–232.

"Detailed Costs." *Office of Admissions, Michigan State University*, 1 May 2017, admissions.msu.edu/cost-aid/tuition-fees/default.aspx.

Elwell, Marelene D., and Martha S. Bean. "Editor's Choice: The Efficacy of Service-Learning for Community College ESL Students." *Community College Review*, vol. 28, no. 4, 2001, pp. 47–61, doi.org/10.1177/009155210102800403.

Eyler, Janet, et al. *A Practitioner's Guide to Reflection in Service Learning*. Vanderbilt University, 1996.

Eyring, Janet L. "Experiential Language Learning." *Teaching English As a Second or Foreign Language*. 2nd ed., Heinle, 1991, pp. 346–357.

Fried-Booth, Diana L. *Project Work*. Oxford University Press, 1986.

González, Norma, et al. *Funds of Knowledge: Theorizing Practices in Households, Communities, and Classrooms*. Routledge, 2005.

Gutiérrez, Kris D. "Developing a Sociocritical Literacy in the Third Space." *Reading Research Quarterly*, vol. 43, no. 2, 2008, pp. 148–164, dx.doi.org/10.1598/RRQ.43.2.3.

Hall, Jonathan. "Multilinguality Is the Mainstream." *Reworking English in Rhetoric and Composition: Global Interrogations, Local Interventions*. Southern Illinois University Press, 2014, pp. 31–48.

Hall, Jonathan. "WAC/WID in the Next America: Redefining Professional Identity in the Age of the Multilingual Majority." *The WAC Journal*, vol. 20, Nov. 2009, pp. 33–49, wac.colostate.edu/journal/vol20/hall.pdf.

Herzberg, Bruce. "Community Service and Critical Teaching." *College Composition and Communication*, vol. 45, no. 3, Oct. 1994, pp. 307–319, doi.org/10.2307/358813.

Hummel, Kristen. M. "Target-Language Community Involvement: Second-language Linguistic Self-Confidence and Other Perceived Benefits." *The Canadian Modern Language Review/La Revue Canadienne des Langues Vivantes*, vol. 69, no. 1, Feb. 2013, pp. 65–90, doi.org/10.3138/cmlr.1152.

Joseph, Michael, and Esther Ramini. "'Glocalization': Going Beyond the Dichotomy of Global Versus Local through Additive Multilingualism." *International Multilingual Research Journal*, vol. 6, no. 1, Jan. 2012, pp. 23–34, doi.org/10.1080/19313152.2012.639246.

Keith, Novella Zett. "Community Service Learning in the Face of Globalization: Rethinking Theory and Practice." *Michigan Journal of Community Service Learning*, vol. 11, no. 2, Spring 2005, pp. 5–24, hdl.handle.net/2027/spo.3239521.0011.201.

Kiernan, Julia, et al. "Negotiating Languages and Cultures: Enacting Translingualism through a Translation Assignment." *Composition Studies*, vol. 44, no. 1, 2016, pp. 89–107, doi.org/10/17239/11esll-2017.17.03.04.

Ladson-Billings, Gloria. "Gloria Ladson-Billings Reframes the Racial Achievement Gap." *National Writing Project*, Apr. 2007, www.nwp.org/cs/public/print/resource/2513.

Lewison, Elise H. "Consuming Development: Responsibility, Citizenship, and the Corporate University." *The Canadian Geographer/Le Geographe Canadian*, vol. 57, no. 3, Apr. 2013, pp. 363–371, doi.org/10.1111/cag.12011.

Lu, Min-Zhan, and Bruce Horner. "Translingual Literacy, Language Difference, and Matters of Agency." *College English*, vol. 75, no. 6, July 2013, pp. 582–601, eric.ed.gov/?id=EJ1014097.

Matsuda, Paul Kei., and Tony Silva. "Cross-Cultural Composition: Mediated Integration of US and International Students." *Composition Studies*, vol. 27, no. 1, Spring 1999, pp. 15–30, eric.ed.gov/?id=EJ585407.

Minor, James M. "Using Service-Learning as Part of an ESL Program." *The Internet TESL Journal*, vol. 7, no. 4, Apr. 2001, iteslj.org/Techniques/Minor-ServiceLearning.html.

Munck, Ronaldo. "Civic Engagement and Global Citizenship in a University Context: Core Business or Desirable Add-on?" *Arts and Humanities in Higher Education*, vol. 9, no. 1, Jan. 2010, pp. 31–41, doi.org/10.1177/1474022209350102.

Ogden, Anthony. "The View from the Veranda: Understanding Today's Colonial Student." *Frontiers; The Interdisciplinary Journal of Study Abroad*, vol. 15, Fall–Winter 2007–2008, pp. 35–55, eric.ed.gov/?id=EJ878378.

Paris, Django. "Culturally Sustaining Pedagogy: A Needed Change in Stance, Terminology, and Practice." *Educational Researcher*, vol. 41, no. 3, Apr. 2012, pp. 93–97, doi.org/10.3102/0013189x12441224.

Pennycook, Alastair. *Global Englishes and Transcultural Flows*. Routledge, 2006.

Pratt, Mary Louise. "Arts of the Contact Zone." *Profession*, 1991, pp. 33–44, https://www.jstor.org/stable/25595469.

"Project Atlas." *Institute of International Education (IIE)*, 1 May 2017, https://www.iie.org/Research-and-Insights/Project-Atlas.

"Public School Review: Willow School." *Public School Review*, 1 May 2017, https://www.publicschoolreview.com/willow-school-profile/48915.

Ratcliffe, Krista. *Rhetorical Listening: Identification, Gender, Whiteness*. 1st ed. Southern Illinois University Press, 2005.

Roman, Leslie G. "Education and the Contested Meanings of 'Global Citizenship.'" *Journal of Educational Change*, vol. 4, no. 3, Sept. 2003, pp. 269–293, doi.org/10.1023/b:jedu.0000006164.09544.ac.

Shah, Rachael Wendler. "It Was Sort of Hard to Understand Them at Times: Perspectives on ELL Students in Service-Learning Partnerships." *Learning the Language of Global Citizenship: Strengthening Service-Learning in TESOL*, edited by James M. Perren and Adrian J. Wurr, Common Ground Publishing, 2015, pp. 169–195.

Singh, Michael, and Eira Sproats. "Constructing Local/Global Pedagogies: Insights into the Learning Experiences of International Students." *ANZCIES Conference, Melbourne, Australia, 3–5 Dec. 2004*, pp. 52–64, citeseerx.ist.psu.edu/viewdoc/download?doi=10.1.1.473.8436&rep=rep1&type=pdf.

Sovic, Silvia, and Margo Blythman. *International Students Negotiating Higher Education: Critical Perspectives*. Routledge, 2013.

"Statistical Report." *Michigan State University Office for International Students and Scholars*, 2015, oiss.isp.msu.edu/about/statistics.htm.

Steinke, Mollie Hand. "Learning English by Helping Others: Implementing Service Learning into the ESOL Classroom." *The Journal of Civic Commitment*, Spring 2009, ccncce.org/articles/learning-english-by-helping-others-implementing-service-learning-into-the-esol-classroom/.

Van Rensburg, Wilhelm. "CSL, Multiliteracies, and Multimodalities." *Education as Change*, vol. 11, no. 3, Dec. 2007, pp. 183–189, doi.org/10.1080/16823200709487187.

Ver Beek, Kurt. "International Service Learning: A Call to Caution." *Commitment and Connection: Service Learning and Christian Higher Education*, edited by Gail Gunst Heffner and Claudia DeVries Beversluis, University Press of America, 2002, pp. 55–69.

Warschauer, Mark, and Janice Cook. "Service Learning and Technology in TESOL." *Prospect*, vol. 14, no. 3, Dec. 1999, pp. 32–39, dx.doi.org/10.1080/16823200709487187.

Wheatley, Nadia, and Donna Rawlins. *My Place*. Kane/Miller Book Publishers, 1989.

Zamel, Vivian. "Strangers in Academia: The Experiences of Faculty and ESOL Students across the Curriculum." *Crossing the Curriculum: Multilingual Learners in College Classrooms*, edited by Vivian Zamel and Ruth Spack, Lawrence Erlbaum Associates, Inc., 2003, pp. 3–17.

PART 3

Service Learning and Civic Engagement Pedagogies in Non-US Contexts

8
STUDENT-DRIVEN SERVICE LEARNING
Fostering Academic Literacy and Civic Engagement in Croatia

Rebecca Charry Roje

The positive effect of well-structured service-learning (SL) experiences on students' academic achievement, personal growth, long-term civic engagement, and engagement in academic life has been demonstrated through a significant body of research over the last twenty-five years. However, most of this literature has been dominated by research on students in the United States and US educational institutions, or American students in study abroad contexts (Dyer and Friedman and Gindlesparger in this collection). As higher education becomes rapidly globalized through establishment of satellite campuses and cooperation among institutions of higher education across borders, additional research on the effect of American-style SL experiences on non-American students is necessary, particularly to better understand and avoid the potential for cultural miscommunication and to ensure the success of future projects in situations where diverse cultural values, customs, and beliefs may be at play. As many scholars and educators have noted, transnational education projects that seek to simply "export" American education abroad without careful consideration of local cultures risk reinforcing patterns of cultural hegemony, which can ultimately undermine the institution and the educational project itself.

In order to better understand the effect of SL experiences in American educational institutions operating abroad, in this chapter I investigate the perceptions of students participating in a local service-learning project at an American college in Croatia, where the concept of SL is not well known and is rarely formalized as a part of higher education. Following a review of pertinent literature and contextual background on Croatia, I investigate the importance of students' level of engagement in the conception, organization, planning, and execution of the SL project itself, comparing those who were positioned as drivers of the project with those who played more passive roles. Based

DOI: 10.7330/9781646421237.c008

on the results of students' exit surveys and written reflections, I argue for the importance of student leadership and autonomy in planning and executing SL activities. This goal is particularly important in transnational contexts where the local culture traditionally values the authority of institutions and teachers and positions students as relatively passive consumers who are expected to simply absorb information.

In this context, I argue that students' sense of their own authority (what Aksakalova in this collection calls "authority of knowledge making") is itself a form of academic literacy that is essential for success in higher education. Student-driven SL projects can help students see themselves as authors and creators, not only of texts, but also of experiences that engage and benefit the academic institution and the wider local community.

THE SERVICE-LEARNING TRADITION

The educational strategy of service learning unites students, educators, and community partners in active service experiences related to students' field of study. Through experiential learning (as opposed to theoretical classroom study), students become active participants in creation of experiential knowledge rather than passive consumers of information. The service-learning movement can be said to have arisen in response to older traditions of charitable donation or volunteering, in both academic and personal or social situations, which can be fraught with dangers of paternalism and may actually create greater hierarchical distance between the donor and the recipient. (Endres and Gould; Pasquesi). In true service learning, students are not simply "donors" or "volunteers" but rather humble learners who are expected to dedicate their time and energy in service of others and, in return, they strengthen their knowledge of the community, the subject they have studied, and themselves. Thus, service learning is understood as a mutual relationship between equals, which benefits all involved.

A rich collection of literature has demonstrated the positive impact of well-structured service-learning experiences on college students' academic achievement, personal growth, social relationships, and long-term civic and political engagement (Conway et al.; Celio et al.). Service-learning experiences can strengthen students' skills in several areas, including critical thinking, moral reasoning, teamwork, emotional intelligence, tolerance, empathy, and intercultural competence (Scott and Graham), while also benefiting educational institutions through improved student retention and deeper student engagement in campus life (Kuh et al.; Bringle et al.; Astin and Sax). Additionally, students' own social engagement and friendship networks can be strengthened through these experiences (Teymuroglu).

In reviewing both successful and less successful SL experiences, several elements have been highlighted as key to achieving these long-term benefits. Essential elements of successful service learning include clear links between the service experience and the academic curriculum as well as well-structured written reflection activities during and after the project (Smith et al.; Celio et al.).

While students, educational institutions, and local communities have widely embraced service learning as potentially beneficial to all stakeholders, the movement has not been without its critics, and several studies have pointed out potential pitfalls in the organization and execution of SL activities (Whitley and Walsh). In particular, the tension between mandatory and optional service has been an ongoing debate with some studies showing mixed results concerning the effect of mandatory service on long-term civic engagement (Henderson et al.; Sokal et al.; Bennett; Kackar; Stukas et al.). The logistical challenges of communication and implementation of a project, as well as cultural and institutional challenges of power sharing among students, faculty, and community partners have also been well documented (Astin and Sax; Felten and Clayton; Larson and Drexler; Bialka and Havlik).

Moreover, even thoughtfully designed projects may unintentionally reinforce social hierarchies and stereotypes and may even increase the cultural deficit or perceived gap between privileged donors and underprivileged recipients (Sperling; Endres and Gould; Pasquesi). Avoiding or mitigating these risks has been a particular focus of current service-learning research.

The effectiveness of the SL experience may partly depend on the level of ownership and leadership taken by students, as opposed to faculty or community partners. Student empowerment is considered high when students have an active role in conceiving and organizing the project, perhaps through conducting a community-needs assessment, reaching out to community partners, and arranging logistics. Research suggests that such student-driven SL experiences can improve their tolerance of "other" groups, self-concept (as empowered and effective agents of change), and long-term political and civic engagement more effectively than projects that are typically conceived, organized, and directed by faculty and/or staff (Morgan and Streb; Larson et al.; Billig et al.).

However, most studies on the level of student empowerment in an SL project, as well as the vast majority of literature on SL in general, have been dominated by data from US educational intuitions and US students. This is not surprising, since the SL movement itself is widely considered to be historically rooted in the United States and traces its theoretical roots as far back as the nineteenth century. John Dewey's emphasis on practical experience as a crucial element of education has been reenergized in recent decades through newer US-based SL institutions, most notably the establishment of Campus Compact in 1985, which has grown from three original founding universities to include more than four hundred educational institutions. As the concept of SL has been widely embraced, some form of service learning is now part of the curriculum at hundreds of US colleges and universities. Many of these programs do include an international component, often a study abroad model in which American students travel to an international location to perform a service activity with a community partner located outside the United States. Such programs have been shown to increase intercultural competence and tolerance among American students visiting other cultures (Cavanaugh et al.; deWinter in this collection).

SERVICE LEARNING: A GLOBAL PRACTICE

While the literature is still dominated by research on US educational intuitions with a study abroad approach, there have been fewer studies on SL programs outside the United States in which non-US students serve their own communities in hopes of fostering long-term civic engagement. The need for additional research on international populations seems clear since service learning is no longer (and perhaps never really was) a US concept but rather a global practice. As early as 1993, SL strategies were successfully adopted at Roehampton University in England, while the early years of the twenty-first century saw the growth of notable SL programs such as at the Dublin Institute of Technology, Ireland (Gamble and Bates). Baltes and Seifert described SL in Germany as "in its infancy" in 2010, with some fifty primary and elementary schools participating in a nationwide program. That same year, the National Citizen Service Programme was started in the United Kingdom, bringing fifteen- to seventeen-year-olds to a three-week residential service and teambuilding experience during school holidays, with some 75,000 participants recorded in 2015. Birdwell et al. note the partial success of this program, calling for increased participation and emphasizing more significant results in fostering "social mixing" among students than in achieving long-term civic engagement. In 2014, the foundation of Europe Engage, a three-year project of the European

Union, began linking universities and SL administrators to share best practices and offer training, networking, virtual platforms, and publication and research tools (europeengage.org/).

As the concept and practice of SL spreads outside of the United States, particularly through US-based educational institutions with globalized reach, including satellite campuses and transnational educational partnerships, the challenge of discovering, understanding, and mitigating the US-specific cultural viewpoints necessarily imbedded in these programs has gained attention. Iverson and Espenschied-Reilly caution against "importing" US concepts of SL, from terminology to conceptions of power and privilege, without regard for local contexts. For example, they note that even the term "service," which generally has positive connotations in the United States, has negative connotations of punishment or even penal servitude in Ireland (6). Umpleby and Rakicevik detail obstacles to SL implementation in the former Soviet Union and Europe, including lack of knowledge, reluctance to engage in "extra work," which is unpaid on the part of both faculty and students, political party allegiance, which may influence choices of "acceptable" community partners, curriculum restraints imposed by government, and lack of instructor freedom. Significantly, they note that SL is more common in individualistic cultures such as the United States, whereas in collectivist cultures, the ties of family, tribe, and religious group may be perceived to negate the need for organized service programs.

Surveying the variety of SL pedagogies currently developing throughout Europe, as well as the need for additional investigation into the role of student empowerment in SL projects outside of the United States, I use this study to focus on an SL project incorporated into a first-year academic literacy/orientation course at a four-year undergraduate college in Croatia. I argue that high levels of student engagement in the project design and execution can be particularly useful in helping transnational educators strengthen students' academic literacy and civic engagement. In particular, student-driven service learning can build students' sense of themselves and authors and co-creators of knowledge, engage with their own local communities, and recognize the complexity of societal problems. In addition, US-based institutions can use student-driven service learning to strengthen students' ties to the institution and combat negative perceptions of the institution as paternalistic or neocolonial. Before examining original data on students' roles in and attitudes toward the project itself, I first consider the specific history and culture of Croatia.

EDUCATION AND SERVICE LEARNING IN CROATIA

Since declaring independence from the former Yugoslavia in 1991 and recovering from the four-year Homeland War that followed, the Republic of Croatia has emerged as a stable, western-oriented parliamentary democracy in a successful but continuing transition from a semi-planned socialist economy to a market-oriented economy. With a current population of about 4.2 million, Croatia joined NATO in 2009 and became the twenty-eighth member of the European Union in 2013. The population is quite homogenous in race (white) and religion (Roman Catholic) with small populations of ethnic minorities, including Serbs and Muslims.

Some insight into Croatian culture and attitudes can be gained from national scores of Geert Hofstede's classic six dimensions of culture. Croatia scores high (73 out of 100) on Hofstede's power distance index, indicating a strong preference for traditional authority figures, and an acceptance and even preference among the population for hierarchy, or unequal concentration of power and authority (compared to the United States, which scores 40). Croatia is also a highly collectivist culture, with a low individualism score (33) compared to the United States (91). Croatians exhibit relatively high levels of uncertainty avoidance (80) compared to the United States (46), revealing a preference for familiar, rule-based situations over ambiguous situations requiring improvisation.

In keeping with Croatia's conservative and traditional culture, educational experiences tend to emphasize the authority of state institutions, teachers, and textbooks. As is true in many neighboring Balkan countries, learner autonomy, student choice, teamwork, project-based learning, and student evaluation of instructors remain relatively rare. Relationships between professors and students in state universities are often distant and formal (Jelenc et al.; Mikelic Preradovic). Given this context, fostering student empowerment and leadership in an academic setting is both a challenge and a necessity.

Although the concept of service learning as a formalized component of higher education curricula is not well known in Croatia, a strong tradition of humanitarian service, civic awareness, and charitable donation informs the culture in both private and public life. As far back as the Middle Ages, the independent city state of Dubrovnik, an aristocratic republic, made special provision for the care of orphans and the poor. In addition to the role played by state institutions, particularly during the socialist era of the twentieth century, religious organizations in this majority Catholic country have for decades played a crucial role in involving the public in humanitarian service. In more recent times, a host of nongovernmental organizations have been created to address issues of public welfare, from environmental and historical conservation, to consumer protection, to women's rights.

These public service traditions, often organized by the church or the state, or privately within families, have not been directly connected to formal education in Croatia until very recently. Some of the first efforts at experiential education in Croatia were organized on an internship or career-focused model that would benefit educational institutions, students, and employers. These early programs were seen as a potential solution to chronic problems of low graduation rates, low motivation, and poor study habits among students, as well as reliance among professors on large, ex-cathedra lecture classes in which student participation was nearly impossible. SL was cited in particular as a potential solution to poor connection between institutions of higher education and to industry/actual employers (Mikelic and Boras). Among the first practitioners of SL in Croatia, Jelenc et al. reported on a program for fourth-year students at the Faculty of Information Sciences at the University of Zagreb. Since the concept of service learning was still quite unknown, only fourteen students actually participated. Motivated mostly by hopes of benefitting their career development through relationships with community partners, they entered the program with "low expectations." In turn, researchers noted low levels of support from the community for the project, and recorded students' "bitter disappointment" when very few members of the public showed up to attend their final presentations at the conclusion of the SL course.

Despite these early obstacles, modest SL programs have been established and continue to be implemented annually at the Universities of Zagreb, Rijeka, and Osijek. The University of Zagreb has joined Europe Engage, the SL network of the European Union.

Although various forms of SL are slowly becoming known to more educators, many challenges remain, and SL projects in Croatia remain sporadic and loosely coordinated (Mikelić Preradović). In fact, a multi-nation comparison by Haski-Leventhal et al. in 2010 found that Croatian university students reported very low levels of volunteering and service-learning experiences compared to students from other countries surveyed. Of the fourteen nations from which they collected data, only Japan reported lower levels of service learning or volunteering experiences (169). My investigation into the role of student empowerment in an SL project occurs within this cultural and historical backdrop.

SERVICE LEARNING WITHIN A FIRST-YEAR EXPERIENCE COURSE

In this study, I investigated a service-learning experience incorporated into a first-year orientation course at RIT Croatia in Dubrovnik, a global campus of Rochester Institute of Technology, a private research university in Rochester, New York. While the student body is primarily local (from Croatia and neighboring countries), the college atmosphere is clearly American-style, both within the classroom and outside the classroom. Professor-student relationships, academic policies, expectations of academic honesty, extracurricular activities, and classroom practices are, in general, based on US educational cultural norms and traditions. For example, relationships between students and professors tend to be less formal, and private consultations during office hours are encouraged. Teamwork, project-based learning, and student choice in project format and topics are common, which is noticeably different from most students' reported previous experiences in local high schools.

As part of the American-style culture within the college, the academic curriculum provided by RIT in Rochester is taught entirely in English, which serves as the lingua franca of a multicultural community that includes students and faculty from around the world. Although all students have studied English since elementary school, and must demonstrate competence in English in order to enroll, the vast majority have never before lived or studied in an all-English environment. Many report culture shock, along with some level of fear and even embarrassment in the first year due to their insecurity with using English. A variety of academic support services, including individual assistance in the Writing Lab, peer mentoring, and remedial courses, are designed to assist struggling English-language learners. In addition, to prevent students from avoiding English out of discomfort or fear, the college actively encourages using only English in the classroom as well as in email correspondence, college events, and faculty office hours.

To help incoming students adjust to the American-style culture of the college and build academic literacy skills perhaps lacking in their previous education, a non-credit first-year course is required of all students in their first semester. In the course, students are encouraged to proactively visit instructors during office hours, participate in class discussions, take advantage of extracurricular activities, and strengthen their study habits. Among the skills developed in the course is students' sense of autonomy, empowerment, and proactive engagement that many lack. This weekly, one-hour, pass/fail course also strengthens students' ties to the college community, providing practical information on college resources, an introduction to staff members and their roles, a personal introduction to faculty and peer advisers, and emphasis on study skills.

In order to strengthen students' sense of authority, leadership, and empowerment, as well as ties to the college community, the course also included a service-learning project designed by the first-year students as a group. Course material included theoretical readings and an introduction to the concept of community needs assessment. Emphasis was placed on the following:

- meeting real needs in the community;
- engaging with local residents in a meaningful way;
- collecting input from those to be served; and
- logistical planning, including transportation, equipment, and recruiting of participants.

Students discussed the benefits of service for student participants as well as the community served and the college institution. Students who had previously participated in service experience, either in high school or through religious or community organizations, shared their stories.

Although first-year students were familiar with the concept of volunteering, and some had had positive experiences with it through religious or community organizations, few students came to the course aware of the distinction between volunteering or charitable donation and service learning as an educational experience that benefits the learner. Therefore, after a brief introduction to the concept of service learning through class discussion, students were assigned to conduct an informal community needs assessment as a precursor to selecting a community partner. The goal was to give students a significant level of authority and autonomy in constructing their own SL experience as a group. The service event itself would eventually be open to all students at the college to participate, but the first-year students were positioned from the outset as the drivers and organizers of the event.

For the needs assessment, first-year students worked in teams of two or three, interviewing local citizens and collecting their suggestions for addressing unmet needs in the community. Students documented their interviews in writing and submitted their notes. In the following class meeting, students discussed the results of the needs assessment as well as logistical constraints and organizational needs. Although many positive suggestions from the needs assessment were discussed, students were nearly unanimous in their support for an ecologically themed event that would assist residents in the nearby region of the Pelješac peninsula to recover from devastating forest fires, which had destroyed wide swaths of forest in the summer of 2015. These fires received widespread media coverage locally, and although there were no injuries to residents, the fires caused extensive material damage and had a negative impact on the local economy, which depends almost entirely on tourism. Students were particularly enthusiastic about the project because it responded to a timely need and to a specific catastrophic event, rather than an ongoing problem such as poverty or hunger, which some of them saw as intractable. Ultimately, students saw the fire-recovery event as an opportunity to respond to an urgent need that existing lay organizations in the community had not yet recognized. They were excited to be the first to do so and proposed their idea to college leadership.

After approval, a small group of students volunteered to serve on an executive committee, which met periodically for the next six months to plan the event with assistance from college faculty and staff. This committee contacted local authorities, who became partners in the event, lending on-site expertise and assisting with specific site selection, scheduling, and task selection. The committee finalized a plan in which students would be divided into teams, each assigned to clean up a particular stretch of beach that had been inundated by both seaborne trash and natural debris that had washed downhill following the fires. A local diving club accepted the invitation to participate in the event and clean underwater areas. Local residents volunteered to cook and serve lunch, providing an important point of contact with the community. The executive committee solicited donations from local intuitions for bus transportation, while the college covered the cost of supplies.

The following semester, in the weeks leading up to the event, student committee members visited classes with a short presentation of photos and a video they had made showing the fire damage. They encouraged their peers (second-, third-, and fourth-year students who had not participated in the site selection) to sign up for the event.

The service event was tied to academic material in the course Ecology of the Dalmatian Coast, in which nearly all students who participated in the orientation course were enrolled the following semester. Connections between the course material and the service event were built both before and after the service event. In preparation for the event, students participated in a field trip to observe the natural processes of forest fire recovery. By hiking through forests that had begun to recover naturally from fire, students built their knowledge of the environmental concept of ecological succession, which had been introduced through reading material and class discussion. Course learning also focused on how humans positively and negatively affect the natural environment. Discussion topics included the introduction of invasive species by humans as well as humans' role as facilitators of natural recovery of autochthonic species through appropriate interventions. The specific history of the Dubrovnik region was also discussed from an ecological perspective, helping students to understand the roles played by various civilizations in the region from the ancient Greeks to the Austro-Hungarian Empire of the nineteenth century. In preparation for the service event, students discussed concepts of erosion, soil substrates, and the roles of wind and sea currents in dispersion of trash particles and the degradation of plastic waste into micro particles—a particular concern for marine ecology.

On the day of the event, students not only participated in the cleanup, but also several students gave statements to members of the local press who had been advised of the event. One student on the executive committee also filmed a video, which was later set to music and published on YouTube. After the service event, students submitted brief written statements reflecting on their experience. This reflection was built into the ecology course in which they were enrolled. In follow-up class discussion, students were encouraged to contribute ideas for planning future events based on scientific principles they encountered in class.

Throughout the process, faculty and staff were purposely construed as facilitators rather than as drivers of the project. In addition, emphasis was placed on maximizing meaningful and respectful contact with members of the community served. Some local community members were positioned as experts (particularly members of the diving club, who directed the underwater cleanup) or supervisors to whom the students reported. On the other hand, local residents without specialized skills also contributed by cooking and serving lunch to the students. Students therefore experienced both serving and being served—a crucial element in moving away from traditional volunteering experiences that may reinforce a sense of privilege or even condescension and toward a vision of mutual service among equals.

The service-learning experience afforded an opportunity to investigate the role of student engagement and leadership of the project and its relation to students' perception of benefits they received from the experience by collecting data through exit surveys and analysis of written reflections.

DATA COLLECTION: STUDENT EVALUATIONS

At the conclusion of the service project, a total of sixty-two students (27 males and 36 females) participated voluntarily in the study by completing a confidential, anonymous survey. Informed consent was obtained from the students. Participants were divided into three groups based on their level of engagement in the planning and organization of the project, as follows:

- The most empowered group ($n = 7$) participated in the first-year orientation course (needs assessment) and the ecology course in the following semester and served as co-organizers of the project over a period of several months, as members of an executive committee along with college faculty and staff, student government, and community leaders.
- The middle group ($n = 25$) participated only in the first-year orientation and ecology courses.
- The least empowered group ($n = 30$) consisted of second, third, and fourth-year students who simply participated in the one-day service event as volunteers. They were not involved in any aspect of the planning or selection of the community partner.

The vast majority of students were citizens of Croatia and neighboring countries. Five students were Americans on a one-semester study abroad experience or were students of Croatian descent who had spent most of their lives in the United States and American educational institutions.

In order to measure student perceptions of and responses to the service event, participants from all three groups voluntarily completed an anonymous survey consisting of twelve five-point Likert scale items, five multiple-choice demographic items, and two open-ended questions inviting general comments. The survey was administered in English and completed by students immediately following the conclusion of the event. The first part of the survey consisted of statements about the service event with which students were asked to agree or disagree on a five-point scale, where 1 = strongly agree and 5 = strongly disagree. Each statement asked students to note their perceptions of the effects of the service activity in a specific area. These included:

- degree of benefit to the community served
- increased knowledge of the community served
- students' self-knowledge
- knowledge of the related academic course material
- feelings about the academic institution
- civic engagement
- teamwork skills
- overall personal development
- career development

The last three statements asked students whether they would like to participate in another similar event, whether they believed that such events should be included in college curriculum, and how strongly they considered their participation to be voluntary rather than required.

Survey results were digitized, and mean values and standard deviation were calculated for each question. One incomplete survey was discarded. In addition to the survey, students' written reflections were analyzed and provided greater insight into students' perceptions of the beach-cleaning service event.

Overall, data from the exit surveys and written comments show that a large majority of all students found the event beneficial. However, those students who were more deeply integrated into the planning and organizing of the event perceived the most benefit and reported the strongest intrinsic motivation for participating. Students in the least empowered outer circle of involvement perceived fewer benefits from their experience and were more likely to feel coerced into participating. Differences between male and female answers were not statistically significant.

Participants generally agreed with all the statements on the survey and seemed to feel that the event succeeded to some degree in every measure. Agreement was strongest with the statement that the event made them **feel good about being part of the educational institution** ($m = 1.58$, $SD = 0.714$). Other areas in which students reported strong agreement included **civic engagement** ("Today's event helped me see how people can work together to solve problems in their community"; $m = 1.73$, $SD = 0.657$) and actual **benefit to the community served** ($m = 1.73$, $SD = 0.772$).

The lowest levels of agreement were found with statements regarding benefit to **career development** ($m = 2.42$, $SD = 1.064$), **self-knowledge** ($m = 2.32$, $SD = 0.937$), and **knowledge of the community** ($m = 2.29$, $SD = 1.046$). Higher standard deviation values for these areas may indicate a greater split of opinion among various groups of participants.

Comparison of Three Populations: Low, Medium, and High Levels of Student Empowerment

In general, the more deeply students were involved in the selection, planning, and organization of the event, the more benefit to themselves and others they perceived. In all but three of twelve questions, results followed a pattern of strongest agreement with the statements provided among the inner circle of most-involved students, slightly less among the middle group, and still less for the outer circle of least-involved volunteers.

The greatest differences among the three groups were noted in the area of whether service activities **should be included as part of a college education** (high-involvement inner circle m = 1.43, low-involvement outer circle = 2.17), **increased knowledge of academic subject** (high involvement inner circle m = 1.71, low involvement outer circle = 2.4), **and increased knowledge of the community served** (high voice inner circle m = 1.86, low voice outer circle = 2.53). While most students overall agreed that they would like to participate in another similar service experience (m = 1.82 SD = 0.95), depth of involvement also correlated directly with this answer (high involvement m = 1.57, medium involvement m = 1.72, low involvement m = 1.97). The exceptions to this pattern were seen in response to statements related to self-knowledge and civic engagement. In the area of self-knowledge, students in the middle group reported the strongest agreement (m = 2.2), while students in the high and low groups reported nearly equal levels of slightly weaker agreement (m = 2.4).

In the area of civic engagement, the middle group again reported the strongest level of agreement (m = 1.52), slightly higher than the high voice group (m = 1.57), but both groups agreed more strongly than the low voice group (m = 1.93). One possible explanation for this difference is that the inner circle, who actually got a close-up look at some of the difficulties involved in the scheduling and logistics behind the event, had more reservations about the difficulty of "working together." The middle group did not see or experience the schedule conflicts, logistical problems, delays, and weather contingencies involved.

While a large majority of students seemed satisfied and enthusiastic about their service experience, a small number of students responded negatively. These outliers are worth investigating for clues as to how service learning can go awry. As many researchers have noted, poorly designed SL programs can actually discourage students from civic and college engagement in the long run. The most negative student was a third-year male who strongly disagreed with almost every statement on the survey. Notably, he was a member of the outer circle, or low-empowerment group. His comments indicated that he felt coerced into participating because points were given in the environmental science course for attending the event. He suggested to future organizers, "Don't let any class make this mandatory or offer extra credit points." Additional negative responses came from two first-year females who also answered neutrally or disagreed with most questions. These, too, were on the outer circle of involvement. Only five students (8%) said they would not like to participate in a similar event in the future. Of these, three were in the outer-circle, low-empowerment group. Two were in the middle group. Of these, one commented, "task too big," perhaps indicating frustration at the amount of ecological devastation she saw, and the limited power students had to mitigate it.

Comments and Student Reflections

Two open-ended questions at the end of the survey invited participants to comment on the most positive aspect of their experience and to offer suggestions for improving future service activities. Out of sixty-two respondents, thirty-three (53%) provided feedback about positive aspects of the event. Of these, twenty-four respondents (73%) cited **teamwork and strengthening of social bonds within the college community** as the best parts of the experience, using words like "bonding," "friends," "group," "team," "classmates," and "professors." An additional eleven comments (33%) cited the effectiveness of the service itself, using words such as "helping" and "community" or "locals." When asked to provide suggestions for improving the event, only thirteen respondents out of sixty-two (21%) chose to write comments. Of these, six comments were related to organizing additional similar events and improving recruitment and student participation.

In addition to the survey comments, students were asked to reflect on the service-learning experience by posting comments on a digital discussion board in their environmental science course. Analysis of these short, unstructured personal essays ($n = 20$) suggests that students felt that the SL experience succeeded in increasing their awareness of members of their local communities ("This trip helped us realize the seriousness of the problem [that people in this part of] Peljesac are facing"). Additionally, some of them made connections between their SL experience and their future roles as global citizens who would be able and willing to solve similar problems elsewhere. In a short essay titled "Togetherness and Hope," a first-year female in the inner circle of highly empowered participants wrote:

> This event strengthened our community and relations with each other—as colleagues, friends, and also as *citizens*. Maybe we cannot change negligence of other people at present, but we can always show them what is right and influence them that way. We can and thus we should support each other at tough situations like this one. (emphasis added)

Other students responded by writing about the long-term root causes of community problems rather than simple reactive actions. "This problem should not be solved by cleaning every time new trash comes, but to prevent it from the source," wrote another female from the middle group.

Interestingly, nearly half of student reflections (nine out of twenty) mentioned the importance of government, even though no official government agencies had been directly involved in the event or specifically mentioned in the preparations. While students clearly saw a role for government in the life of the community, attitudes toward government ranged widely. Some students seemed passive and distant ("it's a shame the government hasn't done more") or cynical ("the EU is a useless organization"), while others demonstrated some insight into and interest in actual legislative processes ("the government should put stricter restrictions and laws regarding this problem") or sounded emphatic calls to action for citizens to push government bodies into action from the ground up.

Overall, student reflections showed that they saw the SL event as a starting point, or entryway into a larger conversation, rather than an end in itself. Few felt that the work had been completed or the problem solved. Some were discouraged that the trash they had worked to remove would soon be replaced by new waste and worried that their work had been in vain. Some even voiced feelings of frustration or powerlessness ("the government should do something about this") or attempted to place blame for the problematic environmental conditions they saw. However, this concern in itself can be viewed as positive in the sense that, even after the event was over, many were still thinking about the relationships between themselves, their fellow citizens, and their government, as an area ripe for improvement and exploration.

DISCUSSION AND CONCLUSION

Due to the self-reported nature of the data and the small sample size, particularly of the "inner circle" of highly empowered students, these results can be considered preliminary and in need of further testing. A further limitation is the short-term nature of the service event studied (one day rather than an ongoing series of events or intensive extended experience). Significantly, Bowman et al. note that short-term service learning has been shown to have equal effect on "orientations towards equality, justice and social responsibility" as long-term projects (20). In addition, it is possible that students may have been biased in favor of positive answers out of a desire to please professors and compliment and support the institution.

Nevertheless, results of this investigation suggest fertile ground for the growth of SL pedagogies in similar contexts, particularly for the importance of student empowerment and leadership in ensuring a range of positive outcomes of service-learning experiences. Like their counterparts in the United States and elsewhere, Croatian students who contributed their voices to the planning and organization of a service experience clearly participated more enthusiastically and felt that they learned and contributed more than those who simply "showed up" to volunteer at an activity conceived of and organized by institutional authorities.

In the context of Croatian (and Balkan) culture, which is generally accustomed to and accepting of traditional hierarchies, the very act of putting students in greater control of planning and designing the experience may be, in itself, a mildly subversive move, upending established traditions that place students in positions of low power. In this sense, a student-driven service experience can be an important tool to build the sense of empowerment and creative authority that students need for success in higher education. While some students, particularly in transnational education in traditional social contexts, may resist the invitation to create knowledge as authors of original ideas (rather than simply absorb and repeat information transmitted by teachers) in written contexts, they may be more likely to embrace the invitation to exert their own authority in student-driven service-learning experience, since the event centers on producing concrete action first and written texts later.

This investigation revealed several areas ripe for additional research. One in particular is whether sustained high voice SL experiences can, over time, combat student citizen feelings of apathy, pessimism, and powerlessness in the face of social problems. This may be particularly important in cultures where citizen engagement is low, where social, economic, or environmental problems are seen to be intractable and inevitable, where skepticism of government is high, and where placing blame is more common than problem solving.

In addition, the service-learning experience as an area in which the use of the native language is welcomed and, in fact, necessary, rather than discouraged, is worthy of further investigation. By privileging the native language, this service experience is a notable exception to the college's usual "English, please" policy. It's plausible that the freedom and encouragement to use their native language contributed greatly to students' sense of their own authority and leadership, particularly since their skill in the native language placed them in a privileged position compared to American faculty and staff who lack fluency in the native language and depend on students to assist with contact with the local community.

In this context, student-driven SL experiences can be useful, even as a starting point, to open students' eyes to new possibilities for greater engagement with community and greater appreciation for complex causes of problems. In addition, these experiences encourage a new way of looking at education and the role of educational institutions. When students strongly agree that these SL experiences belong as part of their curriculum, they demonstrate support for a view of education as much more than a passive absorption of a body of knowledge, but as an active experience in which they shape their own futures as global citizens.

In the current climate of global political instability and the rising tide of nationalism and isolationism that is deeply skeptical of transnational projects and liberal ideologies, the small chorus of student voices reviewed in this chapter may help transnational educators find our way forward. This limited study demonstrates that service-learning projects can, in fact, even now, strengthen students' commitment to transnational education and help them become engaged and active citizens in their own communities. However, it seems more imperative than ever to avoid even the perception of paternalistic or neocolonial intentions, particularly in societies less familiar with the concept of service learning, skeptical of the efficacy of grass roots social change movements in general, and suspicious of "foreign" educational institutions. In navigating this difficult terrain, empowering students and giving them greater control over their own service-learning experiences may be a critical tool. High levels of student leadership increase enthusiasm for the project and combat perceptions of being coerced into service activities. These students, empowered and entrusted by an American institution to become agents of positive change in their own communities, responded not only with a sense of loyalty toward the institution and a strengthening of bonds within it, but also with a broader and more optimistic view of their own futures as global citizens who can effect change locally. The students who took the greatest ownership of this service-learning project seemed to feel that their local identities were not threatened but rather strengthened by engagement with an American institution and taking action in their own communities through that very institution.

In the years ahead, US influence and engagement abroad is likely to decline, while anti-American, and anti-democratic sentiment will likely rise. We can expect transnational projects of all sorts to come under increasing pressure from stakeholders on all sides. Focusing on student-driven service learning as a truly local expression of humanistic values, and consciously incorporating high levels of student involvement into transnational service-learning experiences, will be key to finding our way forward.

WORKS CITED

Astin, Alexander W., and Linda J. Sax. "How Undergraduates are Affected by Service Participation." *Journal of College Student Development*, vol. 39, no. 3, 1998, p. 251, eric.ed.gov/?id=EJ569834.

Baltes, Anna M., and Anne Seifert. "Germany: Service Learning in Its Infancy." *The Phi Delta Kappan*, vol. 91, no. 5, 2010, pp. 33–34, doi.org/10.1177/003172171009100509.

Bennett, Jeffrey. "The Impact of Mandatory Community Service and Social Support on Urban High School Seniors' Civic Engagement Orientations." *Theory and Research in Social Education*, vol. 37, no. 3, 2009, pp. 361–405, doi.org/10.1080/00933104.2009.10473402.

Bialka, Christa S., and Stacey A. Havlik. "Partners in Learning: Exploring Two Transformative University and High School Service-Learning Partnerships." *Journal of Experiential Education*, vol. 39, no. 3, 2016, pp. 220–237, eric.ed.gov/?id=EJ1110382.

Billig, Shelley H., et al. "The Relationship between Quality Indicators of Service-Learning and Student Outcomes: Testing the Professional Wisdom." *Advances in Service-Learning Research*, vol. 5, edited by Susan Root et al., Information Age, 2005, pp. 97–115.

Birdwell, Jonathan, et al. "Active Citizenship, Education and Service Learning." *Education, Citizenship and Social Justice*, vol. 8, no. 2, 2013, pp. 185–199, doi.org/10.1177/1746197913483683.

Bowman, Nicholas A., et al. "Sustained Immersion Courses and Student Orientations to Equality, Justice, and Social Responsibility: The Role of Short-Term Service-Learning." *Michigan Journal of Community Service Learning*, vol. 17, no. 1, 2010, pp. 20–31, hdl.handle.net/2027/spo.3239521.0017.102.

Bringle, Robert G., et al. "The Role of Service-Learning on the Retention of First-Year Students to Second Year." *Michigan Journal of Community Service Learning*, vol. 16, no. 2, 2010, pp. 38–49, hdl.handle.net/2027/spo.3239521.0016.203.

Cavanaugh, Cathy, et al. "Kilimanjaro: A Case of Meaningful Adventure and Service Learning Abroad." *Journal of International Students*, vol. 5, no. 4, 2015, pp. 420–433, eric.ed.gov/?id=EJ1066268.

Celio, Christine I., et al. "A Meta-Analysis of the Impact of Service-Learning on Students." *Journal of Experiential Education*, vol. 34, no. 2, 2011, pp. 164–181, doi.org/10.1177/105382591103400205.

Conway, James M., et al. "Teaching and Learning in the Social Context: A Meta-Analysis of Service Learning's Effects on Academic, Personal, Social, and Citizenship Outcomes." *Teaching of Psychology*, vol. 36, no. 4, 2009, pp. 233–245, doi.org/10.1080/00986280903172969.

Croatian Agency for Science and Higher Education. "Access to Open Data." *Agency for Science and Higher Education*, 1 September 2017, https://www.azvo.hr/en/about-ashe/access-to-open-data.

Croatian Bureau of Statistics [Drzavni Zavod za Statistiku]. "Higher Education in 2015." ISSN: 1331-7784, 2016, Zagreb.

Endres, Danielle, and Mary Gould. "'I Am also in the Position to Use My Whiteness to Help Them Out': The Communication of Whiteness in Service Learning." *Western Journal of Communication*, vol. 73, no. 4, 2009, pp. 418–436, doi.org/10.1080/10570310903279083.

Felten, Peter, and Patti H. Clayton. "Service-Learning." *New Directions for Teaching and Learning*, vol. 2011, no. 128, 2011, pp. 75–84, doi.org/10.1002/tl.470.

Gamble, Elena, and Catherine Bates. "Dublin Institute of Technology's Programme for Students Learning with Communities: A Critical Account of Practice." *Education + Training*, vol. 53, no. 2/3, 2011, pp. 116–128, doi.org/10.1108/00400911111115663.

Haski-Leventhal, Debbie, et al. "Service-Learning: Findings From a 14-Nation Study." *Journal of Nonprofit and Public Sector Marketing*, vol. 22, no. 3, 2010, pp.161–179, doi: 10.1080/10495141003702332.

Henderson, Ailsa, et al. "Political and Social Dimensions of Civic Engagement: The Impact of Compulsory Community Service." *Politics & Policy*, vol. 40, no. 1, 2012, pp. 93–130, doi:10.1111/j.1747-1346.2011.00341.x.

Hofstede, Geert H. "Cultures and Organizations: Software of the Mind." *Cultures and Organizations: Software of the Mind*, McGraw-Hill, 1991.

Iverson, Susan V., and Espenschied-Reilly, Amanda. "Made in America? Assumptions About Service Learning Pedagogy as Transnational: A Comparison Between Ireland and the United States." *International Journal for the Scholarship of Teaching and Learning*, vol. 4, no. 2, 2010, pp. 1–19, doi.org/10.20429/ijsotl.2010.040215.

Jelenc, Lara, et al. "Implementing Model of Service Learning in Teaching Strategic Management Course." *An Enterprise Odyssey. International Conference Proceedings Journal*, 2008, p. 381.

Kackar, Hayal Z. *High School Students' Initial Reasons for, Experiences during, and Intentions to Continue Community Service.* ProQuest Dissertations Publishing, 2010.

Kuh, George D., et al. "Unmasking the Effects of Student Engagement on First-Year College Grades and Persistence." *The Journal of Higher Education*, vol. 79, no. 5, 2008, pp. 540–563, doi.org/10.1080/00221546.2008.11772116.

Larson, Erik, and John A. Drexler. "Project Management in Real Time: A Service-Learning Project." *Journal of Management Education*, vol. 34, no. 4, 2010, pp. 551–573, doi.org/10.1177/1052562909335860.

Larson, Reed, et al. "A Comparison of Youth-Driven and Adult-Driven Youth Programs: Balancing Inputs from Youth and Adults." *Journal of Community Psychology*, vol. 33, no. 1, 2005, pp. 57–74, doi.org/10.1002/jcop.20035.

Mikelic Preradovic, Nives. "Service-Learning in Croatia and the Region: Progress, Obstacles and Solutions." *Journal of the Washington Academy of Sciences*, vol. 94, no. 4, 2011, pp. 33–38, www.washacadsci.org/Journal/Journalarticles/V.97-4-service_learning_in_Croatia.pdf.

Mikelic Preradovic, Nives and Damir Boras. "Service Learning: Can Our Students Learn How to Become a Successful Student?" *28th International Conference, Information Technology Interfaces, 19–22 June 2006, Cavtat, Croatia*, doi.org/10.1109/iti.2006.1708494.

Morgan, William, and Matthew Streb. "Building Citizenship: How Student Voice in Service-Learning Develops Civic Values." *Social Science Quarterly*, vol. 82, no. 1, 2001, pp. 154–169, doi.org/10.1111/0038-4941.00014.

Pasquesi, Kira. "Navigating Difference through Multicultural Service Learning." *New Directions for Student Services*, vol. 2013, no. 144, 2013, pp. 37–45, doi.org/10.1002/ss.20067.

Scott, Katharine E., and James A. Graham. "Service-Learning: Implications for Empathy and Community Engagement in Elementary School Children." *Journal of Experiential Education*, vol. 38, no. 4, 2015, pp. 354–372, doi:10.1177/1053825915592889.

Smith, Bradley H., et al. "The Development of a Service-Learning Program for First-Year Students Based on the Hallmarks of High Quality Service-Learning and Rigorous Program Evaluation." *Innovative Higher Education*, vol. 36, no. 5, 2011, pp. 317–329, doi.org/10.1007/s10755-011-9177-9.

Sokal, Laura, et al. " 'This Course Is Like Paying to Volunteer' Or Is It? Effects of a Mandatory Service-Learning Course on Teacher Candidates" ["Ce Cours s'Apparente à Payer Pour Faire Du Bénévolat » Ou Est-Ce Le Cas? Conséquences d'Un Stage d'Apprentissage Communautaire Obligatoire Sur Les Candidats à l'Enseignement."]. *McGill Journal of Education*, vol. 51, no. 1, 2016, pp. 597–614, doi.org/10.7202/1037361ar.

Sperling, Rick. "Service-Learning as a Method of Teaching Multiculturalism to White College Students." *Journal of Latinos and Education*, vol. 6, no. 4, 2007, pp. 309–322, doi.org/10.1080/15348430701473454.

Stukas, Arthur A., et al. "The Effects of 'Mandatory Volunteerism' on Intentions to Volunteer." *Psychological Science*, vol. 10, no. 1, 1999, pp. 59–64, doi.org/10.1111/1467-9280.00107.

Teymuroglu, Zeynep. "Service-Learning Project in a First-Year Seminar: A Social Network Analysis." *Primus*, vol. 23, no. 10, 2013, pp. 893–905, doi.org/10.1080/10511970.2013.785734.

Umpleby, Stuart, and Gabriela Rakicevik. "The Adoption of Service Learning in Universities Around the World." *South East European Journal of Economics and Business*, vol. 2, no. 2, 2007, pp. 69–74, doi.org/10.2478/v10033-007-0007-z.

Whitley, Meredith A., and David S. Walsh. "A Framework for the Design and Implementation of Service-Learning Courses." *Journal of Physical Education, Recreation & Dance*, vol. 85, no. 4, 2014, pp. 34–39, doi:10.1080/07303084.2014.884835.

9
AN OASIS OF CIVIC ENGAGEMENT?
Considering Critical Dispositions Developed within the American University in Cairo

James P. Austin

As of June 2015, there were more than 270 international branch campuses (IBCs) operating in other countries (Lane and Kinser), an increase from eighty-two such institutions in 2006 (Lawton and Kastomitros). This illustrates the global reach of the Western-style university, with many IBCs originating from the United States. This phenomenon has caught the attention of rhetoric and composition studies, as Schaub, Donahue, and others have expressed concern that non-reflective exports of US-based rhetoric and composition models into other countries may replicate some of the assumptions and consequences of British colonialism and US interventionism.

Recently, rhetoric and composition studies began investigating the development of writing curricula and programs outside the United States (Thaiss). Through this inquiry, the field has engaged critically with the power differentials inherent in the development of US-based writing program models in other countries (Martins). While many scholars rightly warn against the "greed of the corporate university and the colonial reach of Western literacy practices" (Wetzel and Reynolds 95) and the potential for "narrow . . . privileged, Western" dynamics (Martins) in the establishment of US-based approaches in other countries, other scholarship has considered the ways in which US-based program models may serve localized needs. For example, in "Expanding Transnational Frames into Composition Studies: Revising the Rhetoric and Writing Minor at the American University in Cairo," I argued that seemingly unidirectional flows of US-based approaches to writing program independence and curriculum development at the American University in Cairo (AUC) responded to programmatic, institutional, and national exigency. At that time, I called for the expansion of frames within transnationalism and literacy studies into research about

DOI: 10.7330/9781646421237.c009

US-based educational models and writing programs in other countries. Through this expansive framing, he argued, the field can account for many possible interactions of US-based approaches to education and literacy with many kinds of students across several countries and regions. This framing can also account for the ways in which these programs and universities interact with the cultures and communities within which they are situated.

International rhetoric and composition scholarship has focused largely on programs and pedagogies in its critical evaluation of these interactions. As a result, less attention has been devoted to the agendas and experiences of students who flow into these US-based writing programs and courses, as well as the changes that result from students' sustained interaction with ideologies for education and literacy within these US-based institutions.

In this chapter, I argue that interaction with US-based approaches to literacy through essay writing provided five Egyptian undergraduates at the American University in Cairo (AUC), an English-language, US-style university in Egypt, with opportunities for civic engagement in a nation where this form of engagement is often discouraged and can be dangerous (see Aksakalova, this volume, for another study on the impact of approaches to critical thinking on contexts outside the United States, and Bowman, this volume, for another perspective on risk in civic engagement). Such engagement included critiques of political power structures and cultural-religious practices, as well as consideration of the ways in which Islamic charity organizations can better serve local communities. The forms of civic engagement evidenced in the writing of study participants fall into two broad categories: (1) civic discussion based on secondary research, text analysis, and personal commentary, and (2) active engagement with ongoing civic issues in the form of primary research (fieldwork, interviews, and surveys).

Findings in this study suggest that these categories are divided along class and education types; in this study, those who graduated from private secondary schools and came from higher economic classes engaged in discussion, while those who graduated from public schools and lower economic classes engaged actively with civic issues in Egypt. Significantly, these public high school graduates also had prior experience with civic engagement that influenced their educational agendas and writing choices. I argue that education type, class background, and prior experience with civic engagement are correlated in this study, and that this correlation offers a model through which civic engagement can be sponsored in Egypt. In discussion, I consider the limitations of civic engagement at

AUC, an educational space with discrete ideological borders separating it from the rest of Egypt. In particular, I identify how the forms of civic engagement practiced through writing at AUC can cross AUC's physical and ideological borders to permeate community discourse in Egypt, leading to action initiated by Egyptians who have adapted so-called Western literacies for local and national purposes. I also identify some stark limitations in the larger Egypt beyond AUC's borders.

Before proceeding with the study, I offer a working definition of "civic engagement" in this chapter. The term has two primary applications. The first of these is engagement with social, cultural, political and/or economic issues primarily through analytical writing, personal commentary, and secondary research—what I term "civic discussion." This form of engagement, while important, is performed at some distance from the issues themselves and evidences no future potential engagement. The second form is that of "active engagement," characterized by writing and primary research (observations, interviews, surveys). This form is characterized by first-hand interaction with relevant civic issues through primary research and personal experience with the civic issue being engaged in the writing. In this respect, "active engagement" demonstrates more potential to move beyond the page, and the circumstances making this possible offer potential heuristics for future community engagement through what were originally "Western" literacies.

It is important to note that this study focuses on but five participants, so findings cannot be generalized without additional studies that corroborate what I consider the initial findings here. For example, there is no single type of "public" and "private" school experience in Egypt or anywhere else. Still, there are agreed-upon articulations of the "dismal quality of public schools" (de Koning 51) observed in ethnographic research of Egyptian public schools, revealing authoritarian approaches (Naguib) and rote memorization, without comprehension, of state-approved curriculum (Saad). These findings are consistent with my own experiences as an AUC writing instructor; students would often describe the bifurcated nature of public and private secondary schooling in Egypt, differences that would manifest in class and through student writing. Because of the extant scholarship and my own experience, I am confident that the central binary upon which this study rests—the differences between public and private secondary schooling in Egypt—are consistent with reality. It is my hope, however, that this study will inspire others to pursue writing research in Egypt and the Middle East and North Africa (MENA) more broadly, particularly from the perspectives of the writers.

In what follows, I situate this study within literacy studies and transnationalism scholarship. Following this, I analyze data, then follow with discussion that examines the limitations of AUC-based forms of civic engagement in Egypt. In my conclusion, I consider the ways in which AUC-based civic engagement evidenced through literate activity can engage beyond the borders of AUC and assert that these US-based approaches to college writing are forms of transnational literacy, which, as they are utilized by local actors, can engage with many kinds of communities.

FROM COMPOSITION STUDIES TO LITERACY STUDIES AND TRANSNATIONALISM

This study addresses many of the concerns expressed within the international branch of rhetoric and composition studies, particularly regarding the potential deleterious impact of non-reflective exports of US-based rhetoric and composition models into other countries. In this section, I reframe this study within the more expansive paradigms of literacy studies and transnationalism.

The ideological model for literacy developed within New Literacy Studies (Street) does not predict the impact of literacies on individuals and societies but examines through ethnographic approaches the ways in which literacies develop in various settings—even as Street himself is sometimes guilty of essentialist assumptions about global-local literacy power dynamics. Combined with the concept of transnationalism developed in the social sciences (Khagram and Levitt), literacy studies accounts for the factors involved with the movement of literacy ideologies from the United States into other countries—particularly in this study, those found in US composition courses—as well as context-specific interactions of these Western literacies with local languages, literacies, and individuals (Warriner). This approach offers a less deterministic view of the ways in which US-based approaches to education and literacy may develop within other cultures and societies. This also more clearly defines the point of origin for the literacies studied here as belonging primarily within the United States.

In this chapter, I use these frames to consider the ways in which approaches to critical thinking and civic engagement evident at AUC interacted with the agendas and literacy development of five undergraduates. This interaction enabled forms of critical engagement with several kinds of public issues relevant to Egypt in ways that are less common elsewhere in the country. This framing also allows us to account for differences in the forms of civic engagement evidenced by the participants, and the ways in which these differences correlate to sociocultural, economic, and educational difference. This, in turn, offers insight into the ways in which "Western" literacies are appropriated by local actors to serve community purposes.

METHODS AND DATA COLLECTION

For this study, I interviewed five undergraduates enrolled at the American University in Cairo. I used Skype for interviewing and Audacity for recording, and these interviews were subsequently transcribed. Each AUC student provided at least one writing sample from an AUC class. Most subjects were interviewed twice. In the first interview, subjects were asked to provide an educational life history, which covered significant past experiences with writing and literacy (in English, Arabic, and, in one case, French). This interview addressed not only secondary schooling but any significant experience with education and literacy from childhood. The purpose for this interview was to learn about the development of their literacy habits, with particular focus on the topics they addressed in their writing. The second interview, in which one subject did not participate, was a cognitive interview regarding the provided writing samples. In this interview, participants were asked about their writing process, the development of the essay, and their choices of topic and attitude expressed toward the topic. Together, these interviews were used to create profiles of the literacy habits of subjects prior to matriculating to AUC; the sociocultural rules driving and enforcing these habits; the stratification of writing topics and attitudes expressed by language; and consequences for noncompliance of the expected social rules for literacy. Interview findings also allowed me to observe differences in topic and expressed attitudes at AUC compared to prior educational experiences and could also account for what the subjects found challenging (or did not find challenging) about this transition into a site infused with US-based transnational literacies.

The writing samples also allowed direct comparison between the kinds of literacy habits developed through secondary schooling and the changed expectations for literacy at AUC. To accomplish this, I compared the topics each participant wrote about, the attitudes expressed about these topics, and the differences between topic and attitude expression according to schooling background and socioeconomic class. At this point, I divided the participants into two groups: those who graduated from private high schools and those who graduated from public high schools. The reason for this split is to account for the differing ways in which these two groups, who had distinct secondary school experiences with literacy and writing, engaged with civic issues through their school writing. This may, in turn, reveal insights into how Western-based literacies are appropriated by local actors who come from different backgrounds.

RELATING CIVIC ENGAGEMENT AT AUC WITH STUDENTS' PRIOR LITERACY HABITS AND EDUCATIONAL AND CLASS BACKGROUND

In this section, I analyze the findings of interviews of participants and text analysis of the writing samples they provided. My analysis develops along the following themes. First, I account for the Arabic and English language literacy habits reported by participants in their secondary schooling, with particular emphasis on the ways in which schooling enforced strict sociocultural rules governing school writing. This section focuses on literacy differences by language (Arabic, English and, in one case, French) and school type (public and private), the latter of which correlates to socioeconomic differences among the participants. Next, I consider the university writing of participants, focusing on how this writing evidences more engagement with civic issues than secondary school writing, as well as the ways in which participants who graduated from private high schools were more likely to offer cultural critique and vague calls to action, whereas those who graduated from the public schooling system were much more likely to engage with groups and organizations engaged in public discourse or dispute. I consider the reasons for the differences and the implications for civic engagement in Egypt.

Secondary Schooling Literacy Habits

In order to place in context the engagement with civic issues evidenced by participants after coming to AUC, I first consider their literacy habits prior to coming to AUC. In this section, I argue that the literacy habits developed in both Arabic and English (and, in one case, French) discouraged involvement with civic issues within Egypt. I also consider significant experiences that occurred beyond traditional curriculum that allowed for or discouraged civic engagement through writing. In performing this analysis, I consider the ways in which the type of school attended by participants (public or private) and their economic and sociocultural backgrounds affected the ways in which they were taught to avoid the forms of civic engagement through their schooling that they would later encounter at AUC.

Those students who attended the Egyptian public schooling system reported strict social rules governing not only what they were permitted to write about in their school writing but also what kinds of attitudes were allowed to be expressed on these topics. The participants reported that only in their Arabic school writing were they expected to write about Egypt; however, participants reported that it was understood they were supposed to produce reified portraits of an Egyptian nationalist ethos, which would include no acknowledgement of the manifold economic, social, cultural, religious, and political challenges afflicting Egypt. The consequences for breaking these rules, said one participant, was "a big fat zero" on a writing exam—no matter the quality of the writing itself. Likewise, another participant claimed that writing that did not follow the tacit rules would be marked down for errors that did not exist, in order to justify a lower grade.

For students from the Egyptian public schools, writing in English involved general topics meant to satisfy the requirements on the Egyptian national examination administered during students' senior years in secondary school. According to one participant, topics included describing walking your dog, what you did on the weekend, or giving directions to a lost tourist. Moreover, the competence of English instruction was highly problematic. These participants described "learning English in Arabic," where instructors would write words and imitate sounds that were understood by neither students nor teacher or reciting and writing English phrases without any comprehension of their meaning. These phrases could be written on the national examination in response to a general prompt. Another student described being instructed to write "only seven sentences" for any paragraph on any topic, as students were never asked to write more than a paragraph in response to any prompt. These sentences would be numbered and then, after the seven sentences had been written, she would erase the numbers and submit the paragraph to her teacher.

These practices surrounding English language writing instruction are consistent with a wider ambivalence toward English language literacies throughout the Middle East and North Africa. Indeed, throughout the region, there is acknowledgement of the need to learn English as the lingua franca of international communication, while at the same time there is reluctance to embrace the Western values that so often accompany English language acquisition (Al Haq and Smadi; Al-Tamimi and Shuib). These dynamics are consistent with the findings in this study: an acknowledgement of the usefulness of English accompanied by ambivalence toward the uses of English in Egyptian public schooling.

For those study participants who attended private secondary schools, the ideological rules governing English language and literacy learning are, in some respects, quite different for those who attended public schools. One of the most significant differences was their familiarity with Western literature. Indeed, the ambivalence regarding the accompaniment of Western culture with English language and literacies appears absent among those students from private schooling backgrounds. Some participants reported reading and writing literary analysis essays on authors such as Charles Dickens, while others described learning to write five-paragraph essays beginning in middle school. For these participants—including one who attended a French-language school—their ability to access and write about Western literature is a byproduct of their high social and economic status. Interestingly, the literacy habits of those who attended private schools serve a secondary purpose, that of diversion away from issues pertaining to Egypt. As with public school graduates, private school graduates reported no engagement with civic issues pertaining to Egypt.

In this respect, writing Western-style literary analysis diverted private secondary school students away from engagement with civic issues pertaining to Egypt. Instead, they invested in Western-style analysis of European and North American literature, similar to the curriculum of high schools and universities in the West. For those who graduated from private schools, this kind of reading and writing served to mark their status; indeed, it is possible that this reproduction of status through reading and writing about Western literature was among the most important "work" of their school literacies.

This approach was tested during the Egyptian revolution of 2011. According to one participant enrolled at the time in an American-style high school, the school administration gathered students together to actively discourage their involvement with the activities in Midan Tahrir. According to this participant, "we should never support [civil disobedience]. Any kind of behavior that stood against the government, we can't even talk about it." Once the revolution was successful and Hosni Mubarak deposed as president, students were encouraged to portray revolutionaries as national heroes, thereby co-opting the events of the revolution to reproduce the strict literacy rules for producing non-critical, reified school writing about Egypt. Although the methods differed, the expectations were the same for both public and private secondary school students: no engagement with civic issues pertaining to Egypt.

The findings from this section reveal that both public school and private school students were discouraged from forms of civic engagement in their writing, particularly with issues relevant to Egypt. Violating the language and literacy rules had clear academic and social consequences for the participants in this study and at the high schools they attended; participants were aware of consequences and took measures to avoid them. These insights are relevant because they indicate that civic engagement is discouraged in pre-tertiary education in Egypt, particularly when it comes to school writing. These findings further indicate that Arabic was the preferred language for any form of commentary relevant to Egypt at the schools attended by these participants, and that the use of English was relegated for general topics not pertinent to Egypt. Together, these findings underscore the challenges encountered by these participants regarding civic engagement in Egypt. These findings are particularly relevant to the next section, where I examine the forms of civic engagement in the university-level, English-language writing of participants.

Civic Engagement through Writing at AUC

According to study participants, once they began attending AUC, the rules governing literacy practices underwent radical change, particularly regarding the kinds of topics they could address and what they were able to express on these topics. At AUC, participants encountered Western faculty who encouraged them to engage critically with several issues relevant to Egypt. The college writing samples participants provided for this study addressed the following topics: Bassem Youssef, the Egyptian satirist; the practice of female genital mutilation (FGM); a response to the writings of an Arab feminist; a critical profile of the Lifemakers, an Islamic service organization active throughout Egypt; and the efforts of the Egyptian government to displace the population of an island on the Nile River so that the island could be developed. These topics represent significant departures from findings in the previous section regarding high school writing topics and the use of English as the language of engagement with issues pertaining to Egypt. In this section, I analyze the attitudes participants expressed about these topics and identify class and educational background-based rationales for the different forms of engagement evidenced in the writing.

In the following, I describe the topics addressed by writers who graduated from private secondary schools, and the attitudes they expressed about their topics. Each writer is profiled; pseudonyms are used to protect confidentiality. The writing shows engagement with civic and cultural issues ranging from Bassem Youssef to FGM to Arab feminism, but the engagement takes the form of the writers articulating their positions on these issues. Calls to action are vague and "tacked on" to the conclusions of the essays.

Sanaa

In her writing sample, Sanaa wrote about the Arab feminist poet Joumana Haddad. She begins her work by summarizing the main points of Haddad in a writing sample she had been given by her Western instructor. After this, Sanaa expresses broad agreement with Haddad's positions, which include a critique of Western assumptions that Arab women are oppressed and an acknowledgement of the patriarchal nature of Arab societies. Sanaa agrees with these positions and then offers some of her own experiences to support Haddad's positions. Like Haddad, Sanaa claims to have found "liberation in education" by reading Western authors such as Kafka and Nietzsche. These experiences, she claims, led to her abandonment of the Quran.

Sanaa's analysis of Haddad's Arab feminism is predicated upon her prior experiences with reading during her secondary schooling. Sanaa describes previous experiences reading and listening online to Arab poetry at the end of high school. At the same time, she describes finding and listening to TED talks of Arab and non-Arab speakers. She attributes this interest in poetry and TED talks to a teacher who had worked for a short time at her American high school. According to Sanaa, this teacher introduced them to T. S. Eliot and Edgar Allan Poe. This combination of Western poetry and perspectives with modern Arab poetry translated into English was critical, as it allowed her to develop a hybridized, cosmopolitan ethos that she brought to her AUC education and, specifically, her writing about Haddad. This underscores two important findings: First, Sanaa's access to Western literature and literacies was a critical part of her hybridized perspective, which demonstrates one of the ways in which her privileged educational background enabled her to identify with Haddad's non-orthodox views on Arab society; and second, Sanaa's commentary on Haddad is both individualistic and indicates no further engagement beyond the completion of the graded assignment. Like Haddad, she expresses an individualistic stance on cultural issues that underscores her privilege in a culture that often prefers acquiescence to societal norms. Additionally, there is no apparent plan or desire to translate her broad agreement with Arab feminism into tangible forms of protest or reform. There is no civic engagement beyond the page. This places Sanaa's efforts as a strictly text-based form of discussion over civic issues. It should be noted that prior forms of engagement were done privately. For perhaps the first time, Sanaa engages with these hybridized perspectives in a public form—that of an AUC writing classroom. While the magnitude of this "public" forum is limited to that of a single classroom, it nevertheless represents a striking change from her secondary schooling experiences, where any form of public engagement with revolutionaries was explicitly prohibited.

Nour

Nour addressed the topic of female genital mutilation (FGM) in her writing sample. This writing sample may betray the author's strong bias by referring to the practice as a form of "mutilation" (while those who engage in the practice may refer to it differently), but the sample also evidenced research-based approaches to learning the history and scope of the problem, as well as understanding the social, cultural, and religious factors influencing the development of this practice. Nour also provides broad suggestions for decreasing the practice in rural and other religiously conservative areas where the practice is common. She calls for educational campaigns and the "empowerment of women" to help curtail FGM in Egypt.

Nour's engagement with this issue evidences the kind of depth one would expect from a researched academic essay. She uses research to provide history and current context with the practice of FGM. But even a traditional and competently researched argument essay about this topic takes on special significance in Egypt. During the time she was writing this essay, Mohammed Morsi of the Muslim Brotherhood was the president of Egypt. Despite this, she claims not only that the Brotherhood supports FGM but that Egypt witnessed an increase in the practice during the Morsi presidency. She then critiques not only the practice but the Brotherhood for their part in its perpetuation. Like Sanaa, Nour expresses a strong point of view that is, in its own way, out of line with cultural orthodoxy: a public critique of cultural-religious practices. Still, beyond the notable significance of taking on the topic publicly, Nour does little to engage with the issue beyond her own strong critique of the practice. As with Sanaa, her efforts appear to be restricted to the writing of the essay.

Karim

Karim wrote an essay arguing that Abdel Fattah el-Sisi, who was then the most powerful military figure in Egypt, became a fair target for parody and satire for the political comedian Bassem Youssef once el-Sisi became involved in the politics of the country by ordering then-President Morsi to resign the presidency (el-Sisi is now the president of Egypt). By assuming this stance, Karim takes issue with what he describes as the commonly held opinion that the military should be exempt from critique and ridicule. However, because el-Sisi had become a political figure, Karim argues, the exemption from public skepticism was no longer valid. In the end, Karim believes the Egyptian public should gain "a sense of humor" about public scrutiny of the military.

Hidden beneath the surface of this claim, however, is the peril inherent in any public discussion of presidential politics and the military, especially when one expresses an attitude that does not reflect the literacy norms for public discussion on these topics. When Karim comes to the defense of Bassem Youssef, who later quit his television program amid tension with the government, he is indirectly critiquing the nature of public discourse that makes a defense of Youssef's creative freedom necessary in the first place. This public discourse is itself a reaction to the practices of the Egyptian government in response to criticism. That said, there is no indication from the text, or through an interview with Karim, that this critique will lead to further action or engagement.

Among the three participants who had attended or graduated from private secondary schools, there is a form of engagement with civic issues based primarily on commentary and recommendation. In this form of civic engagement, participants identify salient public issues: the status of women in the country, criticizing military figures through satire, and a cultural-religious practice known by many as female genital mutilation. All three cases clearly critique public policy, a departure from the secondary school writing of these participants. These essays, if they had been written in high school, would have likely been considered inappropriate. All three essays end with broad calls to action: creating equality between women and men, using education to help end FGM, and rethinking social rules and laws that forbid critique of public institutions like the military. These broad calls to action are consistent with US-based academic literacies and the genre of academic writing, where calls to action are often included in conclusion paragraphs that look to ground the academic analysis into material social contexts.

As seen from this analysis, three of the five participants in this study engaged in a distant form of civic engagement contained completely within the literacy and genre expectations of Western academic writing. While each participant issues calls to action, these actions are nonspecific and intended to be carried out by others, not the writers themselves. This kind of activity I term "civic discussion." In the next section, we will examine the writing samples of two participants who graduated from the Egyptian public schooling system and consider the ways in which their level of engagement moves beyond "civic discussion."

The two participants who graduated from Egyptian public high schools demonstrated deeper levels of civic engagement in their topics: The Lifemakers, an Islamic charity active in Egypt, and a study of the Island of Gold, a small island on the Nile River in Cairo. While both writers demonstrated research-based engagement with their topics, each conducted primary research. This involved fieldwork, interviews, and creating and analyzing surveys.

Aalaa

Aalaa wrote critically about the Island of Gold, visited the site several times, and interviewed many residents of the island about their disagreement with the Egyptian government's attempts to relocate the island's residents and sell the land to foreign investors. Not only did she present a strong critique of the efforts by the Egyptian government to displace the population living on the island, but she also engaged in primary research in making this argument. Along with classmates and her instructor as part of a composition class project, Aalaa visited the island several times to interview residents. Because of these efforts, Aalaa confronted an issue inherent in primary research: building trust with those whose participation she sought. As she developed relationships, she was able to learn about life on the island in ways secondary research alone could not accomplish.

Farah

Farah wrote about an Islamic charity, the Lifemakers, conducted interviews with administrators, and wrote, distributed, and analyzed the results of a survey. While she cited secondary sources, none of these addressed the organization specifically, indicating that no prior research had been done on this organization. As a result, all the primary research she conducted represented a new contribution. In her essay, Farah addressed challenges within the organization and drew upon interviews and survey results to make recommendations for improving the recruitment and training of volunteers in order to benefit the "illiterate, poor, mothers [and] children" who benefit from the organization.

Farah had first heard of this organization prior to her matriculation to AUC and became involved with the local chapter in her hometown in the Nile River delta region. This involvement drove many aspects of her academic activity at AUC, and she states a desire to become involved with this organization after her graduation from AUC. Of all the participants in this study, Farah's academic interests and agenda for civic engagement are the most intertwined. This reveals not only that it is possible for Western-based forms of literacy to intersect with local individuals, needs, and organizations, but it also provides one model for how this can happen.

These findings show that the participants who came from the literacy and writing backgrounds that are least likely to encourage analysis and critical thinking, and who are in the extreme minority at AUC, evidenced the most active engagement with their topics. A recent institutional study found that roughly 80 percent of an incoming freshman class had graduated from Egyptian private schools, while only 8.2 percent had graduated from Egyptian public schools (Office of Data Analytics and Institutional Research). This strongly implies that the graduates of public schools not only lack the educational, language, and literacy habits of those who graduated from private schools, but that AUC represents a high-stakes opportunity for these students—one for which they are not particularly well-prepared as writers. The opportunities for such students to attend AUC, a university that all study participants held in high regard, are significantly lower. And yet, the students who fit this profile in this study evidenced greater civic engagement in their AUC college writing. In short, the study's participants who fit this profile engaged more and risked more. They practiced primary research and, in Farah's case, saw clear links between their academic work and future forms of civic engagement.

As stated earlier, the writing samples of private school graduates evidenced civic discussion. In two instances, participants expressed support for the views of a controversial public figure and offered broad cultural critiques: of gender norms and the practice of not criticizing the military (and, indirectly, support for satire as a form of engagement with public issues). Another participant critiqued FGM, a religious-cultural practice. While this writer evidenced depth with the topic through secondary research, the writer offered only vague recommendations for solving what she saw as a significant problem. In all three cases, the writers addressed Egyptian issues at some remove: They discussed a relevant issue, offered a personalized response, and prescribed a general solution.

This form of engagement, while limited, should not be downplayed. As I established earlier in this chapter, addressing Arab feminism, the military, Bassem Youssef, and FGM represent marked differences from the secondary school writing topics reported by these participants. Additionally, making strong, personalized claims on these issues also represents a level of engagement distinct from their prior writing, where analysis and critical thinking were typically limited to close readings of Western literature. Still, those abilities were developed in their pretertiary schooling, and at AUC, these participants were able to deploy those abilities to achieve more civically engaged forms of analysis.

The graduates of public schools engaged in primary research in their AUC writing projects. They also had unique experiences in their backgrounds that help account for the particular nature of their engagement with civic issues. Aalaa, for instance, visited the island in Cairo that was the subject of her research. She came to understand the challenge of building trust among the residents she sought to interview. Aalaa had had prior experience with such work; as a middle school student, she had applied for and been accepted into an AUC-sponsored academic program. Through this program, she was exposed to social sciences–based approaches to civic engagement and research. Interestingly, she reported that she was able to acknowledge and investigate many of the social and economic problems within Egypt, a marked difference from her account of traditional schooling. Farah traveled long distances and interrupted her intersession break to conduct interviews with administrators of the Lifemakers. She also composed, disseminated, collected, and analyzed the results of a bilingual survey to volunteers of the organization. She claimed that she had to learn how to create surveys on her own because the scale of her project superseded the expectations for the class. Indeed, she described previous interaction with the Lifemakers in Zagazig, her home city, which inspired both her overall educational agenda and her decision to approach this essay from the scope at which she did. Interestingly, the scale of the project made it impossible for her to complete during the semester it was assigned.

To that end, there is an important bit of context that should be provided to this discussion. In many cases, students who graduated from an Egyptian public school have been awarded one of a small number of highly competitive scholarships specifically targeted at students from the public schools. One of these scholarships, the Empower Scholarship, is available to public school graduates from five governorates and results in a program that promotes "civic responsibility, leadership, cross-cultural competence, professionalism and tolerance" ("Empower Scholarship"). Thus, part of the "authorization" for students from public schools and lower social and economic classes to come to AUC is related to the ethics of service and engagement. Moreover, this also hints at an intensely competitive environment among top students in the public schooling system, who would need scholarships to attend AUC. And while students from public schools communicated the ambivalence with which their families viewed AUC, they also readily acknowledge that an AUC degree represents a rare opportunity for economic, professional, and social mobility in Egypt.

These broad differences in the kinds of civically-engaged writing at AUC, and the correlation to the schooling and sociocultural backgrounds of the writers, beg a larger question with implications beyond AUC: Can writing engaged with issues of public interest result in civic action in a nation where such engagement can be dangerous to individuals? This question is taken up in the conclusion to this chapter.

CONCLUSION: CIVIC ENGAGEMENT IN TWENTY-FIRST-CENTURY EGYPT

In this chapter, I have considered the ways in which civic engagement is discouraged in Egyptian secondary schools, while forms of engagement are much more common at the American University in Cairo. In what ways might these findings be applied to larger efforts for robust civic engagement in Egypt, a nation with significant sociocultural, political, and economic challenges? In considering this question, one must account for the current climate of academic freedom in Egypt. The murder of Italian PhD student Giulio Regeni in 2016 highlights the potential dangers facing those who engage with civic issues the Egyptian government may find sensitive. Regeni had been studying informal labor movements in Egypt and may have been interviewing groups the government considered enemies of the state.

The risk is not limited to academics from other countries. According to an infographic published by Freedom Students Observatory, more than 1,000 students were arrested in Egypt in 2015. Of these, more than 140 students were referred to military trials, 25 were killed, and more than 400 are missing ("Info-graph of Violence against Egyptian students 2015"). The Egyptian government disputes these findings, in part by accusing the reporting organization of ties to the Muslim Brotherhood, which has been formally designated as a terrorist organization. Given this environment, in what ways might research findings from this study shed light on ways to practice civic engagement in Egypt?

Because this study involved only five students, the generalizability of findings to the wider concerns within Egypt, and to the question posed above, is limited. Still, the key finding from this research is that those participants who had a history of prior involvement with civic engagement took more active forms of engagement. Additionally, those students who had come into direct contact with these issues came from socioeconomic and schooling backgrounds not typical for most AUC students. This suggests that students from these "atypical" backgrounds were more likely to come to AUC with an agenda for civic engagement that could be reflected in their writing. For example, Aalaa's experience with an AUC-sponsored program in Beni Suef allowed her to practice social science research and engage with challenges within Egypt. This suggests that research carried out with the support and/or affiliation of AUC may be inoculated against some of the traditional hazards associated with sensitive public engagement. Indeed, AUC has a School of Global Affairs and Public Policy, which touts a "strong belief in the interaction of international and public affairs, [and] an unwavering commitment to ethics and the rule of law" ("School of Global Affairs and Public Policy: Vision and Mission"). Expansion of pre-tertiary programs, such as the one in which Aalaa was enrolled, could help create a more engaged citizenry with the ability to acknowledge challenges and develop some of the tools to investigate and propose solutions to them.

Likewise, Farah's agenda illustrates the potential impact of nongovernmental organizations that are consistent with local, national, and/or regional cultural and religious values. The Islamic ethic of service inherent in the Lifemakers provides it with a locally recognized credibility that no outside NGO or intergovernmental collaboration is likely to replicate: it speaks to the shared values of much of the Egyptian citizenry. Farah's experience with this group in Zagazig prior to her admission to AUC was a formative experience. She enjoyed engaging in service and helping her community, but she also became curious about the way the organization functioned and how, through her engagement with it, she could assist more communities in different ways. Increased recruitment of young people such as Farah into organizations such as the Lifemakers, and inculcating young people into the operations of the group, may help develop additional interest in both the activities of service and the groups that organize such engagement. This may be particularly effective in areas of Egypt where organizations such as the Lifemakers are active—areas with sociocultural, economic, and public schooling realities similar to those of Farah and Aalaa. This underscores another important recommendation: finding ways to increase access and equity for those from all backgrounds who wish to pursue an AUC education, as AUC offers, through its Western-based literacies, avenues for civic engagement.

Finally, this study reveals two important trends regarding civic engagement in Egypt. First, there is a clear and intrinsic interest in civic engagement in the country. All of the students who participated in the study evidenced some form of engagement with nationally relevant issues in ways novel to them. Two students evidenced direct forms of engagement through prior experiences, including Farah, who connected her academic interest in civic engagement with her Islamic values. Likewise, AUC-sponsored scholarships encouraged the development of civic engagement as an ethos and career path. There is a campus organization focused specifically on civic engagement. Given this, it is fair to claim that civic engagement is being practiced within Egypt by local actors who had been influenced by US-based entities such as the American University in Cairo.

The second trend, however, reveals that civic engagement also can be a dangerous activity in Egypt. As earlier data show, there are limits regarding civic engagement in the country. Students can disappear or be jailed for forms of engagement that are perceived, at least by the Egyptian government, as civil disobedience. In other words, this is physically dangerous work beyond culturally specific thresholds. It is entirely likely that the social rules driving topic selection and attitude expression at the secondary school level is reflected again, albeit in a much more consequential fashion, in the enforcement of limitations on forms of civic engagement.

Given these divergent trends, the question becomes *who* can best practice civic engagement and *what counts* within the confines of the present moment in Egyptian history as appropriate. The early findings from this study reveal that Islamic forms of engagement are considered appropriate, as is the kind of social science work done by Aalaa. It seems possible that this work being done by Egyptians may be considered more appropriate than if the work had been carried out by a non-Egyptian or non-Muslim. Indeed, some foreign NGOs have faced resistance from the Egyptian government since President al-Sisi entered office. Likewise, there is a strong possibility that USAID, which helps fund many civically engaged initiatives in Egypt and around the world, will experience budget cuts in the future. Taken together, this may indicate a moment of change regarding civic engagement within Egypt, with an increased focus on local actors and a clear ceiling on the kinds of government-sanctioned activity. Finally, this study offers some insight into the area of the academy where international composition studies, transnationalism, and literacy studies intersect. In this study, as but one example, these fields grapple with the ways in which a form of transnational literacy (US-based approaches to college writing) crossed national borders into Egypt and interacted with individuals in ways that served both the agendas of participants and the ongoing desire for civic engagement in Egypt.

Indeed, one of the most salient findings in this study is that those students with civic engagement in their backgrounds, who brought that agenda to bear in their AUC writing, least fit the traditional sociocultural, economic, and educational profile of an AUC student. These students were able to draw upon their prior experiences through their interaction with the literacy ideologies of AUC in ways that would have been less likely in other tertiary institutions in the country. This raises the possibility that students from this background possess qualities which, when combined with the transnational literacies of AUC by students themselves, can result in greater engagement with civic issues and raises the possibility of engaged action—and increased risk—in the future. It also implies that, despite changes underway, there is still a role for AUC when it comes to civic engagement, inasmuch as the institution, its faculty, and its organization may sponsor local actors.

WORKS CITED

Al Haq, Fawwaz Al-Abed, and Oqlah Smadi. "Spread of English and Westernization in Saudi Arabia." *World Englishes*, vol. 15, no. 3, Nov. 1996, pp. 307–317, doi:10.1111/j.1467-971X.1996.tb00117.x.

Al-Tamimi, Atef, and Munir Shuib. "Motivations and Attitudes towards Learning English: A Study of Petroleum Engineering Undergraduates at Hadhramout University of Sciences and Technology." *GEMA Online Journal of Language Studies*, vol. 9, no. 2, Jan. 2009, pp. 29–55.

de Koning, Anouk. *Global Dreams: Class, Gender, and Public Space in Cosmopolitan Cairo*. AUC Press, 2009.

Donahue, Christiane. "'Internationalization' and Composition Studies: Reorienting the Discourse." *College Composition and Communication*, vol. 61, no. 2, Dec. 2009, pp. 212–243, www.jstor.org/stable/40593441.

"Empower Scholarship." *American University in Cairo*, 2017, www.aucegypt.edu/admissions/scholarships/egyptian-students/empower.

"Info-graph of Violations against Egyptian Students in 2015." *Freedom Seekers*, 2016, freedomseekers.org/en/?p=4240.

Khagram, Sanjeev, and Peggy Levitt, editors. *The Transnational Studies Reader: Intersections and Innovations*. Routledge, 2008.

Lane, Jason E., and Kevin Kinser. "C-BERG Branch Campus Listing." *Cross-Border Education Research Team (C-BERT)*, updated 20 Jan. 2017, cbert.org/?page_id=34.

Lawton, William, and Alex Katsomitros. "International Branch Campuses: Data and Developments." *The Observatory on Borderless Higher Education*, 1 Dec. 2012, www.obhe.ac.uk/documents/view_details?id=894.

Martins, David S. "Transnational Writing Program Administration: An Introduction." *Transnational Writing Program Administration*, edited by David S. Martins, Utah State University Press, 2015, pp. 1–20.

Naguib, Kamal. "The Production and Reproduction of Culture in Egyptian Schools." *Cultures of Arab Schooling: Critical Ethnographies from Egypt*, edited by Linda Herrera and Carlos Alberto Torres, University of New York Press, 2006, pp. 53–82.

Office of Data Analytics and Institutional Research. "Report on the Results of the First-Time Freshman Survey." Office of Data Analytics and Institutional Research, Cairo, Egypt, 2013.

Saad, Ahmed Youssof. "Subsistence Education: Schooling in a Context of Urban Poverty." *Arab Schooling: Critical Ethnographies from Egypt*, edited by Linda Herrera and Carlos Alberto Torres, University of New York Press, 2006, pp. 83–108.

Schaub, Mark. "Beyond These Shores: An Argument for Internationalizing Composition." *Pedagogy: Critical Approaches to Teaching Literature, Language, Composition, and Culture*, vol. 3, no. 1, 2003, pp. 85–98, read.dukeupress.edu/pedagogy/article/3/1/85/29280/Beyond-These-Shores-An-Argument-for?searchresult=1.

"School of Global Affairs and Public Policy: Vision and Mission." *The American University in Cairo*, 2016, http://schools.aucegypt.edu/GAPP/Pages/Vision.aspx.

Street, Brian. "What's 'New' in New Literacy Studies? Critical Approaches to Literacy in Theory and Practice." *Current Issues in Comparative Education*, vol. 5, no. 2, 2003, pp. 77–91, www.tc.columbia.edu/cice/pdf/25734_5_2_Street.pdf.

Thaiss, Chris. "Origins, Aims, and Uses of *Writing Programs Worldwide*: Profiles of Academic Writing in Many Places." *Writing Programs Worldwide: Profiles of Academic Writing in Many Places*, edited by Chris Thaiss et al., The WAC Clearing House, Parlor Press, 2012, pp. 5–22.

Warriner, Dorris S. "Transnational Literacies: Examining Global Flows through the Lens of Practice." *The Future of Literacy Studies*, edited by Mike Baynham, Palgrave Macmillan, 2009, pp. 160–180.

Wetzel, Danielle Zawodny, and Dudley W. Reynolds. "Adaptation across Time and Space: Revealing Pedagogical Assumptions." *Transnational Writing Program Administration*, edited by David S. Martins, Utah State University Press, 2015, pp. 93–116.

10

EXPERIENCES LEARNED FROM FOSTERING A CRITICAL AND CREATIVE WRITING CULTURE AMONG YOUTH IN QATAR

Sadia Mir and Ian Mauer

The Young Writers Program is a regionally significant program that aims to foster a creative and critical second-language English writing culture in Qatar. The program started in 2014 as a collaborative between the US Embassy, Doha, and the Ministry of Education and Higher Education in Qatar and consists of an annual writing competition with an awards ceremony, a series of student workshops led by writing specialists and observed by classroom teachers, and finally, a print journal publication distributed nationwide across Qatar. This is a local initiative aimed at giving students a chance for civic engagement on a global scale through writing (Bringle et al.; McIlrath and MacLabhrainn). Writing prompts are inspired by quotes from prominent Qatari voices, for example, Her Highness Sheikha Mozah bint Nasser Al Missned, wife of the former Emir of Qatar and the chairperson of the Qatar Foundation for Education, Science and Community Development, among other notable leaders. Meanwhile, the US Department of State's Bureau of Education and Cultural Affairs (ECA) has a mission to "build friendly, peaceful relations between people of United States and the people of other countries through academic, cultural, sports and professional exchanges" ("Bureau of Educational and Cultural Affairs").

This program, then, in the current particular geopolitical turbulence in the MENA region, offers an academic and extracurricular avenue for positive cross-cultural collaboration, which focuses on the support and development of Qatari youth through English creative writing and composition education. In 2016, 80 percent of Qatari K–12 schools nationwide participated in the program, which promotes the integration of language teaching and social and civic responsibility through the choice of writing topics that focus on global citizenship, social equity,

DOI: 10.7330/9781646421237.c010

and education. For example, in the 2015–2016 academic year, taking quotes from Sheikha Mozah, the high school writing topics asked students to reflect on global citizenship and the right of access to education around the world. In addition to the focus on writing skills development, the program has branched out to addresses current challenges foreign language teachers face in second language writing engagement in Qatar, such as the reluctance of students to use the second language beyond communicative purposes. The program engages students both inside and outside of the classroom context by providing young writers with a stage and a platform to present their work to their peers and to the wider Qatari community. It enriches the students' experience of second language writing while giving classroom teachers and administrators new perspectives on current writing pedagogy. In an environment where there is limited use of English for creative purposes, the program encourages workshop participants and competition winners alike to build and be part of a community of creative writers. Significantly, as writing specialists of this program, we have come to realize that the program has provided an opportunity for civic engagement through critical and creative writing, as well as a unique gateway to understanding and addressing the complexities of teaching and learning of English language education in Qatar.

CONTEXT

Located in the Arab Gulf of the Middle East, Qatar is a small country with big ambitions. Since the end of the First World War, the people of the Gulf have risen in geopolitical importance due to their fortuitous wealth in and exploitation of nonrenewable oil and natural gas resources. The Gulf is home to the three biggest offshore oil fields in the world. This includes the incredibly large Sanafiya oil field, which is just off the eastern coast of Saudi Arabia and is estimated to contain a reserve of more than fifty billion barrels of oil (Pentland). Although lumped together into one geographical area for the purpose of identification, the modern nation states that have emerged from within the gulf region are distinct in many ways and were divided up along borders that often contradict the local realities of family, kinship, and tribal ties.

When the long-standing Ottoman Empire was partitioned at the end of World War I, huge chunks of the Middle East were divided into "spheres of influence" between Britain and France by way of the Sykes-Picot agreement of 1916. This partitioning left the soon-to-emerge nation states of the Gulf under direct British influence: Qatar and the other Gulf states were designated as protectorates under the well-established British Residency, which lasted for over two hundred years (Olson). Despite the Gulf states being linked by an overarching British influence, the various nations of the Persian Gulf differ in the languages they speak (Farsi vs. Arabic), religious beliefs they adhere to (Sunni vs. Shi'a), and the type of jurisprudence with which they practice their religion (Wahhabi vs. Maliki). What this means, in effect, is that there are strong linguistic, religious, and conservative value differences that divide the region. The geopolitical context that Qatar finds itself in is rather complex, and it is no surprise that Qatar wants to put itself on the map as an internationally established country.

The Gulf state of Qatar has pursued this by using the hydrocarbon revenues discovered since 1949 to rapidly modernize in all areas, from infrastructure and healthcare to arts and education. With great insight, Qatar has made the development of a knowledge-based economy a central priority (*Qatar National Development Strategy 2011–2016*). In support of education for its citizens, Qatar has invested considerably in the education sector. In 2001, Qatar commissioned the RAND Corporation to evaluate its K–12 schooling and provide recommendations on how to build a world-class education system to meet the needs of a transitioning society. Out of these recommendations, a newly structured government agency, the Supreme Education Council (SEC)—the precursor to the Ministry of Education and Higher Education in Qatar—was established. It was created to oversee K–12 public schooling across the country and to address state concerns of students acquiring the academic proficiency necessary to succeed in postsecondary education and enter the global labor market.

The SEC introduced nationwide educational policy reforms and adopted international curriculum systems. In 2005, the RAND Corporation completed a broad-based evaluation of the education reforms. It was observed that public schools under the direction of the SEC were moving toward more student-centered pedagogy wherein students' needs were the focus of instructional practice. Among other documented changes, class sizes were lowered to more manageable sizes, and teachers were encouraged to engage students in higher-order thinking-based cognitive activities rather than rote learning. Students seemed to respond positively to these changes, and parents also seemed to favor these new models of learning (Zellman et al.). There was a notable shift in teaching philosophy and practice across the K–12 public schools that seemed to garner progressive outcomes.

Progress has been made. However, while there is an effort to build creative writing communities across the region (MENAWCA), Qatar has yet to fully realize its goals, specifically regarding English language education in Qatar. Creative writing in English has yet to flourish widely. This is because English has been positioned primarily as a language for academic, business, and pragmatic purposes, and it is generally being taught within these parameters. This understanding of English is widespread in the Middle East and North Africa and is echoed by Austin in his study of US-based educational models and writing programs in Cairo, Egypt, in "An Oasis of Civic Engagement." It is worth noting that Qatar's education system was traditionally shaped within a religious framework and influenced by the country's Bedouin ancestral roots. The transmission of Islamic knowledge, through the Quran, the Hadith, and the Sunnah, was established as a foundation of learning. This delivery of revealed knowledge created a particular educational culture. Certain instructional methods became more prevalent in the classroom and persist through the present, such as rote learning and memorization, where critical inquiry and analytical skills development was less emphasized (Rostron 223). Furthermore, there is little engagement in the use of English outside of the classroom walls beyond what students may watch on TV or be exposed to on the Internet.

These challenges have not gone unnoticed. Recently, the SEC underwent restructuring and was renamed the Ministry of Education and Higher Education in Qatar. With a refocused vision, the ministry has partnered with numerous key educational stakeholders, including the US Embassy in Doha, Qatar, to further broaden curriculum. Together, these two partners have collaborated on an elaborate portfolio of educational outreach initiatives, which includes the "Young Writers Competition." This annual creative writing competition, launched in 2014, has the aim of encouraging K–12 youth to write for fun. The hope is that enjoyable writing will support the development of a creative writing culture in Qatar that extends beyond the school and out into the community and will ultimately support English language proficiency among youth in Qatar, a country that is in rapid modernization, and has launched itself on the global landscape. The US Embassy's focus is also on the promotion of shared cultural values: These students, by developing the ability to think and write critically, will reject harmful false narratives and extremist thinking ("Fact Sheet: The White House Summit on Countering Violent Extremism"). The Young Writers Program has shown itself to be a type of civic engagement that is possible in the cultural context of the Arab Gulf within the political context of the State of Qatar.

PARTICIPANTS IN THE YOUNG WRITERS PROGRAM

The Young Writers Program (YWP) was initially developed to target K–12 students learning English in Qatari schools. However, in addition to the students, teachers have also been recognized as a target group since they determine how the students interact with English in the classroom on a daily basis and could benefit from exposure to the writing program. Another indirect target group of the program is the community as a whole. Qatar is a collectivist society (Rostron 221), and community involvement was identified as a necessary criterion to help support the initiative and to enable long-term sustainability.

In the first phase of the program, based on the understanding that creative and socially conscious creative writing in English was by large a new approach to writing in the public schools, careful planning and specific engagement with stakeholders was necessary to elicit interest from the target audiences. Lead English coordinators from all independent (or public) schools across the country were invited to attend the pre-competition orientation sessions. In 2015–2016, three separate sessions were held (for grade five, eight, and ten teachers). The lead coordinators, in turn, returned to their respective English faculty to promote the competition in the schools. Next, a select number of schools were chosen to participate in the series of intensive writing workshops. In 2015–2016, one boys' school and one girls' school were selected. Twenty tenth-grade students participated from each school. The ministry selected one urban girls' school located in central Doha and one boys' school from Al Khor, an outlying municipality of Qatar. Then there were the numerous students that submitted their work to the writing competition. Before submission to the writing competition, there were large-scale, school-wide writing competitions at each of the participating schools, which led to two final submissions per school entered in the national competition funded by the US Embassy. In 2014–2015, 104 schools participated in the writing competition. This provided the competition with 208 student submissions. The following year, the competition received 240 submissions from 120 schools nationwide, 80 percent of total schools. These numbers were unprecedented and significant considering the regional educational context as outlined earlier and were evidence that this program had tapped into an existing curiosity into a few possible overlapping areas, such as creative writing in English, writing as a means of civic engagement, as well as community participation and engagement.

THE COMPETITION

Launched in 2014, and notably the first of its kind in the country, the Young Writers Competition is an annual initiative with a mission to encourage students to engage in the process of writing in a personal, critical, and creative way. Students are encouraged to have fun with the art of writing as a means of self-expression, exploration, and civic engagement from a local, regional, and global perspective. They are asked to think critically about topics in education, culture, and society. They are given the opportunity, first and foremost, to express themselves, with an emphasis on telling stories about themselves, their personal experiences, and their communities. Students are provided with specific topics from which they are asked to write creative fiction or nonfiction, which can include short stories, personal essays, or poetry.

In the past two years of implementation, the task to engage in socially conscious creative fiction and nonfiction initially seemed challenging for some students, many of whom were struggling to simply express themselves in English by spelling words correctly and formulating complete sentences. Others lacked motivation to take part in a competition and saw the writing as work outside of their formal academic responsibilities. However, the program had an embedded focus on individual authorship and original voice, which encouraged participants to write whatever they could from their own knowledge base. This step away from English language as a formal method of communication to English language as a creative and personal form of self-expression of their subject positions led to a shift of perception. Further, this shift of perception of the writing experience as an avenue for meaningful expression appealed to some students. One student reflected on her experience in the competition by writing the following:

> At first when I started, I didn't know what to write, so I decided to look at my everyday life and reflect what I lived into my writing, because I learned what is better to write than my own experience.
> —Grade 9 student participant, 2014–2015 Young Writers Competition

The logistics of the writing competition itself is straightforward. The competition launches near the start of the academic year with a submissions deadline at the start of the second semester. To use the 2015–2016 academic year as an example, the competition launched in October, with the submissions deadline the following February. The Ministry of Education and Higher Education selected three grades (five, eight, and ten) to span primary, preparatory, and secondary school levels. All schools across the country were encouraged to participate. The prompts fell under two distinct themes: education and global citizenry. The premise was simple: students choose a topic and write something in adherence with certain word counts and related guidelines, such as the writing rubric with which the winning submissions are evaluated. The top fifteen winning submissions were then published in the *Young Writers Journal*, a print anthology of their creative work that was distributed to all schools nationwide.

A jury of writing specialists and educators within the community selected the winners. The rubric utilized was made available to the teachers and was explained during the student workshops to highlight individual expression and creative engagement with the topic over grammar and mechanics. Finally, the student winners were recognized at a celebratory event at Virginia Commonwealth University in Qatar, where the three best submissions for each participating grade were honored and prizes awarded. Virginia Commonwealth University in Qatar, established in 1998, was the first American post-secondary institution satellite campus to form Education City, an initiative developed by Qatar Foundation for Education, Science, and Community Development. Education City has grown to include other American educational institutions such as Carnegie-Mellon University, Cornell University, Georgetown University, and Texas A&M University. The programs offered through these satellite campuses claim to be extensions of their various institutions, committed to parallel requirements, student expectations, and academic vigor. VCU-Qatar, in particular, is fully accredited by the National Association of Schools of Art and Design, The Southern Association of Colleges and Schools, and the Council for Interior Design Accreditation. The Ministry of Education and Higher Education has claimed that these satellite campuses "create an environment of reform and progress without losing strong Islamic values" (qtd. in Eastwood 446). Participating students, their families, and distinguished community members were invited to the institution to celebrate the young writers. At the 2015–2016 event, past student winners participated in the awards ceremony, giving their thoughts on what the program has meant to them and how it affected their ideas about and relationship with writing. At this event, the US Ambassador in Qatar, Dana Shell Smith, referred to the program as "of the utmost importance to our Embassy—education and cultural diplomacy are foundational pillars of our mission here and around the globe" ("Young Writers Receive Awards from US Ambassador"). As stated earlier, community support was a key factor in long-term sustainability, in consideration of the existing functional view of English language education within a collectivist Qatari society.

The awards ceremony was followed by an additional writing workshop to help the student winners prepare their work for print publication in the *Young Writers Journal*. The *Young Writers Journal* is an annual print anthology of the winning student entries. It is distributed to all schools and major educational bodies across Qatar to use within their respective curriculum, giving the students a platform to present their work to a large, appreciative audience. Here, students were given an opportunity to become active creators of knowledge, or authors contributing culturally relevant and representational material reflective of their own lived experiences and environment of the Middle East.

Although this initiative started as a creative writing competition, it has expanded to address the needs of the K–12 educators and learners, incorporating student and teacher workshops, and focus group sessions.

THE WORKSHOPS

As previously mentioned, the scope of the competition expanded to address wider concerns of how civic engagement through creative arts could be encouraged and how K–12 teachers could help the students with this focus. In the teacher program orientation sessions, teachers were given curriculum materials specifically targeting the writing prompts and addressing ways to engage the students with the topics of global citizenry and education. These materials covered the typical stages of the writing process from brainstorming to drafting and revision. The aim of the teacher orientation sessions was to provide classroom English teachers with tips and strategies on teaching critical and creative writing composition and offered opportunities for reflection in/on action for the teachers (Schön 128). Teacher support was essential to the success of this program. As a result, the student writing workshops were open for observation and critical feedback in terms of regional applicability and pedagogical perspectives. They were designed to support teachers who were already incorporating creative writing in the classroom, as well as active and interactive teaching methodologies, and offer alternative instructional strategies for teachers who continued with the rote learning and memorization model. These workshops opened an avenue to discuss challenges faced by the teachers in the classroom.

The student writing workshops aimed to facilitate the two dimensions of teaching writing: the writing craft itself, incorporating the standard stages in the writing process, technique, and skill, as well as the authorial confidence and expression of the self. These two dimensions are unique, significant, and interconnected. Whereas knowledge of the craft is integral and related to issues of language and syntax, addressing writing solely on the basis of error correction is problematic. This "craft-centered approach" (Newman 5), which focuses on the final polished product, is often the teaching methodology used in Qatari schools. Possibly as a result, in the 2014–2015 cycle of the program, a substantial number of entries submitted were plagiarized. The notion of error-free writing superseded creative original thought. As well, this approach, often described as the traditional approach to teaching writing, values a perfection of grammar and sentence structure and can be detrimental for the emotional state of students and their learning. A focus on criticism and solely correcting the elements of the craft can negatively impact student progress. Studies have also shown that a lack of confidence and self-defeatist attitude can result in lowered expectations of achievement (Good and Brophy 269).

To address this concern, the sessions focused on a balance of the craft-centered approach to teaching writing with the affect-centered approach. The latter student-centered method of teaching writing focuses on personal development and using writing as a form of self-expression and deemphasizes error correction for original authorial voice. The affect-centered approach seeks to establish a supportive environment of trust within which students can experiment with the writing process, form, and content. Perfection is less important. Creative and critical thought is accentuated through sample instruction, activities, and assessment models provided in the sessions. From this approach, the craft of writing can be viewed as a vehicle to process their unconscious thoughts and as a medium for negotiating their reactions to the world around them. Researchers have looked at this approach as a way "to help create vital human beings . . . [and] to encourage creative responses to a complex world" (qtd. in Newman 6). The balance of both writing approaches addresses the aims of the Young Writers Program: to develop critical and creative writers who possess the technical skills of the writing craft to reflect upon their subject positioning regarding issues of civic engagement, civil responsibility, and global citizenship.

In addition to working with teachers, this series of workshops was a way of working with the students directly. The workshops encouraged students to write with originality and to think critically and creatively. The sessions were one-hour-long interactive lessons designed around the writing competition's task of reflecting and interpreting the two quotations on education and global citizenship through a fiction short story or poem or a nonfiction short story or personal essay. The workshops encompassed a range of specific learning experiences to highlight the main stages of the writing process and also looked at the four writing forms mentioned above. Students were introduced to the typical writing process stages of pre-writing/planning, composing, feedback, and revision activities in the course of the workshops. Students had opportunities to reflect on the themes as a means of civic engagement through composition and were encouraged to locate their reflections in context of their own lives and experiences. This instructional approach considered both product and process of creative writing. Throughout the workshops, emphasis was placed on what it meant to write creatively: the expression of individual opinions, emotions, reactions, and the telling of personal real or imagined narratives.

Activities that students were given ranged from simple brainstorming and planning sheets, to delicate peer feedback sessions with other students. While sticking with traditional writing activities, there were also thought-provoking classroom practices that challenged the students to incorporate their own reactions, voices, and experiences into their writing drafts. Two such activities were a picture prompt activity and a five senses activity. In the picture prompt activity, a number of provoking images depicting varying social, political, and cultural issues from around the globe were displayed. Students were asked to write down the first English word that each picture evoked. Then they were asked to write down how each picture made them feel. In the five senses activity, students were asked to close their eyes and picture a time when they had learned something important that made them want to change to become a better citizen. They were asked to picture it, envision the smells in the air, the sounds around them, the taste of anything they might have eaten, or the feeling of anything they might have touched or felt. They were guided through this activity through a series of scripted questions. The aim of the activities was for students to think more critically and to explore creative articulations of their thoughts and ideas.

Additionally, the students were also asked to complete an opinion questionnaire. This questionnaire was designed to determine how the students viewed the workshops, whether they enjoyed them, whether they felt they were of value to the advancement of their English, and if they thought the workshops would help them in the competition to come. The questionnaires were brief. They consisted of ten questions, each with a five-point Likert scale response choice ranging from strongly agree to strongly disagree. They were administered at the end of the workshops in order to get insight into questions on student motivation and to track any emerging trends that might appear over time as the Young Writers Program developed. The questionnaires were also a way to adapt and respond to the needs of the students by relaying those findings to the writing specialists and the respective education stakeholders in order to better support English language curriculum within Qatari schools.

In addition to the focus on students, English teachers from the respective schools and of the respective classes were invited to observe the workshops. The conversations were over the applicability and usefulness of the activities as well as how the teachers perceived the students to be responding to them. At the end of the workshops for the 2015–2016 school year, the observing teachers were invited to give feedback on how they felt the workshops impacted the students, whether the workshops fit with their teaching objectives, and if there were areas in which the workshops could be improved. The teachers were given questionnaires and interviewed semi-formally. They felt that the workshops had a positive impact, fit well with the course objectives—despite being very different for some—and were enthusiastic about incorporating further prompts and objectives in future workshops.

The student winners were also asked to attend a winners' writing workshop where they could prepare their work for publication in the *Young Writers Journal*. As young authors, the students readied their work to be shared with a nationwide audience. These students were also asked to reflect on their opinions of the Young Writers Competition; on what it means to them to be young writers in Qatar; and on how the competition has affected their ideas about writing in English. A tenth-grade student reflected: "The writing competition improved my imagination and it gave me ideas on how to let people know how writing can change the world."

DISCUSSION OF IMPACT ON STUDENTS AND TEACHERS OF WRITING IN QATAR

This program has served as a window into understanding the realities and needs of both teachers and students in K–12 education in Qatar in terms of English language education. Through the year-long roster of activities, the Ministry of Education, US Embassy Doha, and the writing specialists have been given numerous opportunities to gather firsthand accounts from K–12 teachers on the obstacles faced within the classroom. As the writing specialists, we aim to use the discussions and gathered information to further enhance the program to meet the needs of the intended populations. In the first two years of implementation, we have come to gain a clearer picture on some of the needs and challenges within the classrooms and for civic engagement beyond. Below are a few of these challenges.

One challenge facing the students is what is functionally a foreign language–learning environment rather than a second-language environment. Learning to write is difficult enough, but these writers have the added complexity of needing to learn to write in English. As is well documented, learners in the Arab world have difficulty with English orthography, so much so that their literacy often lags behind their communicative ability (Bowen). The literacy issues are primarily due to differences in the writing systems, especially regarding the marking of vowel sounds. In Arabic script, short vowels are not written, but readers can guess the correct short vowel sound from context. In English, however, there is a complex system of long, short, and diphthong vowels that vary widely in terms of spelling. This difference creates a major cross-linguistic transfer issue, and Arab students develop what is referred to as "vowel blindness" in English (Ryan). In addition to orthography itself, there are often different levels of English language ability within the same classroom. Even with a differentiated learning approach, teachers can find it extremely difficult to address the array of student needs suitably. Different levels of exposure to the English language, English literacy in the home, or the differing amounts of English used outside the classroom create a challenging learning atmosphere. Moreover, the students also have different levels of exposure to English literacy at home or in the community. These problems make it difficult to teach writing in class because there are underlying language issues that hinder motivation to write and need to be addressed. One particular outcome of this obstacle is that many of the students and teachers spend a disproportionate amount of time on the spelling component, leaving little time to reach the higher order objectives of creativity and exploration through writing.

Furthermore, teachers have expressed frustration over student disinterest, or lack of motivation, in regard to English writing. This is in part due to the systematic difficulty with English spelling and literacy, but also extends far beyond literacy into areas such as the learning environment, the social milieu, and extrinsic versus intrinsic motivation—what Dornyei refers to as the "ought-to L2 self" rather than the "ideal L2 self." Perhaps in part due to the lack of opportunities to engage meaningfully in English discourse, students often see English as a means to an end in achieving high grades—as merely part of what they must do to advance their education or career. English language education, especially in regard to writing, has not had the chance to become a tool for personal, creative, and critical expression of thought in this environment. Essentially, students are less likely to be motivated to write creatively without programs in place to allow for this type of engagement. Therefore, creative expression, risk taking, and a desire to interact with English language speakers are dishearteningly low. Instead, students tend to be more motivated by achieving levels of English that open doors to better opportunities and higher status among their peers. This extrinsic motivation, or what they feel they "ought to" do, seems to be the more typical driving motivation for students in the Gulf region. Because of this, the product-oriented approach to writing makes more sense, where the end result is valued more highly than the actual process of learning to write creatively. However, based on the positive engagement with the Young Writers Program, we contend that it can be through the creation and development of programs like the YWP that this type of writing for creative and critical thinking can take place. The results of the motivation questionnaires showed the students were strongly in favor of the workshops and competition. In addition, the winners were likewise enthusiastic about writing and connecting with the community, as well as grappling with their position in wider global issues. As addressed in Charry Roje's chapter, "Student Voice in Transnational Service Learning: A Study in Croatia," students who participated in the planning and organization responded more enthusiastically to the experience. In this regard, using student feedback to modify subsequent years of the Young Writers Program seemed to have a positive result. Similarly, providing students with tangible actions, like titling the print publication, assisted in improving youth ownership of the program. Increasing student voice became a key component of the program as we observed mixed initial student engagement.

In the first year of the writing competition, students were asked to choose between writing a fiction short story, a poem, or an academic essay. A high number of plagiarized academic essays received indicated a challenge. To address this unexpected outcome, we highlighted the fact that the winning entries from Year 1 were not all perfectly grammatically structured pieces of writing; rather, they were representative of the writers' grade levels. We showcased the stories with engaging and unique content. We emphasized stories that centered on personal experiences and/or passions. For Year 2, we modified the message. The academic essay was eliminated. Students could choose from two categories: fiction (short story and poetry) or nonfiction (short story and personal essay). The affect-centered approach to teaching writing was emphasized. The notion of a strong authorial voice was emphasized. We underlined how the students were their own experts with insights worthy of sharing and that speaking from their own point of view was valid and meaningful, and their perspectives of the world around them were of value. Furthermore, while technical skill, organization, and language concerns remain fundamental building blocks of writing and components of the assessment, they should be balanced with originality and unique content and ideas. This shift from craft-centered to affect-centered writing was designed to foster the development of a community of young, active global citizens and creative writers actively contributing to the body of current locally relevant literature.

In regard to teachers, some have commented on the lack of time to indulge in creative writing activities. While these activities are considered as valuable and meaningful to some teachers, they are difficult to implement. Many curriculum standards need to be met in the limited time allotment for English instruction. Teachers, therefore, often at first-glance, label creative writing instruction as "extra" and non-essential. The standards-based education model is relatively new to Qatar; this model was implemented during the education system overhaul in 2002. The standards themselves are both content standards (what students should be taught in each grade) and performance standards (what students should know by the end of each grade), but do not dictate the curriculum itself nor the pedagogical approaches (Brewer et al.). In response to these concerns, we, as the writing specialists, tasked ourselves to align the creative writing competition and associated activities to the curriculum standards. To address time constraints and an understandable worry about "sticking to the curriculum" and focusing on the standards, it is necessary to demonstrate how this form of writing is not an add-on, but, in fact, also a part of the standards the teachers are tasked with covering. The competition can serve a dual purpose when framed accordingly. In regard to English language teaching, writing supports language acquisition as learners experiment with words, sentences, and larger chunks of writing as a means to communicate their ideas effectively and reinforce target grammar and vocabulary (Bello). Additionally, the feedback received from the teacher was that the workshops covered plenty of the curriculum standards. The teachers interviewed overwhelmingly supported this type of initiative for engaging students and were excited about adapting and expanding it in their classroom practice.

In addition to incorporating teacher input, the YWP has highlighted a few additional areas for teacher capacity building. During the student workshops, the English teachers informally observing the series of workshops facilitated by the writing specialists reacted positively to the teaching methodologies used. We propose that this element of the program be formalized into its own expanded professional development opportunity. Not only do we want to address student needs but also teacher needs. The student workshops can serve a dual purpose: to reach students directly and to serve as model lessons for interested instructors. These teachers can then duplicate the workshops and share their knowledge with the wider community of practitioners in order to support long-term sustainability of a creative writing community and a program with long lasting civic engagement.

CONCLUSION

In its short-term existence to date, the competition has quickly become a vehicle to understand the needs of teachers, learners, and the community. In this regard, we envision this competition continuing as a meaningful long-term complement to K–12 English language education and a way for students to use their English locally but with a global outlook. Notably, it is a collaborative program with an opportunity to connect key educational stakeholders to support critical thinking and English language skills development in youth in Qatar. As the writing specialists, we hope the Young Writers Program can encourage youth to critically consider pressing global issues and articulate their ideas in an engaging way and allow them to join the larger community of writers.

At each turn in its brief run, new expansion possibilities have surfaced for the YWP, from additional training in creative writing instruction in second language–learning environments to professional development on how to design standards-based lessons inside the classroom. Outside the classroom, possibilities from a public community launch of the *Young Writers Journal* to open-mic readings of original culturally relevant and representational work by youth all create much-needed positive associations for the students toward the craft of creative writing in English—both in Qatar and beyond.

The Young Writers Program has shown itself as a positive force for creative writing and civic engagement. At the conclusion of the first cycle of the competition, when asked, the student winners reflected positively on their participation in the competition. A tenth-grade student wrote:

> Participating in this competition has inspired me to write more and more, and it has made me realize my writing talents. I've also learned that quality is better if I take time writing and revising, and sharing it with others. . . . [The competition] was an exciting experience that I'll never forget. I feel proud of myself.

We hope this program can also serve to support the development of a vibrant community of young writers within Qatar and to help transform perceptions of English language as being predominantly a functional language for communication purposes to also being considered an enjoyable and effective means for limitless creative and critical self-expression.

WORKS CITED

Bello, Tom. "Writing Topics for Adult ESL Students." *31st Annual Teachers of English to Speakers of Other Language Convention, Orlando, Florida,* 1997, www.ericdigests.org/1998-1/skills.htm.

Bowen, Helen. "Spelling It Out! Accounting for Spelling Difficulties for Arab Learners of English. Foundations for the Future." *HTC Ma'rifa,* 2011, pp. 85–98, marifa.hct.ac.ae/files/2011/07/Spelling-it-out-Accounting-for-Spelling-Difficulties-for-Arab-Learners-of-English.pdf.

Brewer, Dominic J., et al. *Education for a New Era: Design and Implementation of K–12 Education Reform in Qatar.* RAND-Qatar Policy Institute, RAND Corporation, 2007, www.rand.org/pubs/monographs/MG548.html.

Bringle, Robert G., et al. *International Service Learning: Conceptual Frameworks and Research.* Stylus Publishing, 2011.

"Bureau of Educational and Cultural Affairs: What We Do." *United States Department of State, Bureau of Educational and Cultural Affairs.* eca.state.gov/about-bureau. Accessed 20 Aug. 2016.

Dornyei, Zoltan. "The L2 Motivational Self-System." *Motivation, Language Identity and the L2 Self,* edited by Zoltan Dornyei and Ema Ushioda. Multilingual Matters, 2009, pp. 9–42.

Eastwood, Brent M. "A Note on the New Face of Citizen Diplomacy: Education City and American Universities in the Middle East." *American Foreign Policy Interests,* vol. 29, no. 6, 2007, pp. 443–449, doi.org/10.1080/10803920701777010.

"Fact Sheet: The White House Summit on Countering Violent Extremism." *The White House.* United States, Office of the Press Secretary, 18 Feb. 2015, www.whitehouse.gov/the-press-office/2015/02/18/fact-sheet-white-house-summit-countering-violent-extremism. Accessed 20 Aug. 2016.

Good, Thomas L., and Jere E. Brophy. *Looking in Classrooms.* 4th ed. Harper, 1987.

McIlrath, Lorrainne, and Iain MacLabhrainn. *Higher Education and Civic Engagement: International Perspectives.* Ashgate, 2007.

MENAWCA 2012. Proceedings from: *Connecting Writers Across Borders.* Doha, Qatar, 2012.

Newman, Beth. *Teaching Students to Write.* 2nd ed. Oxford University Press, 1995.

Olson, James S. *Historical Dictionary of European Imperialism.* Greenwood Press, 1991.

Pentland, William. "World's Five Largest Offshore Oilfields." *Forbes: Energy,* 7 Sept. 2013, www.forbes.com/sites/williampentland/2013/09/07/worlds-five-largest-offshore-oil-fields/.

Qatar National Development Strategy 2011–2016. Qatar, General Secretariat for Development Planning. Gulf Publishing and Printing Company, 2001, www.mdps.gov.qa/en/knowledge/HomePagePublications/Qatar_NDS_reprint_complete_lowres_16May.pdf.

Rostron, Magdalena. "Liberal Arts Education in Qatar: Intercultural Perspectives." *Intercultural Education,* vol. 20, no. 3, 2009, pp. 219–229.

Ryan, Ann. "Learning the Orthographical form of L2 Vocabulary—A Receptive and a Productive Process." *Vocabulary: Description, Acquisition and Pedagogy,* edited by Norbert Schmitt and Michael McCarthy, Cambridge University Press, 1997, pp. 181–198.

Schön, Donald A. *The Reflective Practitioner: How Professionals Think in Action.* Basic Books, 1983.

"The Sykes–Picot Agreement (1916)." *Crethiplethi,* 13 Dec. 2009, www.crethiplethi.com/the-sykes-picot-agreement-1916/historical-documents/2009/. Accessed 18 Aug. 2016.

"Young Writers Receive Awards from US Ambassador." *VCUQatar,* 21 Apr. 2016, www.qatar.vcu.edu/news/young-writers-win-plaudits. Accessed 18 Aug. 2016.

Zellman, Gail L., et al. *K–12 Education Reform in Qatar.* RAND Corporation, 2011, www.rand.org/pubs/reprints/RP1428.html.

11
GEOPOLITICAL TURBULENCE AND GLOBAL CIVIC ENGAGEMENT
Forensics of an Unfulfilled Fulbright Suggest Challenges Ahead

Jim Bowman

Compelling stories of transnational civic engagement in higher education—like those we hear firsthand from colleagues and in the news and archives of college publications—encourage us to pursue opportunities to do meaningful academic work in diverse global contexts. The positive outcomes from faculty experiences in other societies as part of research grants or teaching fellowships abroad come in several forms. Home institutions of faculty who travel can benefit tremendously, especially for students whose professors return with rich experiences, knowledge, and networks that subsequently inform their teaching, scholarship, service, and possibly advising. Further, societies that host visiting scholar-teachers profit from a diversity in disciplinary and pedagogical perspectives. Finally, disciplines and professional spheres of influence stand to prosper when research, teaching, and program development is informed by global perspectives. The field of writing studies stands to gain substantially from experiences working with students and scholars of different national and cultural traditions. Assumptions about literacy, writing, and rhetoric receive much-needed second looks as foreign faculty peers and students engage and question our knowledge and pedagogies. And, as the ever-growing number of international conferences in writing and rhetoric demonstrates, the notion that writing studies represents an exclusively North American interest is fictive. Our field and its professional membership, its conferences, its professional journals, and so forth, is increasingly transnational.

Clearly, well-designed and sustainable programs that are sufficiently supported by relevant stakeholders can significantly impact many people in the United States and across borders. The cover story to such initiatives is undoubtedly appealing. Unfortunately, it masks some unpleasant realities and challenges facing many of us involved in global exchanges.

Creating and maintaining the programs that support global exchanges of scholars and students can be exceedingly difficult work, not only in terms of resource investment but also in risks associated with foreign travel and transnational relationships.

The dangers may be familiar to people involved in such efforts, but they are likely to be more acutely experienced in our present times as an epoch of populist nationalisms, nativist rhetoric, and troubling insularity sweeps across the globe. As of this writing, a US government led by President Donald Trump has raised suspicion about the motives of our institutions and people. According to polling by the Pew Research Center in 2019, "a growing share of people around the world see US power and influence as a 'major threat' to their country" (Gramlich and Devlin).[1] A travel ban targeting millions of people who reside in predominantly Muslim countries has had a chilling effect on foreign students and scholars within the United States and those seeking to travel to US institutions. President Trump's "America first" rhetoric and policymaking has had a predictable effect on global attitudes. Perceptions abroad of the US people and government have suffered considerably. In short, recent geopolitical developments make the work of global civic engagement more difficult—and arguably more necessary if the United States values its role as a leader and positive force in the world of higher education. Successes of the past may give us hopeful reminders that such challenges, though perhaps more acutely experienced in the current historical moment, are hardly new.

In this chapter, then, I reflect on the personal successes of several Fulbright-Hays Study Abroad experiences in Turkey and Cyprus from 2004 to 2007, as well as the loss of a recent Fulbright Scholar grant to Turkey, to demonstrate how national and international politics affect local projects and transnational relationships in higher education. Like the other projects in this collection, as well as the pedagogical and scholarly work of many others in our field, I speak as a scholar and teacher of rhetoric and writing studies invested in global affairs and determined to support civic engagement and stronger relationships among US faculty, students, and institutions in their engagement with peers of societies abroad. The particular unfulfilled Fulbright experience at the center of this reflection, for example, would have involved the study of civic engagement practices—many dealing with writing and literacy issues central to graduate and undergraduate education majors at a Turkish university. I had also proposed to teach an academic and professional writing course tailored to these same education majors, informed by my teaching experience in professional and disciplinary writing. As this collection demonstrates, our expertise as writing studies professionals can mean working outside writing programs and English departments and across campus with other departments, programs, and administrative units that share an interest in global civic engagement (see, for example, Gindlesparger et al. and deWinter).

Those in academic institutions who remain invested in global engagement have to prepare for complicated geopolitical developments, and when possible, find ways to work through or around these inevitable obstacles. Even more, though, people and programs in the United States and around the world must be nimble in order to respond quickly to dramatic events and rapidly shifting geopolitical trends. Such an assertion betrays the difficulty of the task, not only in terms of rearranging careful plans and precious resources but also, and more importantly, in terms of triaging the emotional damage that subsequently affects the architects and participants of suspended programs. In such cases, professional relationships and networks remain undeveloped, and opportunities to be enriched by contact with people around the globe slip away. Such a nimble subject is not constructed easily, but the tools and possibilities for design become clearer through reflection on difficult experiences. Though the very real national and international politics that intersect with global civic engagement affect our efforts in ways beyond our control, viable alternatives remain for those determined to connect people and institutions of different countries in mutually beneficial exchanges.

GOVERNMENT-SUPPORTED GLOBAL CIVIC ENGAGEMENT: FULBRIGHT PROGRAMS PAST AND PRESENT

My own recent experiences as an advocate for global engagement offer a window into the volatility of our times. While at the University of Arizona, I participated in three Fulbright-supported summer experiences as a grant-writer and cultural guide for US schoolteachers learning about Middle Eastern societies: I helped to lead Fulbright-Hays teacher education trips to Cyprus in 2004 and 2007 and to Turkey in 2005. The positive outcomes from these experiences invigorated curriculum for these teachers' US classrooms and inspired me to seek future opportunities that would support university students in the United States interested in the region. In my own work as a professor of rhetoric and composition at a private liberal arts college, these efforts have proven difficult, despite a good deal of student interest. In recent successive years, two separate short-term foreign study trips to Istanbul, Turkey, were cancelled due to anxieties about the stability of the country and fears of foreign travel associated with terrorist attacks. I reluctantly declined a separate Fulbright Scholar teaching grant to Turkey that I was awarded in 2016, to be discussed below, after exhaustive deliberations with peers in Turkey and among colleagues and family regarding security and the political climate within the country. These challenges provide the impetus for the reflections of this chapter.

Government-funded programs like those offered under the umbrella of Fulbright provide an intriguing window into the uncertainty of our times. The program was started in 1946 and has consistently received bipartisan support in Congress. It remains popular in the United States and around the world in large part because it has managed to balance its aims for forging long-term relationships through cultural and academic exchange with its more immediate diplomatic and short-term policy objectives (Bettie 370). Before the US presidential elections of 2016, it would have seemed to many unthinkable that Fulbright programs would be considered an unnecessary luxury by a US president and Congress, especially in light of global conflicts and uncertainty. However, populist movements hostile to traditional approaches to governance and foreign affairs have unsettled a great many givens of US priorities and commitments. Although Fulbright was not among the first major budget cuts suggested by President Trump upon taking office, other initiatives focusing on better global relations were not so fortunate. In their reporting for Bloomberg, Syeed and Wadhams write:

> The administration focused many of the [proposed budget] cuts on "soft power" initiatives that found favor under former President Barack Obama. It called for reducing Educational and Cultural Exchange Programs, *other than the well-known Fulbright scholarships*, and eliminating funding to organizations such as the East-West Center in Hawaii.... The proposal drew rebukes from some outside groups, including the Bill & Melinda Gates Foundation. (emphasis mine)

Despite long-running struggles over which entities administer the programs and whether they should focus on a mission of "information activities" or cultural exchange, Fulbrights have largely remained free from partisan territoriality.[2] Confidence that such programs will exist indefinitely into the future may be unwise, regardless of how a Trump administration and other anti-globalist elements within the US government affect efforts at engaging the world. Isolationist attitudes will not likely disappear anytime soon given the ways in which they have been fueled by continued threats posed by terrorist attacks, foreign wars, and mass migrations. Despite the obvious need for government action and leadership on these problems, private organizations such as the Bill and Melinda Gates Foundation may be operating with considerably less government support for their priorities. Universities, too, could be compelled to invest in opportunities outside government funding sources to build programs for foreign engagement. I very much remain an advocate for promoting Fulbright-Hays cultural trips, the Fulbright Scholar, and Fulbright ETA programs, and others like them, yet I recognize that they are vulnerable to vicissitudes of global upheaval, which would make abstract long-term value and some of their inherent contradictions more difficult to justify.

FULBRIGHT-HAYS TRIPS AND THE NERVOUS PRODUCTION OF GLOBAL AWARENESS IN CONFLICT ZONES

Generalized sentiments about the poor state of geopolitical affairs in the era of Trump and Brexit may feel justified in the moment, but they could also be said to demonstrate selective amnesia about bitter conflicts and tense political climates of the past. My own three Fulbright-Hays projects to Cyprus and Turkey between 2004 and 2007 afford me an opportunity to reflect on the past and, perhaps, to peer speculatively into the future of US civic engagement with the Middle East and the world. At the time of the 2004 Fulbright-Hays trip to Cyprus and the 2005 trip to Turkey, the US government, and to a lesser degree its citizens, were viewed with particularly deep suspicion by many in the region due largely to the invasion and occupation of Iraq in 2003. Though the fallout from this war created tensions within neighboring societies, on a human level, I, unsurprisingly, found that American visitors were typically treated well by people in Cyprus and Turkey. For the US schoolteachers involved, the trips appear to have been hugely satisfying and illuminating. They traveled widely, met with citizens of the visited countries—including leaders of NGOs, academics, and hundreds of ordinary people—and also met US officials, UN officials (in Cyprus), and expatriates from around the world. The teachers submitted detailed curricular plans to incorporate much of what they had learned in classroom lessons to be taught thereafter. The trips were a tremendous success and carry value at the very least for their contributions to better educating US citizens about foreign societies and their challenges. However, each trip produced moments of dissonance and conflict that suggest the extent of the chasms that divide us along lines of national identity and demonstrate the darker side of global civic engagement.

The trip to Turkey in 2005 came at a time when it was impossible to avoid discussing the violent insurgency in Iraq. Turkey and the United

States were at odds over the initial invasion and most people in the society opposed the war and occupation. Further, the United States was at odds with the Al Jazeera news network for their coverage of the fighting, and military and civilian representatives of the US government regularly criticized and even demonized their role in the ongoing violence. Al Jazeera had its Turkey bureau headquarters in Ankara, and during our visit to the capital, the teachers agreed to attend a meeting at their offices to meet their bureau chief to discuss their organization, its work in Turkey, and any questions this particular group of Fulbright-sponsored US citizens might have for them. Though there was some trepidation on the part of the teachers beforehand, they came to a consensus that this was a valuable opportunity to get to know an important player on the global media stage.[3] The visit seemed to go well—our host was gracious, professional, open to our questions, and hopeful that tensions might improve between the United States and the Arab world.

In an informal debriefing with the teachers on the bus after the visit, most of them seemed to be energized about the experience and certainly better informed than beforehand about Al Jazeera's approach to covering news in Turkey and the Middle East. Later that evening, however, I discovered that the consensus was not entirely positive. One teacher was deeply disturbed that we had made this visit and especially concerned that we had insisted on giving the guest speaker a small (and customary) honorarium. To her logic, this was essentially using US taxpayer resources to support an organization hostile to the United States. (Our host did not want the small token of thanks and politely refused several times, but I thought it was most ethical to treat him like other guests on the itinerary.) This participant was upset enough that she expressed a desire to leave the trip and return to the United States immediately. I listened to her concerns, emphasized my intent to better understand the perspectives of media and individuals in the region and to provide us with enriched experiences that help us explain to our students and society how our country is understood by people in the Middle East. She remained on the trip and became more comfortable during the remaining itinerary, but I was given pause by how deeply and emotionally global conflicts affect us as individuals, especially as we draw nearer to their proximity. I also imagined distorted headlines in certain media outlets of how Fulbright money had been channeled into the coffers of the "mouthpiece of Al-Qaeda," as some US officials and media regularly referred to Al Jazeera at the time. Though this disagreement was certainly significant, it was the final night of a subsequent trip to Cyprus two years later that continues to haunt my faith in the ability of human connections to transcend the bitter challenges of unresolved conflict.

Cyprus bears the unhealed scars of a long-ago war, and hope for change typically feels unwarranted amidst entrenched discourses of nationalism. As one might expect in a local conflict that was of great interest to Turkey, Greece, the United Kingdom, and the United States, among others, the people of Cyprus tend to be suspect of the motives of outsiders who take an interest in the conflict. Nonetheless, most people on the island, despite their own politics and personal histories, are reasonably welcoming to visitors. That had certainly been the case for a young, flirtatious Greek Cypriot male waiter at an outdoor pizza parlor near our hotel south of the Green Line in Nicosia. Members of our group, most of whom were women of different ages, had frequented a place where this humorous and personable young man had taken our orders and treated us to much-needed laughter after long days of seminars, bus rides, and unrelenting midsummer Mediterranean heat.

As we finished up our meal on the final night, one of the teachers mistakenly produced Turkish liras from her purse and set them on the table to settle the tab. This innocent error became evidence of her and our group's visits north of the Green Line to the Turkish community. The waiter's face changed immediately, and within moments, he was cursing and shouting about this disgusting, dirty money, how it showed that we had been to the Turkish-controlled side of the island, how dare we do this, what a betrayal, and so forth. Though we had learned a great deal about the conflict between the Greek and Turkish communities over the past month, this was still a shock to absorb, coming from someone who seemed to know us and like our company. In the hotel lobby, still jittery from having been part of a small-scale public spectacle, we talked about his reaction and how deeply this conflict has traumatized the people of Cyprus—and how, upon the smallest triggers, no one can escape its fallout. Though the island has seen very little fighting since 1974, the symbolic violence carries on with vigor among many in Cyprus. This is one of the "safe zones" in the region, where correspondents set up homes, where young couples from Israel and Lebanon elope, and where a small UN force in the hundreds stands between soldiers who far outnumber them by thousands on both sides. After weeks of travel and study, we better understood why more than a few political scientists and policy experts hold the island up as a testament to effective peacekeeping operations, though our group could not help but see its beauty as tragically compromised, as a place where a cynical peace has reigned, reluctantly, for decades. Global engagement, even in success, can be bittersweet, and we could not help but feel that the people of both communities needed more support from people on the outside to help them bridge their differences.

THE FULBRIGHT PLAN FOR TURKEY: IMAGINING CIVIC ENGAGEMENT AMIDST POLITICAL TURMOIL

In the years after the Fulbright-Hays trips, I moved on from the University of Arizona to a new position as a faculty member at St. John Fisher College, a liberal arts college in western New York. Globally minded scholarship, teaching and curriculum development, and writing program leadership roles at my institution have prioritized work that explores encounters with difference and how these encounters shape writing and our ideas of the world. As the pre-tenure phase of my career wound down and thoughts turned towards sabbatical and next steps, I turned my attention toward an opportunity that could position me for years to come with a valuable set of personal and professional experiences and connections.

The Fulbright grant proposal to Turkey in 2015 took several intensive summer months to arrange and write, and its conception was many years in the making. The scholarship leading up to my current academic position focused on travel writing, rhetoric, Turkish studies, civic engagement, and service learning. In my current position, I have been fortunate enough to pursue teaching and research interests in all these areas, leading to my application in summer 2015 for a Fulbright Scholar grant to Turkey. With a background in rhetoric and composition and some academic expertise in the cultural and political affairs of Turkey and Cyprus, I had ample directions to pursue that connect to my teaching and scholarship. In the end, I decided to develop a Fulbright Teaching Scholar proposal to teach about service learning and experiential learning in a faculty of education at a Turkish university. My proposed responsibilities would be to teach electives for education majors and graduate students and provide future educators an opportunity to develop their own potential projects with in-service teachers and community organizations. I chose this over some of my other interests for a variety of reasons. I worried that travel writing could have been misconstrued as insufficiently compelling to Fulbright reviewers, and its more likely fit would be within literature departments. My intent was always to use my expertise in both civic engagement/service learning and writing studies/rhetoric. Hate rhetoric and demagoguery felt too politically volatile as a focus point for research or teaching, especially in a society as polarized as Turkey, where many face retribution and even criminal charges for speech that would be considered constitutionally protected in the United States and other Western societies.

Though civic engagement projects are by no means politically innocuous, I thought that perhaps, given Turkey's deeply divided society and its institutions of higher education, this topic would make sense for pre-service teachers looking for practical, impactful pedagogical training. Though I cannot be certain whether or to what extent this factored into the success of the application, my proposal earned the Fulbright Scholar position for the 2017 spring semester. I began to make arrangements for a semester and summer of teaching, network-building, and program development with rich potential rewards for my institution and career—and, hopefully, for the students and colleagues of my home and host institutions. Of course, the danger of political unrest within Turkey and spillover from the war in Syria were known to me at the time as a threat, but my prior knowledge of the country and region afforded me hope that the risk would be worth the reward.

In the context of our times, the violence in Syria has been ongoing for many years, its horrors and dizzying impact reaching people and nations across the globe: European and Middle Eastern countries have been targeted in terror attacks by ISIS sympathizers, and Syrian (and other) refugees fleeing the violence have dramatically affected domestic politics around the globe. At Syria's doorstep, Turkey, a major backdrop to this chapter, has been among those countries most impacted by the situation in Syria. This turmoil has very much affected Turkey's universities and those abroad involved with higher education outreach to the country, especially students and faculty, myself included.[4]

The proposal itself was a Fulbright Scholar teaching proposal to design and deliver two courses to master's students in a school of education at a large, respected public university. One course would be my version of a civic engagement and service learning–focused elective titled Community Service in the Turkish curriculum, another an academic and professional writing course for education majors. The former would have been taught as a course introducing experiential learning and civic engagement to future K–16 instructors of multiple subject areas. We would study principles and best practices of civic engagement in K–16 in Turkey, the United States, and elsewhere, and students would design projects that they could do in their future courses and schools. I would offer a revised version of the course again immediately after the spring semester in a summer session at another large public institution in a different city in Turkey. After the aforementioned political developments within Turkey, culminating in a failed coup in July 2016, I declined the Fulbright grant and called off the trip. Security reasons were foremost in my mind, but I also feared being an American at a time when the United States was perceived to have had a role in Turkey's troubles. I could not help but fear that my presence would have made me a target of suspicion and someone who would have made my colleagues at the host institution also suspect. In the year since declining, the security situation in Turkey has improved somewhat and President Erdogan has consolidated his hold on power. However, Turkey's relations with the United States and with European countries remain very tense and unlikely to improve anytime soon. Erdogan and the pro-government press hailed the election of Trump as a positive sign in relations, but a host of serious issues remain between the two countries. A visit to Washington in early 2017 not only failed to resolve the most serious issues, but Erdogan's visit was also marked by a violent attack on protesters outside the Turkish Embassy in Washington, creating a new challenge in bilateral relations. Andrew Brunson, a US missionary and longtime resident of Turkey, was detained following the failed coup and spent two years under arrest for what most acknowledge to be strictly political reasons. Erdogan has intimated in public statements that US residents in Turkey will not be guaranteed safety if disagreements cannot be resolved. In an address to his party's parliamentarians he railed against the lack of support from outside countries in his fight against his enemies: "I am calling out to the whole world. I am saying that if you don't help us . . . know that if your own [citizens] fall into our hands someday, you will not be able to get them back" (Zaman). The status quo does not appear promising for government-sanctioned cultural exchange in the near future. In this collection, Myers and Zambrano highlight the importance of building strong connections among faculty of institutions engaged in these sorts of exchanges. However, if visiting foreign faculty nationals are treated with suspicion by the host society's leaders, then there could be risk for all invested parties, including hosting institutions and faculty of both societies.

GEOPOLITICS, EMOTIONAL LABOR, AND THE NECESSITY TO BE NIMBLE

How could circumstances change so quickly? Within a few short years, Turkey has transformed from a stable Middle Eastern democracy with a bright economic future—and numerous programs linking its universities and students to partners around the globe—into a country torn apart by divisions exacerbated and at least partly caused by the discord in Syria. Though the situation is far too complicated to address adequately here, some of the highlights include Turkey's abandonment of the foreign policy of "no problems with its neighbors," starting with the case of Syria, as the then–Prime Minister Erdogan chose to support many militants opposing Syria's President Bashar al-Assad, some of whom included members of extremist organizations such as Al-Qaeda and the Islamic State (IS). Some of these militants have taken root in the country and done significant damage through terror attacks on high-profile targets across the country. Further, the Kurds of Syria have gained control of large swaths of territory on Turkey's southern border and strengthened collaboration with separatist Kurds of Turkey, which has caused tremendous political and security problems inside the country and with Turkey's allies in the West. Regularly occurring attacks inside Turkey by militant Kurds and IS fighters from 2015 through 2016 have unnerved many people of Turkey, as well as potential visitors. Finally, an internal power struggle between the followers of self-exiled religious leader Fethullah Gulen and Erdogan exploded into arrests, harassment, and a failed coup attempt, followed by the arrests and persecutions of hundreds of thousands of people in a post-coup crackdown. Those who have been forced to resign their positions, charged with crimes, and arrested include not just Gulen's supporters, but also many others who oppose the ruling regime in Turkey. Under the pretext of a necessary realignment of higher education in light of the coup attempt, all the deans of Turkey's universities were required to resign and thousands of academics and graduate students have been fired or expelled. The failed coup appears to have been a pretext for the government to act against any people perceived to be hostile to its rule.[5]

Though something close to a worst-case scenario, factors like those mentioned above were always part of the risk in my plans for teaching, research, and global program development in Turkey. While Turkey's troubles from late 2015 to the present may seem extreme, it would be naïve to consider them exceptional in a global sense. Terror attacks have occurred throughout the Middle East, Europe, and North America in recent years. Foreign conflicts can undeniably shape domestic political developments around the world, and even threaten to upend the global economy and the stability promised by entities once taken for granted such as the European Union. What then can be done from the perspective of faculty and administrators looking to develop and maintain programs and exchanges in light of such jarring realities?

No one particular maxim or blueprint could likely cover all possible challenges. The stability of institutions and their ability to function through political turmoil obviously affects sustainability. These basic concerns do not even discuss the freedom of academic faculty and staff and local communities to develop projects meaningful for the schools and community partners. Then there are on-the-ground security concerns, liabilities regarding institution-sponsored travel, and decision-making practices of administrators, faculty, and staff who want to keep people safe. The assumption underlying so much of this global work typically posits US institutions and its government as a source of stability and often comparatively greater resources. In just a short period of time, the Trump administration has taken measures to weaken the State Department and its soft power approach to US influence, leaving future government support for programs like Fulbright far less certain than they had been not long ago. In the face of such challenges, individuals, higher education programs and institutions, and local communities around the world need to appreciate the ways that geopolitical circumstances affect civic engagement projects, including in the United States. An exceptionalist approach—one that assumes our own society to be comparatively stable and more advanced in terms of civic traditions—fails to appreciate important intersections among our partners abroad. Efforts among higher education institutions to develop and sustain global relationships in this climate will likely take a doggedness and creative persistence for the foreseeable future.

In the case of Turkey, the faculty Fulbright Scholar program itself was not suspended, but very few US faculty appear to have ended up there that year, presumably for the same reasons. The large and popular Fulbright English Teaching Assistant (ETA) program, which typically sends dozens of recent US college graduates across Turkey each year to teach English in universities and other schools, was suspended due to security concerns, along with several other programs. In *New York Times* coverage of the State Department's decision to suspend the ETA program, US students expressed disappointment and concern with the development:

> "What's going on in Turkey right now is really extraordinary and definitely something that should be watched closely," said Ms. [Joanna] Birkner, 22, a recent graduate of Bryn Mawr College whose interest in Turkey was piqued by a National Geographic cover of Turkish ruins when she was 17. "Ultimately, I think it's even more of a reason that there need to be young Americans who can speak the language, who can understand the conflict from the ground up." (Hortocollis)

Few appear to dispute the wisdom of the decision. Audrey Williams, a former Fulbright scholar, cited the benefits of US students knowledgeable and connected with Turkey and called for the program and others like it to be put back on track as quickly as possible: "When government-to-government relations founder, the connections between the people of each country keep the relationship humming. At the heart of people-to-people relations are the various exchange programs that allow American and Turkish citizens to improve upon their education while building strong bonds with newfound friends and colleagues." Williams argued that opportunities for language study on US soil should be developed by the US government, universities, and other private agencies in order to maintain opportunities for engagement in the event of political instability.[6]

As I soon discovered, declining a Fulbright means that you are out of the program, and no other awards or opportunities are available. Over a year of intensive planning and preparation was lost. The grant I proposed aspired to produce comparative scholarship about civic engagement practices in Turkey and the United States; co-authored research articles borne of action research projects on civic engagement in Turkey with graduate students in education; collaborative, civic-oriented sustainable relationships, exchanges, even projects between my institution and institutions in Turkey; and planning at administrative levels and with vendors for future faculty and student exchanges between our college and one or more universities in Turkey and short-term study abroad course trips in future summers.

Of course, some of these pursuits' ultimate success was not necessarily dependent on the Fulbright, as they could be initiated and developed through other means. Nonetheless, the momentum for these opportunities cannot be underestimated, not to mention the value of months on the ground in face-to-face contact with students, faculty, and community organizations in Turkey or any other foreign society. However, a sober reflection on the experience suggests not only that meaningful civic engagement can continue, but that practical planning and realistic approaches are needed to realize the promise of global civic engagement.

In a spirit of optimism needed at times to balance the choppy waters of global civic engagement, I have decided to recast my "failed Fulbright" as simply an "unfulfilled Fulbright." Losing this opportunity led to a period of mourning what could have been as well as a willful resistance to capitulate to pessimism. It is also meant to suggest and perhaps encourage resilience against daunting difficulties facing those of us pushing for travel and writing as a means of developing more knowledgeable and culturally aware students and society members.

REALIZING CIVIC ENGAGEMENT OBJECTIVES AMIDST GEOPOLITICAL UNCERTAINTY

What can we learn from difficult experiences of global civic engagement like my own, which are hardly unique in these times? To start, a sense of the practical remains important, especially at the administrative level of program development. Large, geopolitically important countries like Turkey should likely remain simultaneously attractive to foreign faculty and students, as well as politically volatile. Giving up on such partners is short-sighted and hurts everyone involved—faculty, students, and the respective societies participating. Pragmatism, though, demands a coherent strategy to engage, which might mean temporarily suspending face-to-face programs and contacts.

While face-to-face programs and direct exchanges may not be wise or practical, distance contacts—involving the use of video chat and other electronic communications—can help to bridge the isolation and connect students of societies separated from one another through political difficulties. Existing third-party organizations facilitate such exchanges, and many universities create their own programs and partnerships tailored to their particular goals and needs.[7] These efforts can be complicated, time-consuming, and resource-intensive, but they produce results and provide students with connections to one another when circumstances conspire against direct, on-the-ground exchanges and programs. Technological support, grant-writing resources, and networked relationships can help to develop and sustain such efforts.

We need to better promote available options for the study of languages and cultures, such as Turkish and Arabic, within US universities and organizations. Williams mentions the value of this option, which positions US students to be ready for cultural exchanges and travel experiences when circumstances improve. I can understand how this could be a difficult sell to US undergraduate students eager to deploy their knowledge in real-world exchanges and programs. Nonetheless, immersion programs often put students in contact with native speakers of foreign societies and others with deep cultural knowledge and grant them exposure to both culture and language.

To develop a deep network of alternative programs in comparatively stable environments creates options for moments like our uncertain present. Of course, I hasten to add here that no particular region has a monopoly on political stability, and the 2016 US presidential election cycle and results demonstrate that the United States is not immune to game-changing populist political leaders, such as those found in the Philippines and Turkey. The hostility expressed by Donald Trump and his administration toward many countries and people of the world have diminished the United States as a destination for foreign travel. The point would be that such developments should not deter exchange but rather emphasize the need to continue with such programs with the acknowledgement that a diversity of options is needed to maintain opportunities for global civic engagement amidst an increasingly unstable world. To provide an example, I cite the case of a large Title VI–funded Center for Middle Eastern Studies, which had sponsored summer study abroad trips for in-service teachers. As the 2003 Iraq war and more recent conflicts in the wake of the 2011 uprisings in the Arab world diminished opportunities to travel to many countries of the region, they have developed programs to more stable countries, such as Cyprus, Oman, Morocco, and Bosnia-Herzegovina. The State Department's Critical Language Scholarship Program made the decision, before the failed coup attempt, to move its program from Turkey to Azerbaijan.

In my own professional work, my faculty colleagues and I have invested in building curricular and extracurricular programming in Middle Eastern studies on campus. We have also taken the lead suggested by colleagues in other institutions and sought out momentarily more stable cultural study opportunities in places like Morocco, Bosnia, and even in the United States. Some may work out, others may not, and places and contacts once suspended will no doubt rise again. No inoculation exists that can prevent or quickly heal the emotional wounds that occasionally accompany such vulnerable intellectual labor. Yet creativity, nimble design, and pragmatism can afford opportunities to students and faculty who face setbacks due to circumstances beyond their control. A pivot into the nimble will provide us with opportunities that we can control that keep us moving forward toward the overall mission of global civic engagement and the people and institutions that it serves at home and abroad.

NOTES

1. Though these views are linked with attitudes toward President Donald Trump, the research covers a period beginning in 2013. In the case of Turkey discussed in this chapter, the always-complicated relationship took a notable downturn in 2014, when the US President Barack Obama was perceived by Turks to have taken a position that posed an existential threat to Turkey's security.
2. Molly Bettie documents these conflicts and tensions in her essay, "Ambassadors Unaware: The Fulbright Program and American Public Diplomacy."
3. As is typical in our own society, the political views on the war were divided in this group of teachers based on conversations I had with them throughout the trip.

4. The war in Syria has not been the only determinant in Turkey's recent troubles, and I do not mean to diminish the ways that internal conflicts have also fueled Turkey's slide into authoritarian rule. I provide the Syria example in particular because the war represents a case of how events in one region can destabilize neighbors and even countries beyond its borders, as the Syria conflict has done for so many.
5. See the statement of the European University Association on the forced resignation of 1,577 deans and Yavuz Baydar's column "The Purge Turns Turkish Academia into a Slaughterhouse: Turkey into an 'Intellectual Desert'" for more specific numbers of those purged and quotes from those involved.
6. Williams contributed her thoughts to *American Thinker*, a conservative, US-based publication, and she also serves as program director at The Turkish Heritage Foundation, a not-for-profit sympathetic to the Turkish government.
7. Many organizations like Soliya, a not-for-profit that connects post-secondary students from the Middle East to Europe and North America using simultaneous conferencing software and curricular tools, are available to realize global communication across lines of national and cultural difference.

WORKS CITED

Baydar, Yavuz. "The Purge Turns Turkish Academia into a Slaughterhouse; Turkey into an 'Intellectual Desert.'" *Vocal Europe*, 2 Oct. 2017, www.vocaleurope.eu/the-purge-turns-turkish-academia-into-a-slaughterhouse-turkey-into-an-intellectual-desert/.

Bettie, Mollie. "Ambassadors Unaware: The Fulbright Program and American Public Diplomacy." *The Journal of Transatlantic Studies*, vol. 13, no. 4, 2015, pp. 358–372.

Gramlich, John, and Kat Devlin. "More People around the World See U.S. Power and Influence as a 'Major Threat' to Their Country." *Pew Research Center*, 14 Feb. 2019.

Hartocollis, Anemona. "State Department, Citing Security, Suspends Teaching Program in Turkey." *New York Times*, 5 Aug. 2016, www.nytimes.com/2016/08/06/us/state-department-citing-security-suspends-teaching-program-in-turkey.html?_r=0.

Schultz, Lisa, et al. "Global Connections: 'A Tool for Active Citizenship.'" *Development in Practice*, vol. 19, no. 8, 2009, pp. 1023–1034.

Syeed, Nafeesa, and Nick Wadhams. "Trump Seeks to Cut State Department, UN for 'America First.'" *Bloomberg.com*, 16 Mar. 2017, www.bloomberg.com/politics/articles/2017-03-16/trump-seeks-to-slash-state-department-un-for-america-first.

Williams, Audrey. "Year of Carnage in Turkey Derails Academic Exchange with US." *American Thinker*, 29 Oct. 2016, www.americanthinker.com/articles/2016/10/year_of_carnage_in_turkey_derails_academic_exchange_with_us.html.

Zaman, Amberin. "US Pastor Remains Political Hostage in Ankara." *Al-Monitor: The Pulse of the Middle East*, 31 May 2017, www.al-monitor.com/pulse/originals/2017/05/pastor-turkey-jail-plea.html.

Afterword
THE PRACTICE OF KNOWLEDGE MOBILITY
Rewriting Global Civic Engagement

Bruce Horner

This collection addresses, broadly, the intersection and interplay of policy and knowledge mobility. Matters of policy inherently raise questions of knowledge mobility insofar as, at least in theory, policies are thought to draw on or express the implications of knowledge (for example, about writing and its learning and assessment), and insofar as the implementation of policies is itself meant to express the knowledge imagined as inhering in those policies. But just as research on knowledge "transfer" has, if anything, problematized ordinary conceptions of the application of knowledge learned in one domain to another (see, for example, Beach; Nowacek; Yancey et al.), research on knowledge mobility has problematized ordinary conceptions of (writing program) policy. Put baldly, no simple one-to-one correspondence seems to obtain between policy and "practice," nor between either of these and the "knowledge" that either is meant to represent (see Ellis and McNicholl; Fenwick and Farrell). Instead, even in those instances where such a correspondence is avidly sought, other factors and forces intervene; for example, just for starters (as contributions to this collection illustrate), other policies; vagaries of specific institutional, cultural, and government structures and practices; student and teacher characteristics and interests. Consequently, any attempt at achieving such a correspondence is very likely to be an exercise in frustration.

The problematics of the interplay between knowledge mobility and writing program policy are, if anything, exacerbated when the mobility in question is located in a global context, since such a context raises issues of multiple and likely conflicting policies by a far wider range of institutional entities—schools, religious institutions, state actors, NGOs—and conflicting sets of "knowledges" (including, of course, language knowledge) and their mobilization. While those problematics are also present in local and intra-national contexts, and while the "global" is of course present in the "local" (just as monolingual practice takes place in an inevitably multilingual context), still, the location of efforts at civic engagement in a "global" context renders these problematics explicit in a way more easily elided in efforts defined in terms of local, intra-national sites and actors. For example, while scholars in the United States are beginning to confront what appear to be attacks on their intellectual freedom and surveillance of their courses (see Mele; Schuman), efforts at civic engagement elsewhere can be far more volatile in these terms, and have far more dangerous consequences, as Jim Bowman and James Austin discuss in their chapters, affecting not only the forms of participation in civic engagement undertaken but even whether participation of any kind is safe or possible.

The accounts provided here of confronting these problematics reinforce several insights true of all forms of civic engagement through writing programs. First, they reinforce the role that social relations themselves play as a productive force and that institutions such as writing programs play in the maintenance (sustenance and revision) of such social relations—democratic or otherwise. So, for example, Olga Aksakalova, in her chapter "Literacy and Civic Engagement in a Transnational WPA Practice: The Case of Russia," concludes that "a firm institutional support is essential for the productive fostering of a teaching and learning environment where literacy habits are developed in connection with civic habits," and Jim Bowman cautions, by way of contrast, that "[e]fforts among higher education institutions to develop and sustain global relationships in this climate will likely take a doggedness and creative persistence for the foreseeable future," suggesting, albeit by negative example, the ways that institutional structures are both the ongoing products of such efforts and vulnerable to rapid dissipation when those efforts themselves decline.

Further, these chapters reinforce the degree to which those of us engaged in programs of civic engagement by means of writing programs need to adopt a stance of humility in the claims and expectations of what our work might accomplish on the ground, but also the need to give due deference to the kinds of civic engagement that may be and are accomplished by means of what appear to be practices so ordinary and quotidian as to be overlooked as instances of civic engagement at all. For example, as Aksakalova argues, teaching writing as critical thinking and the use of conventions for citing sources—practices pervasive in many US writing programs (at least to go by their mission statements)—can in fact be put to use as a means of performing "a different kind of civic duty" than the one officially prescribed by the state for contemporary Russian schools of "improving the country." Likewise, while the student work producing what James Austin calls "civic discussion," which Austin characterizes as "analytical writing, personal commentary and secondary research . . . consistent with US-based academic literacies and the genre of academic writing," is limited by the fact that it is performed "at some distance from the issues themselves and evidences no future potential engagement," its significance as civic engagement "should not be downplayed." For, as Austin acknowledges, such writing "represents a level of engagement distinct from [students'] prior writing, where analysis and critical thinking were typically limited to close readings of Western literature." Austin clearly prefers student work that he characterizes as "active engagement": work involving "first-hand interaction with relevant civic issues through primary research and personal experience with the civic issue being engaged in the writing." Nonetheless, as he also acknowledges, "civic engagement can also be a dangerous activity in Egypt." Hence, for Austin, "the question becomes *who* can best practice civic engagement and *what counts* within the confines of the present moment in Egyptian history as appropriate" (emphasis in original).

Finally, the accounts here reinforce the ways in which recurring binaries of global versus local, academic versus community, host versus guest, expert versus novice, (native) self versus other, and even teacher versus student are inadequate models for making sense of the dynamics of encounters. So while in one sense the editors' argument for "the value of global engagement and the important role universities can play in connecting people from different societies to respond to twenty-first-century challenges" and their encouragement of "global civic engagement" despite the seemingly growing "obstacles to forging successful programs" are unimpeachable, the fact is that there is no alternative to global engagement. Indeed, we can see instead that the efforts at civic engagement in global contexts occasion the reproduction and revision of the meanings of such engagement and of the relations between any and all of these binary pairings. Contrary to the myth of the tourist, there are no encounters by which the visitor merely observes or enjoys the exotica without changing and being changed. In other words, the distinction Michael Byram makes between tourist and sojourner is an ideological rather than functional distinction (and the same may be said of distinctions between and definitions of the global and local, academic and community, and the like).

Indeed, from this perspective, the qualifier "engaged" refers not to a particular kind of encounter distinct from the unengaged but, rather, a kind of encounter that acknowledges engagement and (in the instances discussed in this collection) attempts a particular form of engagement—"civic." Further, as Aksakalova reminds us, even the definition of "civic" is subject to continual redefinition, constituting, under the Soviet regime, "a uniform, state prescribed . . . position steeped in Communist ideology" and, currently, efforts at "the betterment of Russia." As Joyce Meier argues in her chapter, "Intercultural Complications in a 'Glocal' Community Project," "service learning [can] take on a 'glocal' perspective that attends to the global *as enacted through local participants and their ongoing, complex negotiations* of languages, cultures, attitudes and experiences—both present and past" (emphasis added). The service-learning project she describes upends typical axes of power (in which the West helps the rest and academics help the community) by having (mostly international) students deemed by conventional measures of assessment to be academically deficient work as tutors at a local primary school. And as a consequence, "both parties were experts *and* learners, as the international students were as eager to learn about US culture from the third graders, as the children were to learn from them."

This complication of traditional binaries is also attested to in Susan Meyers and María de Lourdes Caudillo Zambrano's chapter, "Whose WPA? Collaborative Transnational Development of Writing Programs." From a distance, the transnational exchange Meyers and Zambrano describe has the markings of just such binaries: the global North imposing its ideas about writing programs and pedagogy on the global South to bring the latter up to speed. But in practice, as their account illustrates, their own frame of "expertise in specific contexts" has allowed them to acknowledge and *share* specific forms of expertise, the key being that all parties have discarded "expectations about how [such expertise] will be used." That is to say, from a knowledge mobility perspective, they have all granted the likelihood, if not inevitability, that whatever expert knowledge is imparted in either direction will inevitably be transformed in the process of it being taken up, hence "policy" is taken not as *diktat* but as a practice of discovering the possible.

Contributions also complicate the longstanding academic/community project binary. Jennifer deWinter's comparison of the two kinds of Interactive Qualifying Projects students can pursue at Worcester Polytechnic Institute in her chapter on "International Project Centers and Global Civic Engagement" might at first glance seem to reinforce that binary: in terms of demonstrated "ability to communicate effectively in writing and with visuals," "ability to research and analyze problems," and "awareness of social and ethical dimensions of the problem-solving context," as well as "overall writing quality," those student projects that involved off-campus work were judged as superior to those that did not involve off-campus work. But—overlooking the obvious fact that the projects were inherently academic in their sponsorship, primary purpose, and participant population—it seems clear that the off-campus projects were more successful at least in part because those pursuing such projects had greater conventionally academic preparation on campus. This included, notably, as deWinter observes, "training in social science methodology, and ongoing feedback on presentations and writing as the project develops"—preparation that, curiously, those pursuing on-campus projects did not enjoy. Thus, it was the academic on-campus preparation as much as the actual off-campus work that made those projects (academically) successful in the terms valued by the academic institution sponsoring them.

I am suggesting a parallel, then, between an approach to cross-cultural, cross-national (which can be read as international or transnational) engagement in writing programs that recognizes such engagement as the inescapable norm of all work in writing instruction (cf. Lu, "An Essay on the Work of Composition"; Lu, "Living English Work"), on the one hand, and, on the other, what Street has identified as the ideological approach to literacy. That ideological approach does not so much distinguish between ideological and non-ideological literacies but, instead, insists on the inescapably ideological character of all literacy as social practice. The question then becomes not whether to be ideological but what kind of ideology to encourage. Likewise, in the cases described in this collection, the question is not whether to pursue pedagogies and programs of global engagement *per se* but, instead, what kinds of engagement to attempt and how. For even those efforts that might attempt not to engage are, inescapably, forms of engagement, just of a kind that many of us would (rightly) repudiate, just as isolationism is not a refusal to engage in "foreign policy" at all but, instead, a particular kind of cross-national policy: the "foreign policy" of isolationism.

Recognition of the inevitability of engagement might, of course, be used cynically as a means to continue business as usual. But this would mistake the inescapability of engagement with a conflation of all possible kinds of engagement. In contrast, as the contributions to this collection make clear, while there is no possibility of actual disengagement, the forms engagement takes vary significantly, and the differences between them matter enormously. Those differences do not mean that we can prescribe in advance the particular form that engagement in pursuit of specific values should take. Context, of course, always matters.

But even more to the point, those differences are not simply the consequence of contexts in which the engagement takes place. Instead, those contexts are also partly the consequence of the forms of engagement taken up, subject inevitably to change and, hence, difference through the reiteration and revision of those forms. For example, what might appear to be the imposition of a top-down knowledge/policy transmission may not in practice operate that way, as Meyers and Zambrano observe regarding the sharing of expertise they came to practice in their transnational interactions.

And here I will attempt to earn the title of this Afterword: the practice of knowledge mobility means, in effect, not so much the mobilization and attempted transfer of knowledge from context to context, place to place, institution to institution. Instead, it means recognizing and engaging with the inevitable transformations of knowledge, those engaged in its transfer, and the place to which and from which it transfers through the practice of knowledge mobilization. As Meyers and Zambrano observe, "In a shared knowledge economy, it is important to keep in mind that information does not 'belong' to one entity. Rather, it takes on meaning and utility as it is shared and circulated, so it is best for each participant to offer information openly and to trust that it will be used—or discarded—as is most useful." This recognition can help us to both avoid the problematic ethics of *noblesse oblige* missionaryism that have troubled previous attempts at "community engagement" and "service-learning" and engage more productively in, precisely, the engagement and learning and service that our work inevitably entails.

The predominant approach to knowledge transfer has to do with either efforts at the transnational communication of knowledge of the kind Christiane Donahue has cautioned us about or with an individual learner's application of knowledge received elsewhere to a different/new site. That approach has then had to confront the problem of the reification of knowledge inherent to the model, which posits simple transport from place to place, party to party, domain to domain: in short, a model of export/import. This is, of course, the same model of information communication on which the ideology of neoliberalism is founded: one that insists on the friction-free transmission of information, goods, and services. Within the terms of that ideology, knowledge (like information, goods, and services) is a commodity exchangeable in the marketplace. Attempts at global civic engagement based on this model aim at the production and transfer of such knowledge: both the production of "skills" currently valued in the employment marketplace and the ready transfer of those skills from site to site.

This, for example, is the model that appears to underlie Katie Gindlesparger's argument, in her chapter on "The Use of Writing for Transfer in Study Abroad," that study abroad programs can enable students to "learn professionally relevant skills and behaviors" for their future professions. The hope is that those skills and behaviors, once learned, will then transfer to the site of students' future professional work, and that, in fact, the value of study abroad resides precisely in the production of those transferable skills and behaviors rather than in any work accomplished at the site of the study abroad.

The problem, as Gindlesparger herself notes, is that "students don't always transfer the study abroad experience to their majors, or to their future professions." And indeed, Gindlesparger acknowledges that "helping [students] to see how the [study abroad] experience transfers to their professions" is "much more difficult." Much of the chapter addresses how that difficulty may be overcome. Still, the aim is to provide the employment marketplace with workers possessing the skills, behaviors, and habits of mind currently in demand, and the focus remains on how to ensure the production in workers of these skills and their transfer to the workplace. Whether those should be in demand and what use they might be put to is not addressed.

But the corollary to the mobility of knowledge is its mercuriality. The commodification of knowledge obscures its mercuriality by eliding the necessary role played by concrete labor in the ongoing production and value of knowledge. It follows that recognizing the necessary role played by labor in the production and value of knowledge means giving up the pretense of the stability and transferability of knowledge that its commodification poses. And this means giving up the kinds of claims about the value of efforts at global civic engagement that trip all too readily from our tongues about the production and future transfer of skills, dispositions, and so on. Given how firmly entrenched such ways of thinking are in contemporary ideologies of knowledge and learning, this is no easy task.

But several chapters in the collection point toward alternatives in their attention to labor and accomplishments at the site of that labor that knowledge, as mobile practice, entails. In lieu, then, of claiming what efforts at global civic engagement might give students to bring home with them, and in lieu of claiming such efforts bring equally transferable and stable knowledge insights to the community, we can value such efforts, and take them up, in terms of how each and every one rewrites what such engagement might mean for all participants as a consequence and in terms of the labor undertaken in such rewriting.

If any single value can be ascribed to efforts at global civic engagement, it resides in the changed sense of relationship of participants to such engagement that these efforts yield. If, as Raymond Williams insists, "the most important thing a worker ever produces is himself, himself in the fact of that kind of labour" (35; sic), then the most important accomplishment of efforts at global civic engagement may well be the sense of self in relation to the labor taken up that participants in such engagement produce.

We can see this not only in the changed sense of self in relation to English reported by students contributing to the "young writers competition" described in Sadia Mir and Ian Mauer's chapter, "Experiences Learned from Fostering a Writing Culture among Youth in Qatar." Admittedly, the project Mir and Mauer describe has many of the trappings of a conventional literacy contest of the kind that would reward adherence to standardized formulas: essay contests on quotations from none other than "Her Highness Sheikha Mozah bint Nasser Al Missned, wife of the former Emir of Qatar and the chairperson of the Qatar Foundation for Education, Science and Community Development, among other notable public positions." But the project deviates from such contests insofar as the essays themselves are written in English, as a second language, which is ordinarily perceived as something to be taken up only for "communicative purposes." Further, as Mir and Mauer explain,

> The program engages students both inside and outside of the classroom context by providing young writers with a stage and a platform to present their work to their peers and to the wider Qatari community. It enriches the students' experience of second language writing while giving classroom teachers and administrators new perspectives on current writing practices. In an environment where there is limited use of English for creative purposes, the program empowers workshop participants and competition winners alike to build and be part of a community of creative writers.

In other words, unlike creative writing competitions aimed at winnowing the ostensible wheat of creative genius(es) from the chaff of ordinary writing and writers, the program Mir and Mauer describe offers students "in and outside of the classroom context" a way to imagine their relationship to writing and a language (in this case, English) differently: as the ongoing product of their collective labor whose constitution their labor on and with it in fact contributes to, what they can and do continually (re)create through their labor at writing. In the program that developed out of the early competitions, the treatment of writing as the production of error-free prose instruction has given way to a concern with craft and content ("a balance of the craft-centered approach to teaching writing with the affect-centered approach")—specifically, addressing topics of global civic engagement. In this way, writing in a second language comes to be seen by the (young) writers themselves as a "vehicle to process their unconscious thoughts, and as a medium for negotiating their reactions to the world around them"—a significant departure from writing programs aimed primarily at developing transferable skills ostensibly in demand by future employers.

In this sense, Austin's concern about the limitations of writers whose civic engagement appears to fail to extend "beyond the page" understates the work accomplished in the production of "the page" at the site of writing. Admittedly, that work, and the civic engagement it might manifest, is less tangible than the forms of engagement we are predisposed to recognize *as* engagement. But we need not limit ourselves or our students to taking up those forms of engagement that the dominant has defined for and ceded to us. Without discounting those forms of global civic engagement that we are already prepared to recognize as such, we can cultivate the engagement that all writing takes up and shift our attention from attempting to teach global civic engagement toward recognizing, and working on, the kinds of global civic engagement in which student writers are always already inevitably involved. The contributions to this collection demonstrate, above all, the global civic engagement that the work of writing accomplishes and makes possible.

WORKS CITED

Beach, King. "Consequential Transitions: A Sociocultural Expedition beyond Transfer in Education." *Review of Research in Education*, vol. 24, 1999, pp. 101–139, doi.org/10.2307/1167268.

Byram, Michael. *Teaching and Assessing Intercultural Communicative Competence*. Multilingual Matters Ltd., 1997.

Donahue, Christiane. "'Internationalization' and Composition Studies: Reorienting the Discourse." *College Composition and Communication*, vol. 61, no. 2, 2009, pp. 212–243.

Ellis, Viv, and Jane McNicholl. *Transforming Teacher Education: Reconfiguring the Academic Work*. Bloomsbury, 2015.

Fenwick, Tara, and Lesley Farrell, editors. *Knowledge Mobilization and Educational Research: Politics, Languages and Responsibilities*. Routledge, 2012.

Lu, Min-Zhan. "An Essay on the Work of Composition: Composing English against the Order of FastCapitalism." *College Composition and Communication*, vol. 56, no. 1, 2004, pp. 16–50, doi.org/10.2307/4140679.

Lu, Min-Zhan. "Living-English Work." *College English*, vol. 6, pp. 605–618, doi: 10.2307/25472178.

Mele, Christopher. "Professor Watchlist Is Seen as Threat to Academic Freedom." *The New York Times*, 28 Nov. 2016, www.nytimes.com/2016/11/28/us/professor-watchlist-is-seen-as-threat-to-academic-freedom.html. Accessed 26 Dec. 2017.

Nowacek, Rebecca. *Agents of Integration: Understanding Transfer as a Rhetorical Act.* Southern Illinois UP, 2011.
Schuman, Rebecca. "Oh Good, a 'Professor Watch List.'" *Slate,* 23 Nov. 2016, www.slate.com/articles/news_and_politics/education/2016/11/professor_watchlist_is_a_grotesque_catalog_of_left_leaning_academics.html. Accessed 26 Dec. 2017.
Street, Brian V. *Literacy in Theory and Practice.* Cambridge UP, 1984.
Williams, Raymond. *Problems in Materialism and Culture: Selected Essays.* Verso, 1980.
Yancey, Kathleen Blake, et al. *Writing across Contexts: Transfer, Composition, and Sites of Writing.* Utah State UP, 2014.

INDEX

AACU. *See* Association of American Colleges and Universities
Aalaa, 210, 212, 214
ABET, 98, 99, 105
academic freedom, in Egypt, 213–14
Academic Service-Learning courses, 133–34, 140, 141, 146; engagement in, 149–50; students in, 148–49
Academic Service-Learning Fellows Seminar, 134–35
Academic Writing Seminar (Seattle University), 47; interview questions, 61–62
accreditation, engineering programs, 98
Acquaro, Kimberlee, 126
action-based/oriented research, 122–24; methodology, 50–52
active engagement, 200
administration, 6; off-campus centers, 71–72
advisors, faculty, 81, 85
Al Jazeera, 240
Al Khor, 222
Allison, 106
Al-Qaeda, 245
alumni, of Academic Service-Learning projects, 149–50
American University in Cairo (AUC), 198; academic freedom, 213–14; civic engagement in, 199–200, 201–2, 215, 216; Empower Scholarship, 212–13; interviews, 202–3; literacy habits and, 203–6; writing topics in, 206–12
anxiety, international students, 162–63
Anzaldúa, Gloria, 114, 129(n6)
Aprender Hacienco, 135
Arabic language, literacy habits, 203, 204, 229
area studies, training in, 68
Argentina, 49
Arizona, 113; entremundista pedagogy in, 114–15; regressive legislation in, 115–17, 120
Arizona House Bill (HB) 2281, 116, 129(n9)
Arizona Senate Bill (SB) 1070, 113, 129(n8); purpose of, 115–16
Arizona Senate Bill (SB) 1188, 116

Arizona Senate Bill (SB)1266, 116
ARU. *See* University Reflection Area
Assad, Bashar al-, 245
assessment, Interactive Qualifying Project, 74–78
"Assessment of Engineering Students' Curricular and Co-Curricular Experiences and Their Ethical Development, An," 82
Association of American Colleges and Universities (AACU), on study abroad, 95, 138–39
attrition through enforcement, 115, 129(n8)
AUC. *See* American University in Cairo
Austin, James, 27
authoritative state, Russia as, 25, 27–28
authority: in Russian academics, 37; student, 185, 230
autonomy, student, 185, 193, 230
Azerbaijan, 249

bachelor's program, New Economic School, 34–35
Beni Suef, 214
Berlin, James, 26
Bolshevik Revolution, 29
borderlands, 114, 123
Boston, 88
boundary-crossing/boundary-guarding, 101–2; youth and, 114–15
brainstorming, 135
Brandt, Deborah, 50
Brazil, 49; students from, 155
Brazilian National Council for Scientific and Technological Development, 49
Brewer, Jan, 120
bridge writing courses, 155; community projects, 154, 156–57
British Residency, Gulf states, 220
Brunson, Andrew, 244
Bureau of Education and Cultural Affairs (ECA), 218

Cairo, 27
Campus Compact, 180
Cape Town, Interactive Qualifying Project, 71, 73

262   INDEX

CCCC. *See* College Conference on Composition and Communication
Center for Communication and Civic Engagement (University of Washington), 13
Center for Middle Eastern Studies (Title VI funding), 249
Central America, engagement, 135
charity organizations: Croatia, 182; Islamic, 27, 199, 210, 214–15
Chávez Leyva, Yolanda, on Chicana/o histories, 120–21
cheating, in Russia, 30
Chicana/os, 114; histories, 120–21
China: education system in, 166–67; international students from, 152, 154, 155, 161–62, 165
Chloe, on study abroad, 104, 107–8
citation, New Economic School training, 36
citizenship, 16, 121; global, 8, 15, 152, 159; in Russia, 23, 25
civic awareness, Croatia, 182
civic consciousness, 25
civic discussion, 200, 210, 211–12, 253
civic duty, in Russia, 26
civic education, 89
civic engagement, 3, 6, 9, 11, 12, 13, 17, 23, 27, 35, 55, 146, 179, 189, 190, 235, 254, 259; American University in Cairo, 201–2, 206–13, 214; in Egypt, 199–200, 205–6, 215–16; Fulbright proposals, 242–43; and geopolitics, 248–49; global, 4–5, 14, 15, 88–89, 152, 237–39, 243–44; writing programs and, 252–53; youth-driven, 124–27
civic values, in Russia, 24–25
civil disobedience, as civic engagement, 215
classroom observations, 51–52, 54–55
Coalition for Civic Engagement and Leadership, 12
COE courses, 53; at Universidad Iberoamericana, 55–56
College Conference on Composition and Communication (CCCC), 145
collaborations, 3, 7, 107, 113, 115, 118; binational, 44–46, 58–59; Interactive Qualifying Project, 72–73; international, 10, 13, 47; in TESOL presentations, 145–46
college entrance exams, Mexican, 53, 60
colleges, 11. *See also* universities
Colombian Department of Science, 49
Communication Across the Curriculum program (CXC), 81

communication skills, 7, 34, 83; cross-disciplinary, 105; international students, 158–59
communities, 7, 71, 121, 289; college, 191–92; knowledge production, 122–23; participation, 157, 222; working with, 11, 15, 79–80
community projects, 152, 159, 254; bridge writing classes, 154, 156–57; PCW, 162–66; translingual approach, 169, 170; youth-driven, 124–27
competency: cultural, 134; global, 68, 95
composition studies, in United States, 48–49
contact zones, 10, 81; transnational, 167, 169
cooperation, 4, 5. *See also* collaborations
corruption, in education, 29–30
cosmopolitanism, 10
Costa Rica, Interactive Qualifying Project in, 73
Council for Interior Design Accreditation, 224
Council for Writing Program Administrators, 54
creative writing: in Qatar, 220–21, 223; workshops, 225–27
criminalization: of migrants, 115–16; of sexuality, 116–17
Critical Language Scholarship Program (US State Department), 249
critical literacy, 70
critical theory, 122
critical thinking, 9, 12, 24, 146, 252; American University in Cairo students, 201–2, 211; in Russia, 26–27, 34; in Seattle University writing programs, 54–55
Croatia, Republic of, 9–10, 12; Rochester Institute of Technology in, 184–85; service learning in, 177–78, 181–83, 185–92, 193–94
cross-linguistic transfer, 229
Crossroads Collaborative, 111, 117–18, 128; civic and community projects, 124–27; teacher-researchers in, 123–24
Crossroads Connections, 128
cultural enrichment, faculty-student interaction, 87–88
cultures, 68; Croatian, 182, 193; ethical engagement, 82–84; experiencing, 137–38, 144; at RIT Croatia, 184–85; sensitivity, 159; sharing, 160–62, 165–66; working across, 107–8
curriculum, curricular models, 24, 49, 98, 184; binational comparisons, 48(table),

54; Universidad Iberoamericana, 56–57, 65
CXC. *See* Communication Across the Curriculum program
Cyprus, Fulbright-Hayes programs, 236, 237, 239, 240–41

Danilov, Alexander, 29
DEAL model, 157
Decolonizing Methodologies: Research and Indigenous Peoples (Smith), 121
Dewey, John, 180
directors, project center, 84–85
disciplinarity, 97
discourse, discipline-specific, 96–97
Dissergate, 29
dissertations, plagiarized, 28–29
Doctors without Borders, 5
documentaries, Grrls Literary Activism, 126
documents, academic, 28–29
Doha, Young Writers Program in, 222
Donna, Nexus Abroad, 106–7, 108
Dublin Institute of Technology, 180
Dubrovnik, 182, 184, 187
Duncan-Andrade, Jeff, *Urban Youth, Media Literacy, and Increased Critical Civic Participation*, 121

EAP. *See* English for Academic Purposes
ECA. *See* Bureau of Education and Cultural Affairs
Ecology of the Dalmatian Coast, 186
economics, free market, 163; in Russia, 31, 33–34
economies, 97; knowledge-based, 220; Russia, 26
Ecuador, Skype project, 143
Educating the Engineer of 2020: Adapting Engineering Education to the New Century (National Academy of Engineering), 98, 99, 105
education, 16, 28, 116, 120, 135, 207, 231; Chinese system, 166–67; corruption in, 29–30; interdisciplinary, 98–99; internationally competitive, 23–24; pre-professional, 104–5; in Qatar, 200–21; in Russia, 9, 25–26, 33, 37–38, 40(n3); US-based models, 198–99
Educational and Cultural Exchange Programs (US), 238
Education City (Qatar), 224
Egypt, 4, 12, 198; academic freedom in, 213–14; civic engagement in, 27, 199–200, 206–13, 215–16; literacy habits in, 203–6; public and private schools in, 202–3

Elbow, Peter, *Embracing Contraries*, 100
Electronic Village (Honduras), 145
El Salvador, hunger in, 134
Embracing Contraries (Elbow), 100
empowerment, 27; student, 179–80, 188–91
Empower Scholarship, American University in Cairo, 212–13
enculturation, to discipline-specific discourse, 96–97
engagement, 13, 79, 146–47, 199; civic discussion and, 211–12; and context, 255–56; building and maintaining, 134–35; ethical, 82–84; global, 237–39, 253
engineering students, 68, 104; ethical reasoning, 82–83; interdisciplinary education, 98–99; study abroad, 102–3
Engineers without Borders, 5
England, service learning in, 180
English as a Second Language (ESL), cultural sensitivity, 159
English for Academic Purposes (EAP), 25–26
English language, 155, 168, 184, 203, 204; in Qatari schools, 222, 228, 229, 132–33; teaching literacy in, 147–48
English studies, social justice, 14
English teaching assistant (ETA), 239, 246–47
"Enhancing Speaking and Listening through Skype and Facebook: A Multicultural Experience," 145
entremundistas, 111, 112–13, 118, 128, 129(n6); in Arizona, 114–15; on sexuality, 119–20
environment: human effects on, 186–87; sustainability, 133
environmental organizations, Interactive Qualifying Project, 73
Eon Youth Lounge, 125
Erdogan, Recep Tayyip, 244
ethics, 7, 10, 85; feminist, 17; social, 82–84
ethnic minorities, 113
ethnocentrism, 84
Eurasia Foundation, 31
Europe Engage, 180–81, 183
European Union, 4; service learning, 180–81
evaluations, RIT Croatia students, 187–92
Examen Nacional de Ingreso a la Educación, 53
examinations, Mexican college entrance, 53, 60
exchange programs, sustainable, 235–36
exchanges, faculty, 5, 10, 46, 47
exclusionary discipline policies, 116
expertise, sharing, 55

Facebook, 147; transnational use of, 142, 143–45
face-to-face dialogues, 138
faculty, 10, 58, 72, 136, 235; action research, 51–52; advisory role, 81, 85; development, 7, 54; engagement, 149–50; exchanges, 5, 14, 46; New Economic School, 32–33; student interaction, 87–88
faculty directors, 71, 85
faculty-to-faculty engagement, 149
Farah, 210–11, 212, 214
Federal Research University (Russia), Higher School of Economics, 31
Fedyukin, Igor, 28, 32
feedback, on student writing, 80–82
female genital mutilation (FGM), 206, 208, 212
feminism, Arab, 206, 207–8, 212
Fields, Amanda, 127
films, on YSHR, 126
fire-recovery plans, RIT Croatia, 185–86
First-Year Composition (FYC), 45, 100
five senses activity, 227
food security/insecurity, 133, 134, 139; elementary school students, 156–57
Ford Foundation, 12, 31
foreign policy, 4, 255
foreign students. *See* international students
forest fires, Croatia, 185–86
freedom of the press, in Russia, 27–28
Freedom Students Observatory, 213
friendship networks, 179
Fulbright ETA programs, 239, 246–47
Fulbright-Hayes Study Abroad trips, 14, 236; to Cyprus, 240–41; to Turkey, 237–38, 239–40, 243–44, 246
Fulbright programs, 14, 239; Teaching Scholar, 242

Gaddy, Clifford, 29
Garcia, Enrique, 125; *No More Ignorant Love*, 125, 130(n15)
Gates Foundation, Bill & Melinda, 238–39
genres, 95, 101
geopolitics, 4; global civic engagement and, 237–39, 243–44, 248–49; Turkey and, 244–45
George, Ann, 26
Germany, service learning in, 180
GICEOLEM, 49
GLA. *See* Grrls Literary Activism
Global Civic Engagement (University of North Carolina), 13
global exchanges: Fulbright-Hayes trips, 236–40; sustainable, 235–36

globalization, globalism, 4, 153, 177
Global Neighbors, 145
global problems, solutions, 167–68
Global Projects for All (WPI), 69
Global Right, 116
glocalization, 152, 163
Gonzalez, J. Sarah, 124
graduates, continued participation of, 136–37
grant writing, 140
graphic design, 106
Great Britain, in Qatar, 219–20
Group for Inclusion and Quality Education by Taking Care of Reading and Writing in all Subjects, 49
Grrls Literary Activism (GLA), 126
Guatemala, 134
Gulen, Fethullah, 245
Gulf states, Britain and, 219–20
Guriev, Sergei, 32–33
Gutiérrez, Laura, 115

Haddad, Joumana, 207
Herdt, Gil, *Moral Panics, Sex Panics*, 120
High Beginner English classes, 136
higher education, 3, 49, 154; in Russia, 23, 37–38
high-impact practices (HIP), 134
high school, in Qatar, 219
histories, multiple, 120–21
Hofstede, Geert, 182
homophobia, 114
Honduras, 9, 10; collaborative program in, 133–34, 141; collected proverbs, 137–38, 140; Learning-by-Doing and, 135–36; literacy project, 147–48, 150; social media use, 142–45
How People Learn (National Research Council), 100, 102
humanitarian service, in Croatia, 182, 183
humanities, 116
Humanities Service Learning course, 136–37
human rights, 113, 119
hunger, and poverty, 134, 136
Hymengway, Zami, 125

IBCs. *See* International branch campuses
identity, 9, 25, 96, 99
IGSD. *See* Interdisciplinary and Global Studies Division
immigrants, 3, 120; legislative criminalization of, 113, 114, 115–16
imperialism, 121
India, Interactive Qualifying Project, 71–72, 73

individualism, neoliberal, 115
Institute for International Education (IIE), *Open Doors* report, 97
Institutional Review Board (IRB), 73, 80, 82
institutions, sustainability of, 245–46
integrity, academic, 12, 26–27
intellectual property, 27
Interactive Qualifying Project (IQP), 254; alumni survey, 69–70; assessment of, 74–78; ethical engagement, 82–84; goals, 70–71; off-campus programs, 71–72, 78–82; preparatory term, 72–73; project sites, 73–74; sponsor selection, 86–87
interconnectedness, global, 13
intercultural exchanges, 158–59
Interdisciplinary and Global Studies Division (IGSD), 74
international branch campuses (IBCs), 198
international business students, 106–7
International Friends, 135
international students, 4, 6, 152, 171(n1), 236; communication skills, 158–59; isolationism, 165–66; PCW project, 162–65; reflective exercise, 157–58; translingualism, 160–62; tuition costs, 154–55
interpersonal skills, 83
interviews: American University in Cairo, 202–3; Nexus Abroad, 102–9; Seattle University, 52, 61–62
IQP. *See* Interactive Qualifying Project
Iraq, 239, 249
IRB. *See* Institutional Review Board
Ireland, service learning in, 180
ISIS, 243
Islamic State (IS), 3, 245
Island of Gold, 210, 212
isolationism, 166–67, 194, 255

Japan, 88, 183
Jesuits, universities, 47

Karim, 209–10
Katelyn, 106, 108
Kilbourne, Jean, 126
knowledge(s), 7, 34, 50, 97, 113, 115, 125, 190; labor of, 257–58; mobility of, 251–52, 256; production of, 27, 28, 117, 121, 122–23; transfer of, 45, 99–100
Korean students, 155
Kore Press, 126

lab concept, Crossroads Collaborative, 118
labor, knowledge as, 257–58
language, and literacy habits, 203, 229
Last Hunger Season, The (Thurow), 146
Latin America, 135; social media engagement use, 142–45
leadership, 146, 147, 162
learning, 9, 25, 30, 35, 68; community-based, 17–18; outcomes, 14, 53
Learning by Doing: in Honduras, 135–36; impacts of, 148–49
Lee, Jamie A., 126
legislation: anti-immigrant, 115–16; anti-LGBTQ, 116–17; regressive, 113–14, 120
Let's Get Real program, 124
LGBTQ community, 126; legislative discrimination against, 113, 116–17
Lifemakers, 206, 210–11, 212, 214–15
Lincoln, Yvonna, 114
literacy, literacies, 16, 50, 70, 123, 133, 134, 136, 139, 198, 201, 255; academic, 44, 184–85; community, 5, 10, 11; English language, 147–48; in Russia, 26, 39
literacy habits, in Egyptian schools, 202–6, 229
literacy practices, 5–6; New Economic School, 35–36; Russian, 24–25
literary analysis, in Egyptian private schools, 205
Lomawaima, Tsianina, 115
London, 88
London Project Center, 72

Major Qualifying Project (MQP), 69
Martin, Adela, 125
Martin, Londie, 125
Matsuda, Mari, 125, 129–30(n14)
McArthur Foundation, 31
media, Russian, 27–28
Medvedev, Dmitry, 32; anti-plagiarism campaign, 28, 29
Mendoza, Grazzia Maria, 145
Mexican Americans, 155
"Mexican Dichos: Lessons Through Language," 137
Mexico, 34, 44, 49, 54, 60; faculty exchanges, 10, 14
Mexico City, 135
Middle East and North Africa (MENA), 200, 243; English language literacy, 204–5
migrants, 120; SB 1070 and, 115–16
Ministry of Education and Higher Education (Qatar), 221; Young Writers

Competition, 223–24; Young Writers Program, 218, 228
misinformation, and fear, 120
Miss Representation (films), 126
mobility/mobilization, 163; knowledge, 251–52, 256, 257
Moral Panics, Sex Panics: Fear and the Fight over Sexual Rights (Herdt), 120
Morocco, 88
Morsi, Mohammed, 208, 209
Moscow Pedagogical University, falsified documents, 28–29
Moscow University for the Humanities, 23, 24
motivations, student, 229–30
Mozah bint Nasser Al Missned, Sheika, 218, 219, 258
MQP. *See* Major Qualifying Project
Mubarak, Hosni, 205
multicompetent experiences, 169
multilingualism, 170
Muñoz, José Esteban, 115
Muslim ban, 3
Muslim Brotherhood, 208, 213–14
My Place (Wheatley and Rawlins), 164

name exercise, 163–64
National Academy of Engineers, 68; *Educating the Engineer of 2020*, 98, 99, 105
National Association of Schools of Art and Design, 224
National Citizen Service Programme, 180
nationalism, 3, 113, 194
nativism, 113
Navalny, Alexei, 32
needs assessment, 185
neoliberalism, 6, 115, 163, 168
NES. *See* New Economic School
New Economic School (NES), 24, 25, 38; description of, 30–32; faculty of, 32–33; students, 36–37; Writing and Communication Center, 34–35; written and oral communication, 33–34
New Literacy Studies, 201
Newsom, Jennifer Siebel, 126
Nexus Abroad, 98; student experiences, 102–9
NGOs. *See* nongovernmental organizations
Nicaragua, social media use, 143
No More Ignorant Love (Garcia and Vazquez), 125, 130(n15)
nongovernmental organizations (NGOs), 5, 71
Nour, 208
Nuestra Voz, 124–26

Obama, Barack, 238, 249(n1)
Ofer, Gur, 32
off-campus centers, 90(n2); Interactive Qualifying Project, 71–72
Open Doors report (IIE), 97
oral communication, New Economic School, 33–34
outreach, 16, 111

Paige, on Nexus Abroad experience, 104–6
Panama, 135, 143
parents' bill of rights (SB 1309), 116
Paris Agreement, 4
participant observation, action research, 51–52
partnerships, 10, 136; global, 16, 17
passive learning, and plagiarism, 30
PCW. *See* Preparation for College Writing
peer mentorship, 138–39
Pelješac peninsula, forest fires on, 185–86
Pennsylvania, 133, 136
Pennsylvania State University, 13
personal lives, enhanced, 83
Philadelphia, literacy and food security, 133
picture prompt activity, 227
Place at the Table, A (documentary), 146
plagiarism, plagiarism policies, 230; in Russia, 24, 28–30, 34, 36, 37
Plan, The (WPI), 69
poetry, Arab and Western, 207
poetry slams, 125, 126–27, 130(n15)
policy-relevant work, Crossroads Collaborative, 118
politics, 18, 199; Middle Eastern, 243–44; resistance, 117; writing programs, 16–17
"Postcolonial Amnesia: Sexual Moral Panics, Memory and Imperial Power" (Wieringa), 121
poster presentations, 139
poverty, and hunger, 134
power: political, 199; relations, 117, 153–54; in Russian academics, 37, 41(n15)
Preparation for College Writing (PCW), 155; class activities, 170–71; communication skills, 158–59; community project, 156–57, 162–66; Culture Circles, 161–62; translingualism, 160–61
presidential election, 2016, 3–4
Presidents United to Solve Hunger (PUSH), 5, 136, 145
private schools, in Egypt, 200, 202–3, 205–12
problem solving, 13, 254–55

PRODEAC, 49
Producing Good Citizens: Literacy Training in Anxious Times (Wan), 26
programs, service-learning, 10–11
Project Centers (WPI), 72(table); directors, 84–85; sponsor selection, 86–87; students at, 76–77
proverbs, collecting, 137–38, 140, 141
Puar, Jasbir, *Terrorist Assemblages*, 120
public schools, in Egypt, 200, 202–3, 204, 206, 210–11, 212–13
public service, in Croatia, 182–83
PUSH. *See* Presidents United to Solve Hunger
Putin, Vladimir, 25, 29, 40(n6)

Qatar, 12; creative writing in, 220–21; history of, 219–20; teacher workshops, 225–26; Young Writers Competition, 223–25, 232–33, 258–59; Young Writers Program, 218–19, 226–27, 230–32
Qatar Foundation for Education, Science and Community Development, 218, 224, 258
queer world-making practices, 115
questionnaires, student and teacher, 227–28

racial justice programs, Nuestra Voz, 124–26
RAND Corporation, 220
reciprocity, 3, 137
Red de Cultura Escrita y Comunidades Discursivas, 44
reflection, 13. *See also* reflective writing
Reflection in the Writing Classroom (Yancey), 100
reflective writing, 96, 100–101, 157; study abroad and, 108–9, 139–40
Regeni, Giulio, murder of, 213
relationships, 123; power, 153–54
research, 112, 119, 212; action-oriented, 111, 118, 122–24; ethical plans, 85
responsibilities, project sponsors, 86–87
revolution, Egyptian, 205
rhetoric and composition studies, 14, 46–47, 199, 201
Rochester Institute of Technology (RIT) Croatia: academic literacy skills, 184–85; service learning projects at, 185–87; student evaluations, 187–92
Roehampton University, 180
Rostova, Nataliya, on freedom of the press, 27–28
rural areas, service-learning programs in, 10–11

Russia, 4, 9, 12, 253; academic hierarchy in, 38–39; authoritative state in, 27–28; critical thinking and academic integrity, 26–27; educational reform, 33, 37–38, 40(n3); higher education, 23–24; literacy and civic values, 24–25; plagiarism in, 28–30; teaching, 36–37

St. John Fisher College, 242
Sanaa, on Arab feminism, 207–8
Sanafiya oil field, 219
sanitation facilities, Interactive Qualifying Project, 73
San Jose (Costa Rica), Interactive Qualifying Project, 71
Saudi Arabians, 155
scholarships, American University in Cairo, 212–13
scholar-teachers, 235
School of Global Affairs and Public Policy (AUC), 214
schools, 116; China, 166–67; Egyptian, 200, 202–3; Preparation for College Writing project, 156–57, 162–66; Qatari K-12, 218–19, 220, 228–29, 232
Seattle University (SU), 53; action research at, 51–52; binational collaboration, 46–47; classroom observations, 54–55; writing instructor interview questions, 61–62
secondary schools: Egyptian literacy habits, 203–6; private Egyptian, 206–13
Second-language English writing, in Qatar, 218, 222, 223–25
service event, RIT Croatia projects, 185–87
service learning (SL), 5, 6, 10, 11, 13, 15–17, 51, 146, 180, 242, 243; communication skills, 158–59; in Croatia, 177–78, 181, 182–83, 184–87; glocal perspective, 152–53; impacts of, 192–93; international, 7, 14, 167; international students and, 157–58; native language skills, 193–94; student experiences, 139–42, 178–79
student empowerment, 10, 179–80, 243; student evaluations, 187–92; student experiences, 139–40, 141–42; study-away, 83–84
service organizations, Islamic, 206
sex education, 116, 120, 125
sexting, 116, 129(n10)
sexuality, 13, 111, 112; social justice framework, 119–20; youth and, 118–19
Sexuality, Health and Human Rights, 119
Sexuality Research in the United States (di Mauro), 119

sheepherders, Interactive Qualifying Project, 73
Sisi, Abdel Fattah el-, 209, 215
skills, 97; soft, 105–6; transfer of, 104–5, 256
Skype, 59, 202; transnational use of, 142–45, 147
slam poetry, 125, 126–27, 130(n15)
slide presentations, 139
Smith, Dana Shell, on Young Writers Program, 224
Smith, Linda Tuhiwai, *Decolonizing Methodologies*, 121
social hierarchy, 179
social justice, 12, 13, 14, 113; Crossroads Collaborative, 118, 124–26; sexuality and, 119–20
social media: cross-cultural use of, 142–45
social mobility, China, 155
social panics, 113–14
social relationships, 191, 252; power and, 153–54
social sciences, 80, 81, 112, 255; methodology course, 85–86
social sustainability, 133
Sonin, Konstantin, 29
Soros, George, 31
Southern Association of Colleges and Schools, 224
Soviet Union, 28, 181. *See also* Russia
sponsors, Interactive Qualifying Project, 86–87, 89
Squires, Ashley, 26
stability, of institutions, 245–46
stakeholders, 179; in Interactive Qualifying Project, 79–80
"Static to Dynamic: Professional Identity as Inventory, Invention, and Performance in Classrooms and Workplaces" (Brady and Schreiber), 99
STEM universities, 11
stereotyping, 166
Street, Brian, 50
stretch model, Universidad Iberoamericana, 56–57
Student Project Day, 139
students: boundary-guarding and boundary-crossing, 101–2; enculturation of, 96–97; engineering, 98–99; ethical reasoning, 82–83; faculty interaction with, 87–88; grant writing, 140–41; motivations of, 229–30; opinion questionnaires, 227–28; peer mentorships, 138–39; pre-professional education, 104–5; social science methods, 79–80; writing feedback, 80–82. *See also* international students
study abroad programs, 257; Fulbright-Hayes, 236–37; knowledge transfer, 99–100; for professionally oriented students, 95, 97; reflective writing, 108–9; student experiences, 102–8. *See also* Nexus Abroad
study away component: service-learning projects, 83–84; Worcester Polytechnic Institute, 68–69
summer study tours, 14
Supreme Education Council (SEC), 220, 221
surveillance, legislative, 113
surveys: of Interactive Qualifying Projects, 74–78; RIT Croatia students, 187–92
sustainability, 9, 133; exchange programs, 235–36; of institutions, 245–46; lifelong, 147–48
Sykes-Picot agreement, 219
Syria, 3; geopolitics, 243, 245, 250(n4)

Tahrir, Midan, students in, 205
Taiwan, international student from, 165, 169
teacher-researchers, 115, 123–24
teachers, 37; capacity building, 231–32; creative writing workshops, 225–26, 228; Fulbright-Hayes trips, 237, 240–41; Fulbright proposals, 242–43
Teachers of English to Speakers of Other Languages (TESOL), 136, 143; presentations, 145–46
teaching, 111, 226; methodological practices, 79–80; in Russia, 36–37
Teaching English Language Learners, 143
teaching for transfer (TFT), 96, 102
technical writing, problem-solving approach, 135–36
terrorism, 120, 213, 245
Terrorist Assemblages: Homonationalism in Queer Times (Puar), 120
TESOL. *See* Teachers of English to Speakers of Other Languages
TFT. *See* teaching for transfer
Thailand, 88; students from, 155
Thurow, Roger, *The Last Hunger Season*, 146
Title VI funds, 249
Tohono O'odham, 114, 121
tourism, service, 10, 186, 253
training, teacher, 10, 49, 68
transdisciplinarity, 12, 113, 118
translations, in translingual exercise, 161
translingualism: in community projects, 169, 170; international students and, 161–62; PCW course, 160–61, 163–64

Index   269

transnational awareness, 114, 121–22
transnationalism, 198, 201, 254
transnational projects, 194–95
travel ban, Trump's, 236
Trump, Donald, 3, 4, 236, 246; global relations, 238, 248–49
Tucson, 13; racial justice program, 124–26; and HB 2281, 129
Tucson Youth Poetry Slam (TYPS), 126–27
tuition costs, international students, 154–55
Turkey, 4, 14, 38; Fulbright programs, 236, 237–38, 239–40, 242–43, 246–47; geopolitics, 244–45, 249(n1), 250(n4); internal politics of, 243–44
TYPS. *See* Tucson Youth Poetry Slam

United Kingdom, 4, 180; and Qatar, 219–20
United States: geopolitics, 248–49; and Turkey, 239–40
USDA, 135
US Department of State: Bureau of Education and Cultural Affairs, 218; Critical Language Scholarship Program, 249; Fulbright ETA programs under, 246–47
US Embassy Doha, and Young Writers Program, 218, 221, 222, 228
Universidad Iberoamericana, 45; binational collaboration, 58–59; COE courses, 55–56; faculty exchanges, 46–47, 51–52; interview questions, 63–64; Stretch model, 56–57; writing culture, 57–58; writing program, 53–55, 65
Universidad Nacional General de Sarmiento, 49
universities, 3, 4, 7, 11, 44, 198; binational collaboration, 46–47; Russian, 23–24
Universities Fighting World Hunger, 145–46
University of Arizona, 12, 237
University of Buenos Aires, 49
University of North Carolina, 13
University of Osijek, 183
University of Rijeka, 183
University of Washington, Center for Communication and Civic Engagement, 13
University of Zagreb, Faculty of Information Sciences program, 183
University Reflection Area (ARU), 56
Urban Youth, Media Literacy, and Increased Critical Civic Participation (Duncan-Andrade), 121

Vazquez, Alexia, 125; *No More Ignorant Love*, 125, 130(n15)
Venezuelan students, 155
Venice, Interactive Qualifying Project, 71
Vieira, Kate, 50
Virginia Commonwealth University (VCU), 224
volunteering, in RIT Croatia program, 185
voluntourism, 10

WAC. *See* Writing Across the Curriculum
WAC/WID, 55; curricular development, 56–57
Waldinger, Roger, 50
Wan, Amy J., *Producing Good Citizens*, 26
Wardle, Elizabeth, 100
Wellington, Interactive Qualifying Project, 71
Widener University, 148; Academic Service-Learning course at, 133–34
Wieringa, Saskia Eleonora, "Postcolonial Amnesia," 121
Williams, Audrey, 246–47
Worcester Polytechnic Institute (WPI), 72(table), 81, 83, 254; faculty-student interaction, 87–88; Interactive Qualifying Project, 70–78; project center directors, 84–85; social science methods, 85–86; sponsor selection, 86–87; study away component, 68–69
workshops: creative writing, 225–26; professional development, 51–52; Young Writers Program, 226–27
"Works in Progress or How I Stopped Worrying and Learned to Love . . . ." (documentary), 126
World Bank, 31, 135
WPAs, 39(n1); transnational, 24, 38
WPI. *See* Worcester Polytechnic Institute
writing, 16, 36, 85, 103, 111, 140, 229, 252; affect-centered approach, 230–31; AUC students, 206–13; feedback, 80–82; for Interactive Qualifying Project, 76–77; reflective, 8, 96, 100–101, 108–9, 157; in Russia, 9, 33–34. *See also* writing programs
Writing across Contexts (Yancey et al.), 100, 101–2
Writing Across the Curriculum (WAC), 24, 34, 45, 49, 53
Writing and Communication Center (WCC), New Economic School, 24, 34–35, 40(n13)
Writing and Public Life in America course, 156

writing centers, 26, 40(n4), 49, 57
writing competition: in Qatar, 218–19, 221, 223–25
writing culture, development of, 57–58
Writing-Enriched Curriculum (WEC), 55
Writing in the Disciplines (WID), 45, 49, 53; at New Economic School, 24, 34
writing instructors, 95; interview questions, 61–64
writing programs, 65; binational comparisons, 53–55; civic duty, 252–53; knowledge mobility, 251–52; models for, 198–99; political space, 16–17; transnational, 23, 28
writing studies, 9, 14–15
"Written Culture and Discursive Communities Network," 44

Xenophobia, 4, 114

Yancey, Kathleen, 96, 100
Young Writers Competition, 223–25, 228, 232–33, 258–59
Young Writers Journal, 225, 228, 232
Young Writers Program (YWP): affect-centered approach, 230–31; opinion questionnaires, 227–28; in Qatar, 218–19, 221, 222, 229–30, 232–33; workshops, 225–27
Youssef, Bassem, 206, 209, 212
youth, 13; boundary flouting, 114–15; civic and community projects, 124–27; knowledge production, 121, 123; and sexuality, 118–19
Youth. Art. Activism. Summer Camp, 124, 125
youth sexualities, health, and rights (YSHR), 111–12, 117, 118, 123, 124, 126; policies on, 127–28
YouTube videos, 146
YSHR. *See* youth sexualities, health, and rights
YWCA, Nuestra Voz program, 124–26
YWP. *See* Young Writers Program

Zagazig, 212, 214
Zamorano, Escuela Agricola Panamericana (Honduras), 134, 135
Zenkin, Sergei, 30

ABOUT THE AUTHORS

Olga Aksakalova is a professor of English at LaGuardia Community College of the City University of New York. Her research interests include transnational implementations of writing pedagogy, virtual exchange practices and program administration, as well as twentieth-century American literature and autobiography studies.

An assistant professor of English at Central Connecticut State University, **James P. Austin** has published on transnational writing programs and student writers in the Middle East-North Africa. As a 2017 recipient of a CCCC Emergent Researcher Award, Dr. Austin returned to Egypt, where he lived and worked for four years to conduct research on a book-length project about transnational literacies at the American University in Cairo. He has also published multiple short stories and encyclopedia articles.

Jim Bowman is an associate professor of English at St. John Fisher College in Rochester, NY. He does his teaching, research, and public speaking around issues of civic engagement, rhetoric, demagoguery, travel, and Middle Eastern studies. He has led cultural learning tours to Turkey and Cyprus on Fulbright-Hays grants and has been awarded a Fulbright in Turkey.

María de Lourdes Caudillo Zambrano is a full-time professor at Universidad Iberoamericana, Mexico City. She works in the Faculty Development Program and teaches first-year academic writing courses. She earned her PhD in quality and assessment of institutions, programs, and psychopedagogical intervention from Universidad Complutense de Madrid and a master's degree in philosophy from Universidad Iberoamericana.

Rebecca Charry Roje teaches English composition and literature at RIT's global campus in the endlessly fascinating and occasionally absurd town of Dubrovnik, Croatia, where she has lived a surprising international life for nearly twenty years. Her current research interests include applied linguistics, world Englishes, digital communication, and intercultural competence. In addition to numerous publications and presentations, she is the author of a TEDx talk on English language acquisition and the emergence of "Cringlish." She holds a Master of Arts in English from Georgetown University.

Jennifer deWinter is a professor of rhetoric at Worcester Polytechnic Institute, where she simultaneously directs the Japan Project Center and the Interactive Media and Game Development program. She publishes on Japanese media culture and policy, technical communication, and administration.

Patricia M. Dyer is a professor of English at Widener University in Chester, Pennsylvania, where she is the Director of the Writing Center. She teaches courses in linguistics, intercultural communication, technical writing, and methods of teaching English as a second language. She has given presentations at TESOL, CCCC, International Writing Centers Association, Quinnipiac University Critical Thinking and Writing, and the Conference on Community Writing. She has had sabbatical assignments in Honduras, Mexico, and Costa Rica.

ABOUT THE AUTHORS

Tara E. Friedman is a senior lecturer and teaches English at Widener University in Chester, Pennsylvania. She loves to work with individual students in the University Writing Center. She often presents on critical thinking, community literacy, and writing center theory and pedagogy, and her recent research interests focus on twentieth-century novels, ecological resilience and sustainability, and service learning.

Kathryn Johnson Gindlesparger is an associate professor of writing and rhetoric at Thomas Jefferson University, where she directs the writing program. Her research interests include the rhetorical and affective dimensions of administration and professional identity development. Gindlesparger's work has appeared in *College English*, *Community Literacy Journal*, *Peitho*, and *Writing Program Administration*.

Bruce Horner teaches composition, composition theory and pedagogy, and literacy studies at the University of Louisville, where he is endowed chair in rhetoric and composition. He writes about translingual theories of language, transnational approaches to composition, mobility studies, and the work of composition and its teaching.

Writer, editor, organizational leader, teacher, and artist, **Adela C. Licona** is the founder and lead consultant at the Art of Change Agency. With twenty years of experience in higher education in the fields of rhetoric, professional communication, and women and gender studies, she has participated in innovations in shared teaching and leadership in feminist and community-based organizations and consulted for justice-oriented organizations as well as grant-funded collaborations. Working through the principles of what she terms "art as coalitional gesture," she has developed action-oriented participatory projects as community connections and interventions. She is a member of the Colectiva Fronteristas Border Art Collective, professor emerita of English at the University of Arizona, and editor emerita of *Feminist Formations*.

Ian Mauer is an assistant lecturer of English at Sultan Qaboos University in Oman. With a background in linguistics and curriculum design combined with an MA in TESOL, his interests range from English for specific purposes, emerging digital literacies, and the impact of sustained motivation on educational and creative pursuits.

Joyce Meier is associate director of and associate professor in the First-Year Writing Program at Michigan State University. In 2014, she taught at the Harbin Institute of Technology in China. Supported by a generous university grant, her recent work entails facilitating special faculty-student teams that develop videos, curriculum, and pedagogical workshops on asset-based teaching of multilingual learners.

Dr. Susan V. Meyers is an international leader in writing studies, having offered keynote addresses at conferences and workshops in Asia, Africa, and Latin America. Director of Seattle University's Creative Writing Program, she holds an MFA from the University of Minnesota and a PhD from the University of Arizona. Her novel *Failing the Trapeze* won the Nilsen Award for a First Novel, and her monograph, *Del Otro Lado: Literacy and Migration Across the U.S.-Mexico Border*, was supported by a Fulbright Fellowship and grants from the National Endowment for the Humanities and the American Association of University Women.

Sadia Mir is an assistant professor of English at Virginia Commonwealth University School of the Arts in Qatar. She served as the lead writing specialist for the Young Writers Program (Doha, Qatar). She is co-author of *Spring Bloom* (HBKU Press, 2019), a children's book that uses storytelling as a tool to teach mathematics. Her interdisciplinary research interests include storytelling pedagogy, community writing, and multimodal documentary literary and media practices.

Stephen T. Russell is Priscilla Pond Flawn Regents professor and director of the School of Human Ecology at the University of Texas at Austin. He is an expert in adolescent and young adult health, with a focus on sexual orientation and gender identity. He is on the governing board of the Society for Research in Child Development, a fellow of the National Council on Family Relations, and past president of the Society for Research on Adolescence.

www.ingramcontent.com/pod-product-compliance
Lightning Source LLC
Chambersburg PA
CBHW031100080526
44587CB00011B/760